Estimating Capital and Operating Costs in Urban Transportation Planning

Estimating Capital and Operating Costs in Urban Transportation Planning

AURELIO MENENDEZ

PRAEGER

Westport, Connecticut
London

Library of Congress Cataloging-in-Publication Data

Menendez, Aurelio.
    Estimating capital and operating costs in urban transportation
planning / Aurelio Menendez.
        p.   cm.
    Includes bibliographical references and index.
    ISBN 0-275-94219-8 (alk. paper)
    1. Local transit—Estimates—United States.   2. Local transit—
United States—Planning.   I. Title.
    HE4456.M46   1993
    338.4'068'1—dc20   92-9806

British Library Cataloguing in Publication Data is available.

Library of Congress Catalog Card Number: 92-9806
ISBN: 0-275-94219-8

First published in 1993

Praeger Publishers, 88 Post Road West, Westport, CT 06881
An imprint of Greenwood Publishing Group, Inc.

Printed in the United States of America

The paper used in this book complies with the
Permanent Paper Standard issued by the National
Information Standards Organization (Z39.48-1984).

10 9 8 7 6 5 4 3 2 1

A mis padres

The easiest thing of all
is to deceive oneself,
for what a man wishes
he generally believes to be true.

—Demosthenes

Contents

Tables and Figures   ix

Acknowledgments   xi

1. Introduction   1

2. Transportation Planning in a Changing Environment   13

3. Case Studies   27

4. The Technical Process of Estimating Costs   75

5. Decision Making: Perspectives, Elements, and Problems   97

6. Putting the Pieces Together: A Framework for Cost Estimating   121

7. Conclusions   153

8. Recapitulation: Some Views with Hindsight   165

Bibliography   171

Index   185

Tables and Figures

Tables

1.1. Estimated and Actual Construction Costs per Mile,
Selected Cities and Technologies   4

1.2. Capital Cost Estimates for Buffalo Metro Rail   5

3.1. 1987 Capital and Operating Costs for the Boston Alternatives   36

3.2. Capital and Operating Costs and Daily Patronage
for Selected Santa Clara County Alternatives   46

3.3. Comparison of Capital Cost Estimates for Santa Clara Light Rail   50

3.4. Reasons for Cost Growth in Santa Clara County's LRT, 1984-1988   51

3.5. Capital and Operating Costs and Daily Patronage
for Selected Buffalo Transit Alternatives   58

3.6. Summary of Capital Costs for Buffalo's Light Rail Rapid System   61

3.7. Reasons for Cost Growth in Buffalo's LRRT, 1976-1985   62

4.1. Operating Costs Classification   82

5.1. Costs, Annual Ridership, and Cost-Effectiveness Index   109

5.2. Comparative Statistics from Several Commuter Rail Systems
in the United States   110

5.3. Comparative Statistics from Several Light Rail Systems
in the United States   110

5.4. Comparative Indicators from Several Commuter Rail Systems
     in the United States   111

5.5. Comparative Indicators from Several Light Rail Systems
     in the United States   112

6.1. Table of Utilities: Case 1   133

6.2. Model Structure and Output: Case 1   136

6.3. Model Results: Case 1   137

6.4. Table of Utilities: Case 2   138

6.5. Model Results: Case 2   139

6.6. Table of Utilities: Case 3   140

6.7. Model Results: Case 3   141

Figures

2.1. Schematic Representation of the Alternatives-Analysis Process   17

2.2. General Methodological Framework   23

3.1. Boston's Old Colony Project   31

3.2. Santa Clara County LRT   44

3.3. Buffalo's Rail Options   57

4.1. Schematic Representation of Major Elements of Technical Process   88

5.1. Schematic Representation of Institutional
     and Decision-Making Processes   106

6.1. Actors in the Planning Process   123

6.2. Schematic Representation of Analytical Framework   144

Acknowledgments

An endeavor like the research for a book cannot be undertaken without the support of many people, and more if the book is based on a case-study approach requiring extensive interviews and the gathering of a substantial amount of dispersed information. Because of this, it is not possible to list here the many people that one way or another contributed to the completion of this study. This is not to say that many others, aside from those listed below, deserve less recognition.

I must first thank Prof. Gakenheimer and Prof. Ferreira, of the Massachusetts Institute of Technology, and Prof. Meyer, of the Georgia Institute of Technology. In relation to the case studies, I must thank, in Santa Clara County, David Minister; in Boston, Bob Lepore; in Buffalo, Gordon Thompson; and in Washington, Don Emerson.

I also extend my appreciation to the many friends with whom I have shared the years since I began the research for this book and who made the entire research process more gratifying, particularly, Hugo E. Beteta, Francisco Martin Carrasco, Emily S. Jonas, Marisela Montoliu, and Elena Diez Pinto.

I must also thank very much my wife, Cira Canelas Schütt, who placidly as well as encouragingly gave me the enthusiasm to undertake and complete this book. Her wonderfulness, support, and love deserve my most affectionate consideration.

A very special remembrance goes to Toto and Abuelita, my grandparents, who left this world as I was working on the research for this book, and whom I miss very much and keep alive in my memory.

Finally, I must endlessly thank my parents and my brothers and sisters, Mercedes, Belén, Pablo, Begoña, Rodrigo, and Gerardo, who, far from where I wrote this book but very close to my heart, have been, are, and will always be, the major reason for the efforts that I have undertaken outside my home country. To them, my deepest gratitude for their tireless understanding, support, and patience.

1

Introduction

MOTIVATION

The motivation for this book came from a concern raised because of the discrepancies usually present between the planning estimates of capital and operating costs of transit alternatives and the costs obtained in the final design and construction of the selected alternative. The book presents a framework for the cost-estimating process that acknowledges the interplay among the different actors with a stake in that process and identifies those elements that affect the assumed neutrality of the process and along which a better estimation process could be developed ("better" in the sense that a broader set of elements, in addition to the formal technical elements, is considered; that the tendency to bias the results is reduced; and consequently that the decision is made on the basis of more accurate information).

The importance of improving the estimating process stems from the consequences of a failure in estimating costs that are close to final actual costs. This failure may cause all or some of the following problems:

- Selection of a non-cost-effective alternative, at least from society's perspective—that is, one where the selected alternative yields costs that are larger than the benefits, as these costs and benefits relate to the society as a whole.
- If operating costs exceed revenues by more than expected, proceeds needed to ensure long-term financing will not be available (e.g., to pay back bond indebtedness, cover debt service).
- If capital costs turn out to be much higher, the confidence that project participants place in the planning process and in analysts' attempts to predict inflation and escalation[1] would decrease, and would likely result in delays, anger, and distrust in the construction of the project.[2]
- If either capital or operating costs turn out to be higher than forecast, they may generate problems in raising the additional needed revenues and may create strains with the institutions providing the funds to construct and operate the selected system (e.g., the U.S. federal government).

- If capital costs end up being higher than predicted, they may discourage completing the project as originally designed, and hence may leave out parts of the system; this may, in turn, reduce the initially intended function or functions of the system, decreasing its use, reducing revenues, and generating additional pressures on the operating agency.
- In more general terms, underestimation of either capital or operating costs tarnishes the image of the system (e.g., the perception of poor management practices), decreases its marketability, and discredits the planning process; all these factors may jeopardize subsequent project proposals.
- Underestimation, and the subsequent cost overruns, may embarrass the people who had supported the proclaimed estimates, possibly causing adverse evaluations of their particular accomplishments (e.g., for a politician, cost overruns may lead to an electoral defeat).

Some authors argue that if capital costs were accurately calculated, there would be less incentive for cost control (i.e., if the estimates are closer to actual figures, the constructor will go close to those estimates and then end up spending more than if costs are said to be lower), which in turn would generate more expensive projects.[3] According to this view, underestimation encourages more stringent cost control practices. These authors further state that if the true price of some projects had been known in advance, the projects would have never been undertaken and this would have been detrimental to society's economic well-being, since their benefits have, ultimately, outweighed their costs—even when these costs have ended up being much higher than expected.

The argument about cost control, however, does not apply to the concerns raised in this book. During the planning phase of a project, the decision maker has to decide which alternative to pursue. Therefore, the immediate purpose of the estimation process is not the construction of the transportation facility (that may come later) but rather the selection of the best or preferred alternative among several (although, of course, the selection of the preferred alternative may be influenced by what the possibilities of constructing one or another alternative are). If estimates are biased, the decision will be made, in principle, on the wrong basis, regardless of the consequences at the time of construction. Also, at the time of selecting alternatives, commitments are made among different institutional levels in terms of dividing funding responsibilities, and this would likely be based on capital and operating costs.[4] Finally, lack of accuracy in estimating costs would ultimately affect the bidding process; if estimates are incorrect, the bidding process may be distorted, adding frictions between contractors and administrators during the construction of the project.

The argument about missing the opportunity to construct public works projects is also debatable since the blame, in those cases, would be put on benefit estimating rather than cost estimating, for final benefits are the ones that are argued to be underestimated. In the end, all these arguments can be consolidated into two, considering what the particular actor (e.g., the decision maker) perceives as most important from society's perspective: (1) to perform an unbiased selection process or (2) to underestimate costs (or overestimate benefits) with the aim of keeping ultimate costs low (or of reflecting the perception that benefits ultimately always turn out to be larger) even if the selected alternative is not the best alternative ("best" on the basis of unbiased information and society's preferences). This book follows the former.

In addition to capital costs, operating costs should be carefully calculated and reliable revenue sources pinpointed so that operating deficits do not become burdensome to local institutions. Ideally, the purpose of accurate operating costs is to ensure that a transit system is not built if local governments cannot afford to operate it (considering the extent to which the local political process establishes that operating deficits are adequate). The sources of revenue must be sufficient to pay not only the operating and maintenance costs of the system not covered by revenues or contributions from the different levels of government, but also the local share of the principal and the interest on any bonds issued to pay for the capital costs.

Table 1.1 highlights the differences between the estimated and actual capital costs for various projects undertaken during the past decade in the United States. The actual numbers are adjusted for purposes of comparison to the year when the study was undertaken and costs were estimated. The average building cost index for major U.S. metropolitan areas (as reported in *Engineering News Record*) was the indicator used for the adjustment. Since annual outlays were not readily available, total project expenditures were adjusted by the change in the appropriate building cost index, considering that expenditures incurred in the same fashion as funds provided by the federal government. Percent changes vary from almost 12 percent in the case of Miami's heavy rail system to 77 percent in the case of Miami's people mover. These changes—which include all kind of causes from changes in project scope to those produced by unforeseen inflation—indicate a sizeable underestimation of costs for transit projects carried out in the last decade in the United States.

Table 1.2 indicates the cost estimates at several different times for a transit line in Buffalo, New York. The numbers are in current dollars and constant dollars. Some of the reasons alleged for the changes in cost estimates are provided. Adjustments are made upward along the way to reflect design changes or "unpredictable" additional costs. The question that this table raises is, Would decision makers have selected the same alternative had they known in advance the actual costs for undertaking the selected alternative? Another question is, Why were initial costs so much lower than final costs?

In recent years, a lot of attention has been focused on the performance of existing urban transit systems and the impact of the construction of new ones or extensions of existing ones. Most of these systems have not lived up to their expectations, with projected ridership levels usually overestimated and capital and operating costs underestimated. These disappointments have tarnished the image of transit systems and have put additional pressure on accountability and

Table 1.1
Estimated and Actual Construction Costs per Mile, Selected Cities and Technologies

City	Corridor	Mode	Construction costs ($ millions per mile)				Actual Million $ per Mile Adjust. to Est. Year (c)	Change (percent) ((c-a)/a)
			Estimated (a)	(year)	Actual (b)	(year)		
Buffalo		LRT	$33.28	(74)	$82.66	(85)	$50.2	51.0
Sacramento	Northeast	LRT	4.75	(80)	9.62	(86)	7.7	63.4
Santa Clara	Guadalupe	LRT	13.80	(81)	28.00	(88)	24.0	74.0
Atlanta	A, B, & C	HRT	51.34	(73)	93.28	(86)	64.0	25.2
Baltimore	A & B	HRT	32.14	(73)	70.71	(87)	48.1	49.9
Miami		HRT	39.75	(78)	52.50	(87)	44.4	11.8
Detroit		DPM	41.03	(85)	72.41	(87)	70.6	72.2
Miami		DPM	41.05	(83)	73.68	(86)	72.6	77.0

Sources: Urban Mass Transportation Administration (1988, February); *Engineering News Record* (various issues); own calculations.

Note: The sharp differences among systems with similar technologies is mainly due to the different physical requirements involved (e.g., an underground system costs more than a similar one at grade).

Key: HRT: Heavy Rapid Transit; LRT: Light Rail Transit; DPM: Downtown People Mover.

managerial performance. The frequent gaps between planning estimates and results after the construction of the transportation facility have attracted the attention of public institutions, which have been trying to tackle the issue.[5]

FOCUS

This book focuses on the process of estimating capital and operating costs in the phase of analyzing transit-project alternatives and develops a framework for that estimating process. The framework attempts to show the interaction among the technical aspects involved in establishing capital and operating costs of transit alternatives and the institutional, political, and decision-making dimensions of that process.

The purpose of estimating is to predict, as accurately as possible, a future condition—in this case, a future cost. Estimating is one of the most crucial, controversial, and relevant activities in any planning process for, in principle, based on the estimation of the values of a set of variables (e.g., demand, costs, population), plans are developed and decisions are made. One of the reasons

Table 1.2
Capital Cost Estimates for Buffalo Metro Rail

Study/Year	Proposed System	Current Cap. Cost Estimates ($ millions)	Constant (1971) Cost Estimates ($ millions)	Remarks
Niagara Frontier Mass Transit Study (1971)	11-mile HRT	$241	$241	Estimate based on predominantly aerial alignment.
Buffalo-Amherst Metro Preliminary Design (1974)	11-mile HRT 6.4-mile LRT	$476 $213	$375 $168	Increase due to inflation, 80% increase in underground and refined engineering
Alternatives Analysis/UMTA Grant Application (1976)	11-mile HRT 6.4-mile LRRT	$555 $336	$370 $224	Based on escalated unit costs of 1974 estimate by taking into account different technologies.
Ridership and Operations Analysis/Full Funding Contract (1978)	6.4-mile LRRT	$450	$255	Refined estimates; engineering changes; schedule revised; increased contingencies and insurance.
Forecast Update (1985)	6.4-mile LRRT	$525	$253*	New estimate near completion of project; phased-out station reinstated.
Forecast Update/ Cost to Complete Estimate (1987)	6.4-mile LRRT	$552	$264*	Unanticipated inflation; utility relocation and start-up costs; claims settlements; artwork.

Sources: Niagara Frontier Transportation Authority, May 1987; *Engineering News Record* (various issues); and own calculations.
Note: The constant-dollar column was calculated using the average building cost index for major metropolitan areas in the U.S. as reported in *Engineering News Record*. The values with an asterisk (*) were calculated assuming costs took place in a schedule similar to the disbursement of federal funds.
Key: HRT: Heavy Rail Transit; LRT: Light Rail Transit; LRRT: Light Rail Rapid Transit..

for focusing on the process of cost estimation is that, unlike other aspects of planning, cost estimates have an exact basis for ultimate judgment. We can, eventually, determine how accurate the estimates were (accounting, if necessary, for any changes in project design and/or scope). Unfortunately, however, we do not usually learn much about accuracy until the decision has already been made, the project has been implemented, and it is too late to undo what has been done.

A set of studies related to cost estimating focuses on the technical aspects involved in developing analytic methods for calculating capital and operating costs.[6] In these studies the estimating process consists of a clear and precise sequence of steps: definition of alternatives, identification of components, gathering of unit-cost data, selection of estimating methods, generation of cost estimates for each alternative, consideration of uncertainties, review, and documentation. However, frequently there are deviations from that process: some steps are missing, the order of the steps is changed, and/or the allocation of time and resources is concentrated on a few steps to the detriment of other steps. These deviations may increase the possibilities of generating, accidentally or intentionally, biased estimates, which in turn may lead to inadequate decisions ("inadequate" in the sense that the selection is done on the basis of inaccurate information).

Another trend in the literature emphasizes the institutional aspects of the implementation of transportation plans and how the technical process should be modified to become more effective.[7] This literature indicates that decision makers need good qualitative data in addition to the quantitative data, as well as techniques for identifying problems and constraints in order to improve the effectiveness of the planning process so that plans do not get stalled once they are approved.[8]

Since the period when planning was thought to be a purely technical process, there has been a growing awareness and analysis in the literature of the dynamics of the political and institutional setting within which the transportation planning process is conducted.[9] That setting influences the planning process and generates a picture that differs from the unbiased and value-neutral intention of the technical process. Many factors, such as the interaction among different levels of government, the pressure exerted by interest groups, and the way information is collected and transmitted to decision makers, affect the final outcome and the selection of the optimal alternative ("optimal" in the sense that it is the solution the concerned decision makers think is the best, on the basis of the information generated by the planning studies).

Along these lines, this book investigates how data and techniques can be influenced by institutional and political factors, and how these factors may override the technical process. By bringing together the different perspectives—the technical, the institutional, and the political—the book provides a description and explanation of the dynamics involved in the cost-estimating process in particular and the process of analyzing transit alternatives in general.

One can view this book from at least two vantage points. From one point, it describes a broader framework to look at the cost-estimating process and the processes of analyzing transit alternatives and planning for transportation systems. After the discussion of the motivation for the book and the research methodology in this introductory chapter, Chapter 2 discusses the history of transportation planning and develops the general theoretical framework. Chapter 3 presents the case studies and the empirical findings as they relate to the issues presented in this book. Chapters 4 and 5 each describe one component of that model. Chapter 4 describes the technical, analytic process; it encompasses its elements and techniques. Chapter 5 discusses the theoretical and empirical underpinnings of modern decision-making theory, and puts this theory within the context of the alternatives-analysis and cost-estimation process. In Chapter 6, the two components are brought together to define a framework for estimating capital and operating costs; it introduces the practical recommendations that generate from that framework. Finally, Chapters 7 and 8 present the conclusions to the book.

From the other vantage point, the book is a comprehensive essay on the theory and practice of estimation in transportation planning. The second, third, fourth, and fifth chapters encompass three major sections: a presentation of empirical findings, a survey of past research, and a critical look at this research. As a whole, the suggested framework provides opportunities for strengthening and improving the estimation process of any planning activity.

SCOPE AND METHODOLOGY

As mentioned in the previous section, the book will focus on cost estimating within the process of analyzing alternatives in transportation planning. The alternatives that are analyzed will encompass projects involving fixed-guideway transit systems (e.g., new rail lines, extensions of existing lines, and busways).

The process of analyzing alternatives comes after the system planning phase, during which the particular transportation problems in the (metropolitan) area are identified along with the study corridor. Alternative solutions are proposed for the corridor and subsequently analyzed in order to select the best one.[10] The process of analyzing alternatives is, then, the critical stage during which planning must be carried out at a level of detail deep enough to select the best alternative. It is in this step that pressures from interested parties reach the highest point and decisions are most crucial. The development of the process of alternatives analysis reflects the complexities of the urban transportation planning process and its interdisciplinary nature.

The book focuses on the alternatives-analysis process, as it is understood in the United States, for several reasons. This process involves fixed-guideway systems—heavy rail, commuter rail, light rail, or busways—which have a permanence not present in other transit systems, such as bus or paratransit systems. In fixed-guideway systems, the question of aging facilities, and the impact of the construction of new systems or extension of existing ones, has a higher relevance than in other less permanent systems. Furthermore, spending levels for the construction, maintenance, and operation are usually higher, putting more pressure on the management and planning of these transit systems.

In considering the definition of costs, the book focuses on (1) capital costs (i.e., engineering, right-of-way, construction, vehicles, equipment, and other facilities), (2) operating costs over an extended period of time (including indirect costs such as administrative, overhead, taxes, and insurance), (3) financing costs (e.g., debt service on bonds or short-term borrowing, and special financing fees), and (4) maintenance and repair costs over an extended period of time. (The last three costs will be put, for convenience, under the rubric of operating costs unless there exists a need for further clarification.)

These types of costs, compared to less tangible costs such as travel costs or environmental costs, are expected to be more manageable, more objective, and probably less conducive to influence by interested parties. There are precise methods and techniques to calculate capital and operating costs. Estimators with adequate technical backgrounds are hired by estimating departments for the sole purpose of calculating capital and operating costs. Hence, decision makers can be presented with a straightforward analysis, on the basis of which decisions should be less malleable and more accurate than in areas with more controversial information. This should help isolate the issues from too many interferences and reach more general conclusions.

Lastly, cost information is often an extremely important basis for making a decision about project investments; indeed, it may be the primary determinant for such decision. Even when the final decision is not based on cost information, this information for preliminary proposals is often the major determinant in deciding whether to pursue the project. Key evaluation criteria used in many studies to select a short list of final alternatives include ridership, cost (capital and annualized), and cost-effectiveness measures (annualized cost per new rider and annualized cost per passenger mile).[11]

Cost estimation cannot be investigated and understood without looking at the broader picture of the transportation planning process. Some elements of this process, particularly demand estimation, considerably affect costs. These elements must be kept in mind when investigating the process of estimating costs. By focusing on costs but looking at the broader planning process, one should be able to identify the issues that both particularly pertain to the cost-estimating process and that are more general and applied to other elements of the planning activity and their interactions.

The research approach taken in this book relied upon the investigation of several case studies. The research focuses on an alternatives-analysis process for a fixed-guideway system in the South Shore corridor of the Boston metropolitan area. This case is complemented with two cases from other cities in the United States.

The basic data-gathering techniques in this study were field interviews supplemented by examination of documents (proposals, reports, etc.) and periodic literature (journals, newspapers, etc.). The interviews were conducted with the managers of the transportation projects. In addition, other interviews were held with the consultants involved in the project and the decision makers. Decision makers included individuals from several decision-making levels: municipal officials, members of advisory and control boards, managers of the metropolitan transportation authorities, and elected state officials. Another set of interviews involved people from those levels of government involved in approving funds for the construction of the projects. These interviews involved federal officials at the Urban Mass Transportation Administration (UMTA) and regional administrators of this same federal agency. A number of key people who had opinions on the projects, although they did not participate in them directly, were interviewed as well.

The information is developed and analyzed along two major dimensions: technical and decision making. The technical dimension is examined through an analysis of the components and approaches of cost estimating, and the issues of database management, uncertainty, phasing of alternatives, and organizational setup. The decision-making dimension is examined through the identification and investigation of the behavior of the actors (individuals and institutions) involved in the cost-estimation process, and the analysis of the attributes of the decision-making process, including stages of the process, types of problems, uncertainty of the decision, and role of estimating.

The connection between both processes is examined through attributes such as the timing of costs analyses and its relation to the development of the decision-making process, the action orientation of cost estimates (e.g., the actions that may eventually be taken after a particular set of cost estimates is generated), the communication and interaction among analysts and decision makers, the influences from the political dimension, and the validity of the technical process (including data gathering, interpretation and quality of cost data, and evaluation of cost models).[12] Several of these dimensions are further assessed through the investigation of database-management techniques and the possible improvements that computer-based information systems could bring to the effectiveness of decision making, the performance of sensitivity analyses, and the generation of more systematic ways of obtaining the optimal solution.[13]

A study such as this risks overlooking or neglecting some issues and elements. The transportation planning process, with its myriad of components and interests, is influenced by numerous factors that may affect its final outcome. The diversity of the case studies is an attempt to encompass as much variance as possible to identify the major variables that influence the cost-estimating process. There are, however, other perspectives such as the macro-administrative structure (e.g., a centralized versus a decentralized approach to estimating costs), or a postmanagement analysis (e.g., how construction took place), or differences in the maturity of the project (e.g., how new the project and technology were) that were not followed. Instead, this book looks at the history of the planning of transportation alternatives from the perspective of the actors involved. This process-oriented perspective is shaped by the actors' technical contribution or their personal or political stakes in the construction—or not construction—of the project. Chapter 2 further develops the general theoretical framework that guides this process-oriented perspective.

Within the process-oriented perspective, there are some elements that are difficult to isolate and identify. For instance, people in charge of carrying out the technical process are seldom ready to accept that more emphasis and work were put into a potentially "preselected" alternative, with other alternatives overlooked and probably put into a disadvantaged valuative position; that preliminary cost estimates were possibly done carelessly and with too much optimism; or that perhaps initial preferences affected which data they used and how they undertook the technical process. Some of these components therefore need a careful but unavoidably personal perception that may be subject to criticism. So as to minimize this bias, the research was carry out by questioning as many different people as possible (different in the sense of having different stakes in the process) and scrutinizing documents and newspapers.

CONCLUSION

The underestimation of capital and operating costs in the analysis of urban public transportation alternatives has been highlighted as one of the critical points in the transportation planning process that requires further investigation. A reliable estimate of the costs of constructing, operating, and maintaining each alternative is crucial to an accurate assessment of its cost-effectiveness and financial implications, and hence of its evaluation vis-à-vis other alternatives.

The purpose of this book is to understand why the underestimation process occurs so often and to conclude with an assessment of the degree to which technical work actually contributes to informed decision making. The book develops a framework for the estimation of capital and operating costs including two major dimensions and their components: the technical dimension, with the definition of its inputs, models, and outputs; and the decision-making dimension, with the definition of the actors, organizations, their relationships, and the political pressures that come from external forces and interest groups trying to force desired outcomes. The research methodology consists of a case-study approach. The diversity of the cases helps one to better perceive and define the different components of the framework and to reach a better conclusion for the ultimate objective of the book: the definition of the role of technical analysis in the decision-making process.

NOTES

1. One of the most difficult questions confronting the cost estimator is how to understand and estimate possible changes in costs owing to inflation or escalation. Inflation is the time-oriented increase in costs brought about by rising prices of materials, parts, goods, services, and so on, owing to mismatches between supply and money available to acquire them. Escalation is the time-oriented increase in costs brought about by increases in the amount of resources (e.g., labor, materials, or services) required to complete a project. It may also be caused by the continuous modification or upgrading of a project beyond the planned specifications. Stewart (1982), pp. 223-39.

2. Deiter (1985).

3. See for instance, Merewitz (1972). This author, using a regression analysis of several public works projects, found that cost overruns were positively related to size of project, incompleteness of preliminary surveys, engineering uncertainty, inflation, project scope enlargement, length of time to complete project, exogenous delays, complexity of administrative structure, and inexperience of administrative personnel. He further divides them into controllable and uncontrollable overruns. Among the former, he identifies poor administration, incomplete starting surveys of engineering, and financial and legal problems. Among the latter, he distinguishes inflation, which he rates uncontrollable but often foreseeable, and scope changes owing to unexpected technological problems or construction delays from unanticipated causes such as wars, new laws, or strikes.

4. For instance, in the United States, the Urban Mass Transportation Administration looks at, among other criteria, the financial commitments at the local level and the operating effort to decide to go ahead with a project. Therefore, if capital costs are underestimated, the financial commitment at the local level will appear higher; if operating costs are underestimated, the operating effort will appear good.

5. Pickrell (1992), Pickrell (1989), Ryan et al. (1986), National Cooperative Transit Research and Development Program (1983, December), and Urban Mass Transportation Administration (1980).

6. Clark and Lorenzoni (1985), Bay (1984), Stewart (1982), Calder (1976).

7. Menendez (1986), Wachs (1985a), Jones (1985), Meyer and Miller (1984), Gakenheimer (1976), Hamer (1976).

8. Meyer and Miller (1984) state that "the product of planning can be any form of communication with decision makers that provides useful information in identifying alternative actions and selecting among them" (p. 1). They further state that the types of data should be broadened to include information "relating to the policy, organizational, and fiscal environment of transportation decision making" (p. 10).

9. Johnston et al. (1988), Moore (1988), Catanese (1984), Deiter (1985), Dorschner (1985), Whitt (1982), Altshuler et al. (1979).

10. In the United States, the outcome of the process of analyzing alternatives is called the "locally preferred alternative report." This is the alternative that, if approved by federal government (specifically, the Urban Mass Transportation Administration), will be carried into the preliminary engineering phase and then into final design and construction.

11. For instance, Niagara Frontier Transportation Authority (1976, June). This report indicates that the two areas of overriding relevance (among the several dimensions of transit alternatives) are cost and level of service provided (pp. 4 and 5). Capital cost is crucial in any study of lower capital cost alternatives. Operating cost is, in combination

with capital costs, the critical element in the evaluation of the cost-effectiveness of alternative systems. Also, Urban Mass Transportation Administration (1984), and Ryan et al. (1986) in the guidelines for UMTA's alternatives analysis, indicate how one of the thresholds to approve study funds, and subsequently preliminary engineering and construction, is an index reflecting the ratio of capital and operating costs minus travel savings by new transit riders.

12. Tanaka (1982).

13. Date (1986), Senn (1984), Keen (1981).

2

Transportation Planning
in a Changing Environment

A BRIEF HISTORY OF TRANSPORTATION PLANNING

The history of transportation planning in the last 40 years has been one of a continuous and dramatic change in its conceptual and methodological focus. The 1940s saw the beginning of the development of models that tried to replicate the relationships between land use and transportation. Out of these efforts, the sequential demand model was developed.[1] At that moment, transportation planners were mostly concerned with ways to increase the mobility of the population, and expansion of highway capacity was usually the recommended solution.[2]

By the end of the 1960s, in large part owing to the lack of attention given to the urban environment, the public reacted against the construction of urban expressways and thus precipitated a reexamination of transportation methods and policies. In the early 1970s, the external impact of transportation facilities became a significant planning issue. The objectives of transportation planning, previously expressed mostly in operational terms, began to be expressed in terms of more general criteria including environmental and social factors (e.g., special services to the elderly and handicapped, energy, safety, and equity considerations).[3] In addition, public transit was perceived as a more valid solution to the urban transportation problem. The type of project implemented was no longer dominated by the capital-intensive, large-scale facility, but rather tended to rely more on small-scale, operational improvements.[4] This era also meant an increase in the role of central governments—the federal government, in the United States—in transit investment and operations.[5] In the United States, the federal involvement encouraged the planning of a high number of fixed-guideway transit systems to be constructed in part with federal funds.

Since the beginning of the 1980s, the changes in central government policies (fiscal federalism), along with the failure of some of the transit systems in achieving their expected objectives, have led to a deeper scrutiny of the generation of transit plans and of the activities of transit agencies, as well as an emphasis on accountability. In addition, the participation of private transit providers has been stressed as a way to help improve the transportation problems in urban environments. This continuous change in focus of transportation planning has, for 40 years, produced parallel changes in the procedures and objectives of the relevant organizations.

Out of this environment, a new attempt in the 1980s was made to reestablish a role for long-term transportation planning after the period of reaction to the inadequacies of conventional forecasting model had led, particularly in the United States and United Kingdom, to an increasing emphasis on short-term transportation planning measures. This attempt has led to the development of a strategic framework that acknowledges the changing environment surrounding the transportation planning process, emphasizes the action orientation of plans, and redefines the role of government in providing public transportation services.[6] This framework underscores the organization as the focus of transportation plans, and the need to define its role. In addition, the framework shifts the focus of the planning process by emphasizing the strategic consequences of its outcomes.

This brief historical review illustrates how transit plans and policies have been subjected to the wandering and erratic pressures of national and urban politics and the interest groups that shape transportation policy. The result has been a broadening of the goals that mass transit must accomplish and a confusion as to what mass transit is supposed to do to achieve those goals. All this has been reflected in the planning process.[7] By attempting to achieve so many goals, transit planning has not been able to concentrate on a clear methodology but rather has put that methodology at the mercy of the political environment.

THE PROCESS OF ANALYZING ALTERNATIVES IN TRANSIT PROJECT PLANNING

The development process for major transit investment projects, within which local institutions plan and develop fixed-guideway transit facilities, contains five steps from project conception to construction: system planning, analysis of alternatives, preliminary engineering, final design, and construction. During the system-planning phase, local agencies examine long-range urban development trends, collect travel data, forecast needs, and evaluate transportation policies and investment options. Based on their preliminary assessments of travel patterns and problems, local agencies evaluate a range of alternatives leading to the identification of those that seem to merit further study based on their cost-effectiveness, financial feasibility, or other more general criteria. These alternatives are then studied in detail during alternatives analysis, leading to the selection of the locally preferred alternative in terms of both mode and alignment. This alternative is then further examined during preliminary engineering and final design prior to its construction.

The process of analyzing alternatives focuses on a specific transportation need (singled out during the system planning phase), identifies alternative actions to address this need, and generates the information needed to select an option for implementation. In many respects, the step of analyzing alternatives is key to the project development since the selection of a project initiates the process that will eventually lead to its construction along with the improvements that it will bring about, the costs that will be incurred, and the environmental consequences that will result.

As a response to a perceived need—politically or technically motivated—a local agency investigates the priority corridor in detail and singles out alternative solutions to the transportation problems identified for the corridor. The range of alternatives typically include one or more rail options—which may range from light to heavy rail technologies—a busway alternative, and a transportation system management (TSM) alternative that represents the best that can be done without a major investment in new infrastructure. Sometimes, an alternative consisting of a somewhat novel technology is also included.

The realization of the technical process requires a wide range of skills, including travel-demand forecasting; estimation of capital and operating costs; analysis of social, economic, and environmental impacts; financial analysis; and evaluation. These skills may not be present in a single local or metropolitan agency. In the United States, the metropolitan planning organization is often skillful in analyzing travel demand and land development, but the transit operator may have greater expertise in transit operations, project design, cost estimation, and financial analysis. Either or both may have project management ability.

The necessary blend of technical skills obliges the cooperation of several agencies and/or consulting firms working under the supervision and management of a lead agency—usually a local or metropolitan agency closer to the local decision makers and with the capability of managing the project and supervising its construction if this step is reached. In the United States, many different kinds of agencies have served as the local lead for federally-sponsored transit planning projects. These have included transit operators, metropolitan planning organizations, agencies of city government (e.g., departments of public works), state highway and transportation departments, and regional port authorities.[8]

The perceived need and the identification of alternative solutions initiates the study process and the definition of the participating agencies, their roles, and responsibilities. These agencies agree on the purposes to be achieved with the transportation facility, the issues to be addressed in the study, the boundaries of the study (i.e., what will be investigated), and which data and models will be used for addressing the purposes and issues of the study.[9] In principle, the attempt is to develop a set of analytical methodologies and a set of alternatives for analysis that all participants agree on, before the more detailed technical analysis is undertaken. Once the agreement is reached, the responsible agencies carry out the bulk of the technical analysis including the forecasting of demand, the estimation of capital and operating costs, and the assessment of potential funding sources. The different pieces are put together into a document—in the United States, the Draft Environmental Impact Statement (DEIS)—that is subject to analysis by other potentially interested institutions and the public at large.[10] This step ensures public participation in the decision-making process. Out of this process, one alternative is selected for more detailed study and, if funds are secured, eventual construction.

Higher levels of government provide funding and technical assistance during some or all of the steps of the technical process. These levels of government, at key points, review the local technical work for completeness and accuracy, and acknowledge the methods being used and the results obtained. Between each pair of phases there are decision points, at which time the relevant agencies decide whether to support the continuation of the planning and project development process. Cost-effectiveness, financial feasibility (compared to other alternatives), and local financial effort (i.e., strength of the proposed capital financing plan including provisions to fund potential project cost overruns, and stability and reliability of sources of operating deficit funding) are major considerations at these decision points.

In principle, the purpose of the process of analyzing alternatives is to develop sound and objective information necessary for informed project decision making.[11] Among other things, project decisions (i.e., which option will be the preferred alternative) are based upon realistic cost estimates and financing proposals that take into account the operating expenses of the proposed transit system. The estimating process is therefore crucial. The estimated values for the different variables, and particularly capital and operating costs, may tilt the balance toward one alternative or another. At the same time, the technical process is not performed at sufficient detail to recognize all the necessary engineering and environmental conditions that may affect the project. There is a tradeoff between comprehensiveness and how much can be accomplished. At this stage, only preliminary work is done in the field (to estimate slopes, types of soils, or how many trees must be torn down). Most of the work is performed in an office, based on maps and other cartographic information. Decisions therefore are prone to be controversial and the political process reaches its peak. Political actors and interest groups try to influence the development of the planning process and its results to reflect their points of view on how to address the particular transportation problem.

Figure 2.1 schematically summarizes the different steps of the process that lead to deciding which alternative to pursue. The figure illustrates how decisions made about how to undertake the planning process, which alternatives to consider, and which techniques to apply may all ultimately affect the selection of the preferred alternative. The range of alternatives could theoretically be very

Figure 2.1
Schematic Representation of the Alternatives-Analysis Process

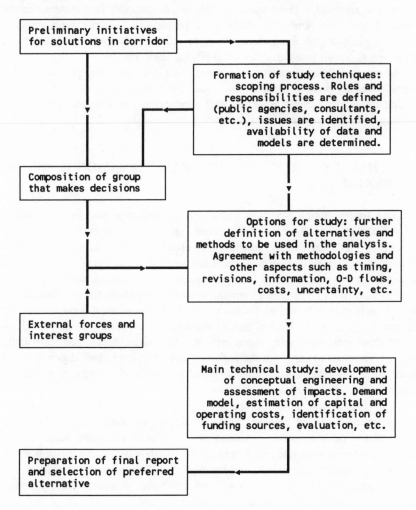

large, but the constraints of the technical process, in terms of how much it would cost and how long it would take to accomplish it, limit the possibilities to consideration of a half-dozen alternatives (or a few more that are variations of the six basic ones). Transportation planners must then analyze that set of alternatives and present the pros and cons of each alternative according to a variety of criteria.

This process is fairly formalized in some countries—for instance, in the United States—and more adhoc in others. The differences among countries stem from a variety of factors, ranging from the cultural environment, to the participatory tradition of the society, to the influence of the central government, and to the assumed role of transit in the urban transportation system. In the United States, the American tradition of politics and district representation fosters a process with a significant level of citizen participation. However, in some areas, transit faces an often inhospitable environment.

In spite of the differences in planning cultures, the basic purpose of the transit planning process remains the same: the identification of which among several alternatives seems to be the more appropriate transit solution to address the transportation problems of a corridor.

THE CHARACTERISTICS OF THE TRANSPORTATION PLANNING ENVIRONMENT

The transportation planning process is an endeavor that involves many individuals and institutions. This broad appeal mainly comes from two directions. First, individuals are concerned about the effects of the construction of permanent, large transportation facilities and the burden on their budgets as taxpayers and as consumers of transportation services. Second, decision makers need to mobilize a large enough constituency to bring about the construction of large transportation facilities. Furthermore, the limits of local finances to fund the construction of this kind of facility force the involvement of other levels of government with their many more interests. Moreover, local agencies usually lack the resources to carry out the various elements of the technical process, and must request involvement of other levels of government and private consultant agencies.[12]

The broad institutional framework enlarges the complexity of the transportation planning process. The high degree of complexity, in both the technical and decision-making components, evolves from several factors, such as the uncertainty associated with the impacts of alternatives, the multiplicity of criteria to evaluate alternatives, and the fuzzy line separating the technical and political processes.[13] These factors affect the different elements of the planning process and, particularly, the cost-estimating process.

Associated with the elements of the planning process at the stage of analyzing alternatives is a considerable amount of uncertainty in both quantitative values and qualitative aspects (such as political uncertainty). This uncertainty has two edges: on one side, planners would choose to know everything with certainty so their plans can be based on facts, not on mistaken perceptions; on the other side, uncertainty—and its associated ambiguity—is the critical element that permits the different actors and audiences in the transportation planning process to articulate their views and play their particular roles.

There usually are not one but several decision processes in transit project planning. Owing to the geographical and financial scope of the projects that are the subject of this book, decision processes affect horizontal and vertical layers of government. On the horizontal plane, several local governments may be affected by any of the alternatives being considered (because they cut across their districts), creating some cooperation or competition among the affected constituencies.[14] Along the vertical, the substantial funds required to construct fixed-guideway transit projects make the involvement of higher levels of government (e.g., the federal level) necessary.[15] Thus, these transit projects usually involve different audiences, which the results of the technical process must address.

THE RATIONAL PLANNING PARADIGM AND ITS CRITICS

The complexity of the planning environment has not deterred planners from aspiring to an ideal comprehensive rational process whereby plans are the reflection of a process that (1) is supposed to be impartial (i.e., actors do not deliberately lean the process toward particular outcomes because personal emotions and values stay out of the process); (2) considers all possible alternatives; and (3) concludes with selecting the optimal alternative. For over 30 years, this rational paradigm has been the major thrust behind the development of the planning field, and particularly of the transportation planning field, in spite of the fact that criticism of the rational paradigm has been abundant.[16] In reality, however, practicing planners accept the cognitive, practical, and political limitations to comprehensive, rational decision making for planning. They also acknowledge that public decisions are not usually made according to the ideal conception of rationality mentioned above and, consequently, adapt planning methods to the characteristics of each particular situation.[17]

The debate over rationality applies to several steps and components of the planning process. There is technical rationality, when methods and data are unbiasedly applied to precisely defined problems (whose definition is also achieved through a rational, scientific process, with all the necessary information and following specific steps). There is also rationality in the decision-making process, whereby the decision maker, if one can be identified, bases his or her decisions on all the information available and the maximization of his or her expected utility. In either case, normative rationality requires both comprehensiveness and impartiality. But comprehensiveness cannot be achieved as soon as the technical analyst or the decision maker wishes to complete the technical study or make a decision within a reasonable period of time and with a reasonable amount of resources. Impartiality is not possible either, because the lack of comprehensiveness gives way to uncertainty and ambiguity, which allow pressures and, ultimately, compromises between the forces and interests that have a stake in the process and its outcomes.

Besides rationality in both the technical and the decision-making processes, we can also identify rationality in how information flows between those two processes. In principle, the decision maker is the recipient of the information rationally gathered and manipulated (calculated) by the technical analyst. The analyst is an impartial technician, while the decision maker is engaged in politics, entrusted with expressing public values. Rationality in the link between the technical and decision-making processes implies that information generation and decisions are completely separate and distinct activities. This rationality cannot be achieved because it would not "engage the emotions or imagination of the potential user,"[18] probably giving way to plans that are not effective (i.e., plans that do not meet the intended goals).

The attack on the planning paradigm began as early as the 1950s with Simon's discussion of the connection between planning and decision making. He stated that no real decision-making process could meet the requirements of normative rationality: complete information and the simultaneous consideration of all possible alternatives. Almost at the same time, Lindblom developed his concept of disjointed incrementalism. According to this theory, alternatives developed in a planning process differ only slightly from the status quo.[19] From another perspective, observers of how planning and administrative decisions are made in the real world placed increasing emphasis on their political context. That resulted in an increased sensitivity to the "politics of planning," a resulting critique of and retreat from comprehensive planning, and the realization that there is a "culture of planning" that is not necessarily rational.[20]

At the same time, organization theorists have suggested that the institutions and organizations where planning takes place and where decisions are made do not conform to the premises of the rational model, either. Organizational decision making and behavior may be the result of bureaucratic politics, organizational "satisfying," or even the simple limits of individual and institutional attention and information-processing capabilities.[21]

These criticisms of the rational paradigm have led several academics to think that the field of planning theory must confront the question of how to resolve the contradictions, in practice, between that paradigm and the realities and constraints of real-world decision making. Forester (1984), focusing on the decision-making side, suggests that "the role of theory may well not be to predict 'what will happen if . . .'; instead . . . [it] may be to direct the attention of the decision maker, to suggest what important and significant variables and actors and events and signals to be alert to, to look for, to take as tips or warnings." Others, focusing more on the interaction between the analysis and decision-making processes, advocate the development of alternative paradigms,[22] paradigms that can be labeled under the rubric of argument-oriented paradigm. In this paradigm, one must look at planning primarily as a communicative action rather than mainly as consisting of two distinct and separate components: analysis and decision making.[23] It provides a useful perspective on the complex interweaving of techniques, information, power relations, and values that are unavoidably embedded in planning practice.

The argument-oriented paradigm underscores the impossibility of achieving comprehensiveness (generality) and advocates the understanding of particular events in their own terms and contexts. In this paradigm, the focus shifts to the identification and confrontation of the needs of particular situations rather than to the generation and application of a comprehensive, universal method. The technical process is not guided by an attempt to achieve objectivity—that is assumed to be an impossible task—but rather is formulated as part of a broader process wherein concepts, data, and methods evolve as the planning objectives change and the myriad of interests interfere with each other and try to reach agreements on how to proceed. According to this paradigm, the outcome of the planning process becomes "objective" as a result of the interplay of and argumentation among the affected interests and the reliance on a variety of sources, not as a result of a supposedly correct method, and the analyst's work as a detached observer. Thus, information becomes "more important in problem defining than in problem solving; more in describing process than predicting outcome; more in saying what happened than in saying what works; more in generating alternatives than in comparing them; and more in negotiating than in providing simple decision criteria."[24]

THE ANALYTICAL FRAMEWORK: AN ARGUMENT-ORIENTED APPROACH TO ANALYZING THE TRANSIT PLANNING PROCESS

Much has been written about transportation planning methods, their application, and how their results can better reflect actual figures. The literature primarily focuses on analytical elements and possible ways to improve them.[25] The drawback is that, although analytical tools are generally available and their improvement and application can be helpful, it is very difficult to explicitly treat the complexities immersed in the urban transportation decision-making process. How effective or how accurate transportation models are cannot be analyzed in isolated technical terms. One must look at the broader transportation planning process including its institutional and political environment.

The disenchantment with transportation planning techniques that surfaced in the beginning of the 1970s arose not so much because of technical errors,[26] but rather because of the high expectations society put on those techniques for solving the transportation problems of metropolitan cities and for addressing a myriad of other goals, and the subsequent perception of its failure in solving those problems and achieving those goals. In the end, the success or failure of technical analyses will not depend on the accuracy or the sophistication of their technical components but rather on the ultimate role assigned to these analyses and how useful they are in making transportation decisions. This is why it becomes crucial to look at the role of transportation planning in decision making and to take an argument-oriented approach to analyzing the transportation planning process, an approach that focuses on how the technical process is undertaken, how the decision-making process unfolds, and how both processes interact with each other.[27] In this approach, the transportation analytic process is viewed as a dynamic iterative one, where the analyst, the decision maker, the transportation system manager, the system user, and those affected by the system are all part of the same process.

The approach followed in this book is an attempt to confront the criticisms of the rational paradigm and put them in the right context. Within the rational paradigm, better techniques and more information would unambiguously lead to more accurate estimates and better decisions. If that paradigm, however, does not fit a particular situation (as seems to be mostly the case in transportation planning), better estimates (or methods to generate more accurate estimates) do not necessarily lead to better decisions. This is because underestimation (or even overestimation) may be an acceptable way of hedging against uncertainty, politics, or social preferences. In this vein, the book investigates the limits of the rational paradigm through analysis of several transit project planning exercises and, after identifying what leads to underestimation, takes into account those limits to suggest some ways to improve the transit planning process (recognizing that those ways may not necessarily conform to the rational paradigm).

An argument-oriented approach places the technical-rational analysis within a broader framework than the decision-oriented one, and better allows one to address and explain the complexities of existing planning processes. The argument-oriented approach expands the framework of the planning process by putting more emphasis on the process of defining the actors, the terms of reference, the "fair" relative comparisons among alternatives, and the set of criteria and/or objectives to evaluate alternatives, considering the possibility of mismatches between decision processes at the local and those at higher level institutional settings. This approach *does not* abandon rational concepts and methods; rather, it views these concepts and methods as dealing with other subsystems (institutions, politics, personalities), and hence integrates them into a paradigm that is more encompassing.[28]

By following the argument-oriented approach, this book also attempts to illustrate how far the prevalent approach can be from a purely rational process, and then proposes ways to redirect the process in terms of the definition of a correct decision-making process. Two approaches can be identified in the literature as normative bases upon which to establish the definition of a correct planning process. The first is to evaluate a correct planning process on the basis of overall moral values of fairness, honesty, public spirit, and impartiality.[29] The second one is to look at how distortions in the process have led to a "planning disaster," in the sense that few or none of the intended goals were achieved.[30] To define a correct planning process is no small task, and it will surface several times in other sections of this book. For now, we can think that a good planning process is such that ensures decisions are made on a good footing—that is, on the basis of the best information we can have—and, to the extent possible, in a democratic way (in the sense that participants have knowledge of the facts and can voice their reactions to the technical process). With these conditions, the ultimate purpose of the planning process is to use society's resources in the proper way, anticipating that eventual implementation of the selected action reflects the predicted effects—that is, estimated costs and benefits—and puts no impossible burdens on any affected group or on the society as a whole.

Figure 2.2 schematically illustrates the general methodological approach of this book. The case studies (empirical framework) allow a view of the transportation planning process from the rational perspective, sustained by the theoretical rational paradigm, and singles out those limits that prevent the achievement of rationality. The identified limits allow for a discussion of the elements that constitute an argument-oriented paradigm that expands upon the elements of rational analysis and decision-making theories.

Figure 2.2
General Methodological Framework

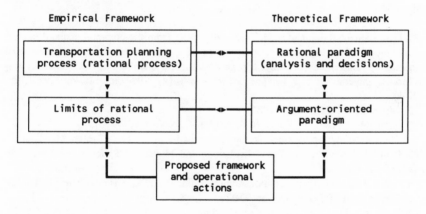

CONCLUSION

This chapter has led to the presentation of the general methodological approach taken in this book, after a brief description of the history of transportation planning, a discussion of the characteristics of the planning process, and an exposition of both the paradigm upon which the prevalent process is based on and a complementary alternative to it.

The history of transportation planning and the discussion of the characteristics of the planning process support the claim that decision makers typically choose means largely on the basis of a broader set of factors, rather than on the basis of technical and empirical considerations. The claim leads to placing the planning process within the realm of an argument-oriented paradigm, whereby the researcher can characterize the planning process with the interrelationships among the technical analysis (information), the constraints and characteristics of the decision-making function (power and politics), and the actors' personal values and beliefs. The argument-oriented paradigm provides crucial insights into the institutional and political factors that shape decisions and influence the technical process.

By designing a framework that makes planners realize the limitations of the rational paradigm, one should be able to generate more correct outcomes ("correct" in the sense described in the previous section), or at least a more responsible and reliable planning process. The purpose of this book, however, is not to abandon or substitute the prevailing rational paradigm; indeed, much of what it has contributed can well be integrated into a more encompassing paradigm. Rather, it proposes a framework that attempts to better serve the realities of the decision process with a planning process that is strengthened with elements that should encourage improved cost-estimation procedures.

NOTES

1. The sequential demand model was a departure from the common demand models consisting of a single equation. It consisted of a number of separate models used sequentially: land-use forecasting, trip generation, trip distribution, modal choice, and traffic assignment. See, for instance, Meyer and Miller (1984), or Morlok (1978), pp. 422-47.

2. Menendez (1986), Allen (1985).

3. Menendez (1986), Altshuler et al. (1979), Gakenheimer (1976).

4. The short-range operational planning was called Transportation System Management (TSM) in the United States. See Gakenheimer and Meyer (1979) for an account of its emergence.

5. The Urban Mass Transportation Administration (UMTA) was established within the U.S. Department of Transportation (DOT) in 1968.

6. See, for instance, Friend and Hickling (1988), Bryson and Roering (1987), Kaufman and Jacobs (1987), Nutt and Backoff (1987), Tomazinis (1985).

7. Menendez and Cook (1990).

8. Ryan et al. (1986).

9. This process is sometimes called "scoping." Although, in principle, it is to be accomplished at the beginning of the planning study, it usually ends up being redefined as priorities shift, interested parties are added to the process, and so on. In the scoping stage, the attempt is to define the terms of reference for the rest of the planning exercise.

10. In the United States, after the public participation process, a new document, the Final Environmental Impact Statement (FEIS), is published including those changes deemed appropriate based on the comments gathered during that participation process.

11. Meyer and Miller (1984).

12. Meyer (1978) identifies almost 40 different types of actors, at the federal, state, and local levels, involved in transportation planning and implementation in the United States (p. 19, fig. 1-1). This institutional structure, with its myriad assigned responsibilities and regulations, has created an "extremely complex environment for coordinated transportation planning" (p. 24).

13. Mahmassani (1984).

14. This aspect is of major importance in the United States, with its district-representative system and weak metropolitan institutions. Metropolitan transportation projects are more likely to cut across several municipal jurisdictions, generating competing interests that may lead to a lack of coordination. The representative system may also encourage pork barreling and weak internalization of costs (which tend to be spread over a jurisdiction larger than the represented district).

15. This premise presumes that private construction of this type of project is usually not feasible for economic, financial, or political reasons.

16. De Neufville (1987), Dalton (1986), Alexander (1984), Forester (1984), Allison (1971). De Neufville states that one of the major reasons for the pervasiveness of this paradigm is the lack of a persuasive alternative and the fact that education of planners tends to focus on the rational paradigm owing to lack of time and resources to expand the curricula to alternative approaches. In the transportation planning field, Gakenheimer (1985), Manheim (1985), Wachs (1985a), and Blanchard (1976), among others, indicate the need to broaden the research agenda in transportation beyond that of the rational paradigm.

17. Forester (1984), Howe (1980).

18. De Neufville (1987).

19. Lindblom (1959).

20. Alexander (1984).

21. Scott (1981), Allison (1971).

22. Ines (1988) labels this paradigm "social-argumentative" (p. 277).

23. Meyer and Miller (1984) follow a parallel paradigm and state that effective planning requires communication with decision makers, providing them with the information they desire and need. The argument-oriented paradigm defines planning in a broader manner as its communicative purpose involves an audience broader than that of decision makers.

24. De Neufville (1987), p. 89.

25. Some examples are Atkins (1987), Obeng (1985), Chomitz and Lave (1984), Walker et al. (1984), Caudill et al. (1983), and Merewitz (1972).

26. Atkins (1987).

27. Faludi (1987) talks about "procedural" planning.

28. Etzioni (1988) calls such an approach "codetermination" (p. 3).

29. Wachs (1985b), Kelman (1987).

30. See Hall (1980) for the history of some planning failures, in the sense of implementing courses of action that ended up generating the wrong effects and adding heavy burdens to the affected societies.

3

Case Studies

INTRODUCTION

This chapter summarizes both the information gathered from interviews held with the parties involved in the different case studies and the documentation related to those case studies. Each section highlights the main issues related to the estimation of capital and operating costs identified in each case. Chapters 3 and 4 develop these issues in greater detail and put them in the context of cost-estimating and decision-making theories.

For each case study, the presentation includes a brief description of the geographical context and an introduction to the case study; a description of the transportation and institutional contexts; a description of the project, projects, or other documentation relevant to the planning and decision-making processes for the particular transportation facility, with reference to the cost-estimation element of those processes; and comments on the case study.

The case studies involve three different U.S. cities. The history in some of these case studies spans a long period of time (almost 15 years, or even longer depending on when we consider were the first serious proposals). As a common ground for these three case studies, it is convenient to briefly describe the U.S. context as it relates to transit development.

Transit Development in the United States

In the United States, the history of transit policy and planning (as well as of transportation, in more general terms) is closely linked to changes in broader federal policy.[1] Until the 1960s, transit was perceived as a local responsibility with both capital and operating costs financed by its users. The social conflicts of the mid-1960s modified federal policy toward transit, which then was presented as an integral part of the new federal commitment to urban renewal and a more "balanced" transportation system. In 1964, direct capital grants to transit agencies were approved for the first time. Also during this time privately owned transit firms began to be transferred to public ownership. Operating costs were covered mostly out of the farebox and expansion of services was modest.[2]

By the early 1970s, attention shifted to new problems, including energy shortages, air pollution, traffic congestion, urban sprawl, and the needs of minority, elderly, and handicapped sectors of the population. The belief that transit was an effective way of serving all these objectives broadened the political appeal of transit assistance, although transit's direct constituency was relatively small. Transit was perceived as an investment that could address and satisfy many perspectives on the urban problem. This situation led to authorization in 1974 of Section 5 of the Urban Mass Transportation Act, which provided for direct payments to offset transit operating expenses.

By 1978, the federal government was funding a greater percentage of the total operating and capital subsidy than were all other government levels combined.[3] In order to gain a broad base of political support for the transit assistance program, new services were expanded and new systems were created in less densely populated areas, where transit could not easily compete with car travel. The transit assistance program became essentially redistributive in nature, with funds flowing from, and back to, local areas on the basis of politically determined criteria (focused on demographics rather than transit service supplied and consumed). These criteria encouraged expansion and the construction of less efficient new transit systems (from a cost-effectiveness standpoint). Social, environmental, and political concerns seemed to govern, rather than costs. Nonetheless, subsidies reversed the trend of ridership decline of the previous decades, although they promoted less efficiency.[4] Transit was given a whole set of social and political objectives, most of them incompatible with operating and financial efficiency.

By the end of the 1970s, there was a general frustration that transit had not been the panacea for urban problems, and had cost too much for what it had accomplished in terms of reducing pollution and congestion, conserving energy, and addressing the needs of particular sectors of the population.[5] Attention then shifted from transit's social objectives to the more pressing issue of its escalating costs. President Reagan's policy of "new federalism" emphasized fiscal prudence and accountability, local control and responsibility for expenditures, and increased involvement of the private sector. These policies were to be implemented by phasing out the federal operating assistance program and the provision of funds for new rail construction. At the end of Reagan's presidential mandate, however, the administration had not been successful in implementing these policies.

As a common institutional setting for the three U.S. cases, the Urban Mass Transportation Administration (UMTA) of the U.S. Department of Transportation plays a major role in all the matters related to urban transit projects that seek federal funds. The UMTA has the responsibility for federal funding of planning, capital acquisition, and operating costs for mass transportation in urban areas. In the projects that it funds, the UTMA establishes standards for the planning process and oversees its development. For example, it requires preparation of an Environmental Impact Statement (EIS) documenting, among other things, the possible environmental consequences that each alternative would encompass if constructed. The UMTA has regional offices to facilitate communication between the local participants and the federal office.[6]

Two major funding sources are provided at the federal level: Section 3 and Section 9 funds.[7] Section 3 are discretionary funds, which the UMTA administrator can allocate as deemed appropriate, while Section 9 funds are specified by formula. The formula includes factors such as the number of bus miles, the population of the area, and the population weighted by persons per square mile, for bus systems and revenue vehicle miles, route miles, and passenger miles for rail systems.[8] Section 3 funds and around 60 percent of Section 9 funds are used for capital investments, and the rest of Section 9 funds are for operating assistance. Most of the funds for new fixed-guideway systems come from Section 3 (discretionary) funds; rail modernization takes about half of both Section 3 and Section 9 funds combined; the rest is appropriated for bus systems (and a small amount for technical planning purposes).[9] Some matching requirements are applied to all the funds in such a way that the federal match for planning and/or capital assistance cannot exceed 80 percent of net project costs, or 50 percent in the case of operating assistance.

For the last 15 years, there has been a growing move away from allocating funds in a discretionary manner and toward a formula-based allocation. Recently, along the lines of the "fiscal federalism" philosophy, UMTA officials at the federal and regional level advocated reducing the discretionary portion of UMTA assistance, leaving most of the funding based on formula. This approach, it is argued, would decrease the uncertainty about federal funding and eliminate most of the political component of the transit funding process. The conclusions of this book will provide some indications about the appropriateness of this approach in improving the transit planning and allocation process.

THE CASE STUDIES

The Boston Case Study

The Boston case study singularly illustrates the struggle of different parties and institutions over the analysis process as its outcome is taken as the basis for decisions. The struggle forced frequent changes in some elements of the planning process such as the alternatives to be considered and the costs to include in each of them. The Boston case also illustrates the difficulties generated by the attempt to use the analysis process to satisfy the needs of different audiences as well as the difficulties generated by the uncertainty associated with some of the technical elements, particularly the amount of funding available. These difficulties forced technical analysts to "dress" the project so that compromises could be reached among the different interests involved in the planning process. Finally, because of all these factors, the case illustrates the challenges for decision makers in their efforts to put the project forward.

Boston's transit system is one of the oldest in the United States (its tunnel section is the oldest), and is fairly well developed with a transit network of buses, trolley buses, light rail, rapid rail, and commuter rail transit covering most of the metropolitan area. In the past ten years, the rail network has been in an extensive planning and construction stage as old lines have been extended (Red Line) or relocated (Orange Line), and new lines have been proposed (Old Colony Project).

The particular investigation in this case study is the Old Colony Project. This project involved analysis of the rehabilitation of commuter rail service south of Boston's central business district (CBD). Service on the commuter rail line had been abandoned in 1959, owing to disagreements over the assessment of operating subsidies and the opening of the Southeast Expressway, a major highway. (Furthermore, in 1960, a fire destroyed a bridge over the Neponset River, which had connected the rail lines to Boston's CBD, thus eliminating the physical possibility of using the rail lines for daily commuting.)

At the beginning of the 1980s, the major transportation planning organizations singled out the corridor, the southeastern portion of Massachusetts, as an area that needed urgent transportation improvements since it was the most rapidly growing in the state, with a predominant transportation demand toward the CBD of Boston (see figure 3.1). At the time the project was proposed, two major thoroughfares (the Southeast Expressway and Route 3) and a single transit subway line (Red Line from Braintree to Boston) provided the transportation links to the CBD.[10] The area was also served by express buses, a commuter boat service, and feeder buses connecting to the transit line stations and the commuter boat service.

Institutional Environment

The agency in charge of managing Boston's transit system is a state agency, the Massachusetts Bay Transportation Authority (MBTA). This agency reports to the state's Department of Transportation, and the director of this department to the governor of Massachusetts. The MBTA, in addition to operating the existing public transportation system, has the statutory responsibility for preparing the engineering and architectural designs for transit development projects and for constructing and operating them within the area constituting the authority (79 cities and towns).[11]

A variety of other state institutions are also involved in the planning, construction, and management of public transportation in the Boston area.

Figure 3.1
Boston's Old Colony Project

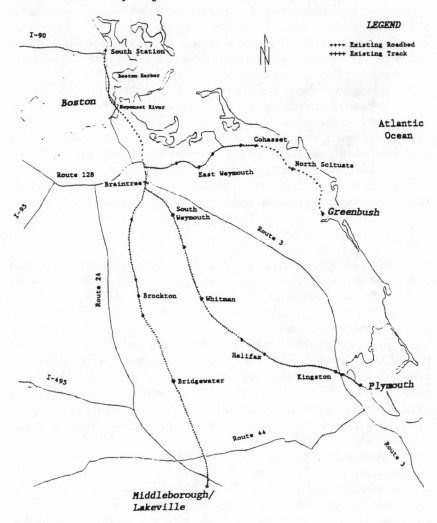

Among them, the Executive Office of Transportation and Construction (EOTC) coordinates the activities and programs of the state transportation agencies, and prepares the capital investment program of the MBTA in conjunction with other transportation programs. The Secretary for Environmental Affairs reviews and approves the programs for the construction of state transportation facilities. Another important state institution is the Massachusetts Department of Public Works (MDPW), which has the responsibility for planning, designing, constructing, and maintaining state highways and their related facilities. At the MBTA, the Advisory Board acts as the regional body in charge of reviewing and approving the MBTA's annual operating budget and mass transportation programs. The Advisory Board consists of the chief administrative officials (or their designees) from each of the 79 member municipalities.[12]

At the local level, the municipal governments have a wide range of statutory powers critical to implementation of transportation programs such as transit facilities and transportation systems management (TSM) proposals. Any state agency in charge of executing these programs must deal individually with the municipal governments. Local governments have statutory powers regarding land use and zoning, and traffic management and parking within its boundaries on roadways that are not federal, state, or county roads. In addition, local officials must initiate requests for federal urban systems projects in their municipality.

Project History

In 1984, as a response to complaints about the unbearable travel congestion in the southeast corridor, voiced by several legislators from districts in the area, the state legislature instructed the MBTA to study the feasibility of restoring commuter rail service in that corridor. The study was going to analyze the possible transportation improvements in the area including rehabilitation for commuter use of the Old Colony lines. In this report, it was stated that "[o]ther possibilities such as light rail or other transit technologies . . . exist but have not been analyzed as part of [the] feasibility assessment." [13] This initial interest in restoring service on the railroad lines gave the posterior studies a suspicious name, "Old Colony Railroad Rehabilitation Project," although, as is explained below, the alternatives also initially included a TSM alternative and a busway and, later, a TSM alternative alone.

In response to the state request, a feasibility study was prepared. It was found that restoration of the Old Colony service would be feasible (with the adequate physical improvements) at a cost of almost $200 million (in 1984 dollars) for the full-restoration alternative. Following the feasibility study, the governor instructed the MBTA to proceed with the necessary environmental studies, officially launching the Old Colony Railroad Rehabilitation Project.

Initially, the environmental studies had to comply only with state regulations (Massachusetts Environmental Policy Act of 1972), since the project was going to be funded with state money. The steps included the filing an Environmental

Notification Form, accomplished in January 1986; preparation of a project scope, issued in October 1986; and publication of the Environmental Impact Report (EIR). But as local officials approached the federal government, and the UMTA agreed to provide technical assistance and to consider possible future federal financial participation, preparation of an Environmental Impact Statement (EIS) was also required, in order to comply with the National Environmental Policy Act (NEPA) of 1972.

The feasibility study estimated commuter rail capital costs at $187.7 million, and annual operating costs between $15.7 and $16.8 million for the full-service alternative.[14] Ridership could reach 9,200 passengers per day by 1990. Local newspapers publicized these figures, which became widespread in spite of the fact that the feasibility study explicitly indicated the shortcomings of the cost figure and the elements that were missing (such as land acquisition costs, and provisions for design, administration, and contingency). The figure however was low enough *to give the project a head start* and push it into the next stage, the process of analyzing alternatives.

By 1985, there were high hopes of returning passenger rail service on the Old Colony lines. For instance, in May 1985, a referendum held in the town of Weymouth indicated that 77 percent of the 10,000 people who voted favored restoration of the commuter rail service, although 53 percent disapproved of using local tax dollars to cover operating costs. With this overwhelming support, by the end of the year the state was hoping to get 80 percent of the estimated costs from the federal government and start track work for the project by 1987.[15] The UMTA, however, was not very receptive because it considered the project a major new capital investment, not a simple rehabilitation undertaking.

Before the formal technical process of analysis of alternatives was initiated, a scoping report was published in September 1986 indicating the range of site-specific and regional-level impacts that would need to be considered in the analysis process. The Secretary of Environmental Affairs had designated the project a "Major and Complicated Project" and appointed an independent body including a wide variety of perspectives and personal and professional interests, the Citizens Advisory Committee (CAC), to review and comment on the technical studies. The CAC basically agreed with the scoping report and emphasized that "safety and security," "traffic and parking," "noise and vibration," "air quality," "land use and zoning," "community disruption," and "consistency with local plans" were the impact categories that would require particularly detailed analysis in the technical process.[16]

At this initial stage of the process, most efforts of the project managers were geared toward keeping the alternatives within the technical limits dictated by federal funding criteria (and, of course, those of the operating agency, the MBTA). For instance, the relocation of the Greenbush line (with monorail technology, as another alternative) on the median strip of a major route in the area—Route 3—was rejected because it would make the project a "new start," a qualification that, in federal terms, meant fewer funds available, stronger competition from other cities in the country, and a lengthier process for approval from the federal government. Federal funds, it was said, would cover only reactivation of *existing* rail lines.[17] In addition, the MDPW opposed that alternative on the basis of technical feasibility.

The Route 3 alignment was not the only concern that surfaced in various community meetings. Other dissenting voices were raised in those communities, particularly near the center of the city, through which the trains would pass without making stops. In addition, the proximity of the tracks to some residential areas and particular types of buildings (e.g., schools) started generating fears of neighborhood disruption and destruction.

By the end of April 1987, the price tag for the project had risen to $387 million. As costs increased,[18] the federal government showed less support for the project, and opposition became more vociferous in some sections affected by the proposed lines. The secretary of the EOTC and the MBTA indicated that the project would be phased, starting with the less controversial lines with service only to Braintree station (the terminal station on the Red line of the subway system), not to South Station (the initially planned terminal in the Boston central business district).

In spite of the fact that the phasing plan also tried to reflect a $50 million annual spending cap—the amount the federal government usually allows states to withdraw from all federal transportation funds per year—the changes angered local legislators and supporters of the restoration, for they thought that the state was retreating from its promise of rehabilitating the whole rail system. They demanded a strong commitment from the state to prove that the full system would eventually be put in operation. That came in the form of a request for funds from the governor of Massachusetts. On May 19, 1987, the governor reiterated his firm commitment to the full restoration and requested $195 million from the state legislature over the next two years for commuter rail service serving 34 cities and towns south of Boston (with a total population of around 600,000 persons in 1980).[19]

At that moment, the estimates indicated that the system would carry up to 15,000 passengers a day when opened in 1993. The $195 million, if approved by the legislature, would cover 50 percent of the capital costs for restoration of full service. The estimates were based on calculations made in the Environmental Impact Report (to comply with State regulations). The more detailed calculation of capital and operating costs required by the federal process would not be completed until December 1987 (later revised in July 1988).

The reason for a 50 percent share was based on the UMTA suggestion that with this share (instead of the statutory 20%) the project will have a better chance of getting federal support (and would probably involve fewer hurdles). A new head of the UMTA in November 1987 challenged the federal support for the project, and eliminated the guarantee of the $195 million federal share. The impasse lasted four months, until March 1988, when new talks between the UMTA and the MBTA officials put the possibility of a 50 percent federal share back in place. The explanation given by MBTA officials was that there existed a misunderstanding between the UMTA and the MBTA as to which type of project they were dealing with: "new start" or "rail modernization." Almost two years after the MBTA had taken precautions to persuade interested parties to stay within the limits imposed by the existing rail network, the UMTA raised the issue again, slowing progress on the project.

The technical analysis included, in addition to the commuter rail alternatives, three other alternatives: a no-build, a TSM, and, by recommendation of MDPW, a busway. The state process required study of the largest and most complicated alternative for its Environmental Impact Report. The UMTA, however, also required analysis of suboptions for the possible total system with enough differences to be able to compare the worthiness of the full system. In the case of the Old Colony project, the suboptions consisted of reconstructing: (1) the innermost line alone (the Middleborough line), (2) this line with the middle line alone (the Middleborough and the Plymouth line), and (3) the innermost line and the shore line (the Middleborough and the Greenbush line). For the correct operation of each of the seven alternatives, two or more modes of transportation were included, such as improvements in the existing bus system and rapid transit Red line, or additional feeder bus lines and commuter boat service.

The different components of the study, from demand estimation, to the calculation of capital and operating costs, to the assessment of environmental impacts, were assigned to different consultant firms in the Boston area. The costing model for both capital and operating costs was based on the principles of ground-up costing, in accordance with UTMA guidelines (see Chapter 4 for a more detailed description of costing approaches). Table 3.1 shows the cost figures generated in December 1987. Capital costs included a lower and an upper bound, and a best estimate (the middle value shown in the table), which tried to reflect the uncertainty of some cost figures. However, the values were calculated based on differences in assumptions about particular items. For instance, the busway variations responded to assumptions about lighting on the busway (the lower bound assumed no lighting; the best estimate, lighting every 200 feet; and the upper bound, lighting every 100 feet) or about the trackwork in the commuter rail alternatives (the lower bound assumed only replacement of existing defective ties; the best estimate, all new wood ties with resilient fastenings; and the upper bound, concrete ties with resilient fastenings). These limited assumptions yielded lower values less than 6 percent lower than the best estimate and upper values less than 0.6 percent higher than the best estimate.[20]

Eight months later, after the confidence of the UMTA had been regained, new figures were generated. At that moment, the busway alternative was rejected on the basis of two major considerations. The operational considerations were that the lower capacity of buses would require an almost constant stream of buses to run during peak hours, interfering with local traffic at grade intersections. In addition, the busway would be too narrow to permit overpassing in the case of breakdowns, and would eliminate the present freight operations.

Table 3.1
1987 Capital and Operating Costs for the Boston Alternatives
(1986 dollars)

Alternative	Annual Oper. & Maint. Costs	Capital Costs (middle values)
No build	$12,926,801	$0
TSM	18,308,663	31,949,640
Busway	18,408,629	102,580,669
Commuter rail		
Middleborough	22,633,791	189,979,064
Midd./Plymouth	26,492,298	282,415,561
Midd./Greenbush	25,108,638	262,353,966
Midd./Ply./Green.	28,957,473	360,975,566

Source: Massachusetts Bay Transportation Authority (1987a and 1987b).

The institutional considerations were that a busway would be incompatible with the objective of modernizing the regional rail network, isolating the Old Colony area from the remainder of the MBTA's extensive rail network. The rest of the capital cost figures were decreased by $1.3 for the last two alternatives (of the list in Table 3.1) and by $1.6 million for the other three —while the annual operating and maintenance costs were reduced by $2 million for the no-build and the last two alternatives and $3.6 million for the other three—owing to elimination of improvements in the commuter boat service component of each alternative (as those improvements affected all the alternatives in a similar way).

As of 1990, the Boston case was ongoing. State and local officials kept working on all fronts to secure approval of federal funding for the full project. Conversations with these officials indicate that they were mostly interested in getting the project moved ahead. These officials stressed the need for the project and praised its advantages, but they were not aware of the technical results (at most they were familiar with overall figures). They further stated that, nevertheless, the study was necessary to validate their predefined preferences and comply with federal regulations.

Comments on the Boston Case

The Boston case, as the rehabilitation or extension of an existing system, highlights some particular characteristics of the transportation planning process. When one is dealing with extension of existing (well-established) transit systems, the constraints on the technologies to be considered are stronger than in other cases. In Boston, alternatives different from the commuter-rail ones never attracted major interest from decision makers. This indifference was reflected in the alternatives under study, and can be attributed mainly to the fact that facilities such as maintenance shops and terminals were already in place to accommodate any additions to the commuter rail network. Furthermore, labor groups in the transit agency would probably have complained if a novel technology had been introduced.

Notwithstanding, the study process could be assessed as more straightforward than in instances of new systems, since information could be gathered from other parts of the existing system. On the other hand, owing to new federal requirements, the analytical study had to be carried out to a more detailed level than in other instances, making the whole technical process a difficult endeavor. Since demand was to a great extent already known from existing commuter rail lines, cost estimation became one of the most important and time-consuming elements of the planning process.

Shifts in the federal stance toward the project further affected development of the technical process. First, the definition of the project—as a "rail modernization" project—limited the range of alternatives to be analyzed. Second, increases in capital costs made the UMTA suggest that the statutory 80 percent federal share would not be easily attainable for the Old Colony Project. Both factors added to the uncertainty as to which level of funds could be obtained from the federal government, and put the MBTA in the position of trying to keep costs as low as possible (and perhaps be as optimistic as possible in estimating ridership).

The decision makers' need to attend to two different audiences further affected the technical process. The major difference between the two audiences was emphasis: the state process was concerned primarily with assessing (and addressing) the full range of environmental impacts and insisted that alternatives (or components of alternatives) be examined whenever they met objectives with less serious environmental consequences; the federal process focused on cost and financing issues and insisted on examination of alternatives that met the basic objectives at less (financial) cost. Therefore, the former process allowed cost increases to meet environmental concerns while the latter tried to encourage limits on capital and operating costs. The clash over criteria upon which to evaluate the projects is also reflected in the differences between what the CAC as representative of community interests deemed the appropriate evaluating categories and, again, UMTA's emphasis on cost measures.

The Old Colony study stressed the lack of transportation capacity to serve downtown Boston from the Old Colony area (in terms not only of highway capacity but also of downtown parking spaces) in the light of urban developments taking place in the corridor (including reconstruction of a major highway—the Central Artery—underground). These concerns, even if not explicitly indicated in the technical report, broadened the constituency affected by the project. On the other hand, the perception of the goals was not always the same across different groups, such as across some communities at the local level (e.g., Quincy, Braintree, Weymouth).

The extent of the project—a rail network of 80 miles of double and single track—increased the number of concerns to be addressed. Station locations and parking lots, for instance, were a constant source of complaints from the affected communities. As a matter of fact, in November 1988, when the DEIS was almost completed, the locations of some stations (e.g., South Weymouth on the Plymouth line) were still undecided.[21] This added to the uncertainty of cost elements and of operating strategies because of constraints generated by the predominantly single-track sections of the system (particularly in the segment closer to the CBD terminal). Nonetheless, supporters of the restoration, probably aware of the effects that community concerns might have on the technical process, indicated that although transportation decision makers (including the governor) could have a difficult task persuading local residents of the advantages of the project, they should also make certain that they do not scale down the plans to meet local concerns.

As to the technical process itself, the slight variations between the lower or upper values and the best estimates indicate that no attempt was made to reflect the uncertainty of cost estimates. The many other documents that had to be generated in order to comply with state and federal requirements (ten volumes, two of which referred specifically to capital and operating costs) and how cost information was organized did not encourage a full sensitivity analysis.

Rather than costs, two other major (and time-consuming) concerns absorbed analysts and decision makers. The first was the relationship with the communities in the corridor so that they could know exactly how the project would affect them and could voice their concerns.[22] These meetings were also a good opportunity for the MBTA to gain support for its proposals. The second major concern involved the cost-effectiveness criterion required by UMTA regulations (this process is explained at greater length in Chapter 4). This criterion had not been publicized by the time capital and operating costs were calculated, but the quietness of the analysts when asked about the criterion [23] leads to the presumption that the project did not fare very well on that regard.[24] This apparent shortcoming of the project probably forced decision makers to increase negotiations with the federal government to reduce the possibility of rejecting the project on that basis, trying to relegate the cost-effectiveness evaluation to a second stage.

The Boston project has not been constructed yet. Its history, however, indicates many of the issues involved in the cost-estimation process and mainly the pressures exerted by different parties and institutions on the technical process in an attempt to reflect their ideas about the purpose and worthiness of the transit project. The next two cases, Santa Clara County's LRT and Buffalo's LRRT, illustrate some similar issues and some other issues from the perspective of two fixed-guideway systems constructed in cities with no previous rail systems in place.

Santa Clara County's LRT

The case of Santa Clara County illustrates the situation in a fast-growing area with conditions unfavorable to a fixed-guideway transit system (e.g., low-density developments or high-income population) but plagued with traffic congestion that ultimately could thwart growth and development in the area. This fear created the belief that it was necessary to avoid the experiences of other cities in the same part of the country (mainly Los Angeles), and try to redirect the land-use patterns in the area. Strong advocates for a fixed-guideway system (basically, a light rail option) at the decision-making level very much determined the survival of the project until its implementation, in spite of the many setbacks that appeared throughout the process.

Unlike the Boston case, Santa Clara County is predominantly a suburban area, with low density and a transit system—a 470-bus fleet operating on 79 routes and limited commuter rail service on the peninsula to San Francisco—that has only lately received some consideration. The county is home to the world's innovative high-tech industry (known as the Silicon Valley), and includes the cities of San Jose and Santa Clara. Growth in the electronics industry here for the past 15 years has been accompanied by similar growth in the population and residential development in the county. This growth has led to high levels of congestion, aggravated by the suburban character of the area.

In 1975, the county's employment base of 502,000 jobs was growing at a higher percentage rate than its population of 1.1 million persons and its resident labor force of 490,000 workers. Countywide, more than 4 million person-trips were being generated daily, only 1 percent of which were on public transit. The region known as the Guadalupe corridor—for it goes parallel to the Guadalupe River—encompasses an area approximately 16 miles long and five miles wide. In the 15 years from 1975 to 1990, the corridor was expected to grow from 360,000 to 420,000 people and from 187,000 (.519 jobs per person) to 383,000 (.912 jobs per person) of jobs. This growth was to generate 50 percent more trips than the 1.2 million trips generated in the corridor in 1975.[25]

The locational imbalance of jobs and housing and, consequently, the predominant southeast-to-northwest travel pattern (from South San Jose to North San Jose and Palo Alto) created delays on the major roads during peak hours. Congestion was exacerbated by continual development in the semiconductor industry during the mid-1970s. In addition, state freeway projects slated for construction by 1970 had not been completed—though the right-of-way had been purchased—aggravating congestion on major highways and arterials, with traffic spilling over onto local streets, increasing intrusion into and disruption of residential neighborhoods. By the end of the 1970s, with growing congestion and climbing gasoline prices, ridership in the bus system almost doubled between 1978 and 1981.[26]

Concerns, however, were broader than for the mere traffic congestion. A 1976 report, the "Santa Clara County Transit District Light Rail Feasibility and

Alternatives Analysis," quoted the then-UMTA Administrator Robert Patricelli, stating that "rapid transit is part of becoming and being a great city." The study concluded that

> Santa Clara County is essentially facing the choice of a future similar to that which exists today in Los Angeles . . . or one which provides the option for some of its urban area—by no means all—to accommodate itself to transportation and urban development characteristics associated with one or more rail lines. . . . In the final analysis, however, the choice is dependent not on technical information alone, but on the unique and special way the County perceives itself and the future toward which it wishes to move.[27]

Other concerns included the perception that residential growth could only occur if the additional transportation capacity were provided. San Jose's plans for some additional 50,000 new dwelling units by 1990 in the south of the city could only be carried out if new transportation facilities were constructed.[28] Furthermore, a rail-based transit system would help encourage growth in the downtown area where revitalization was very much needed. Overall, these concerns amounted to an attempt to not constrain further growth in the area. If transportation improvements were not made, the region would be unable to support the inevitable growth.

Other concerned parties stressed the role of transit projects in developing a diversified transportation system that would prevent any problems in case of oil shortages, and at the same time would meet the travel needs of different segments of the population and of different urban communities. But at the forefront of desires for a major transportation improvement, public officials underscored the attempt to guide land use development and encourage denser development patterns in the process of directing the inevitably expected growth.[29] At some point the proponents of the system said that the preferred transportation system (mainly a light rail line and improvements in highways) could make the Silicon Valley the "Paris of the West Coast." "It will determine more than any other action whether we will be a great community in the 21st century in that it establishes the mode of interurban transportation for the next 100 years."[30] Later, they also indicated that the "[federal] administration realizes that the Guadalupe Corridor project not only is a relatively low cost project, but that it offers a unique opportunity to directly benefit the growing defense, aerospace and electronics industries which are some of the few bright spots in the U.S. economy."[31]

All these concerns fed the perception of a need to develop transportation facilities in the Guadalupe corridor. Development of the transportation system had lagged sharply behind private residential and employment development, and some studies had to be undertaken to provide the evaluation necessary to give local decision makers the required information for choosing the adequate transportation mode to address the travel needs of the corridor.

Institutional Environment

The Santa Clara County Transportation District (SCCTD), the agency that led the project throughout the planning process, acts as the transportation authority in Santa Clara County, with responsibility for planning and operating transit services in the county. The cities of San Jose and Santa Clara, which the corridor of analysis traverses, are responsible for supervising transportation infrastructure investments within their boundaries. The scope of the project, affecting two municipalities, required involvement of several other coordinating agencies. Among these, the Association of Bay Area Governments (ABAG) had responsibility for coordinating planning development efforts in the San Francisco Bay area and was in charge of making predictions about population and employment changes in such area. The Metropolitan Transportation Commission (MTC) was responsible for overseeing performance audits,[32] and for helping allocate state monies and coordinate transit services, fares, and operations among the different transit agencies operating in the area. At the state level, the California Department of Transportation (Caltrans) also had a stake in the process as soon as the SCCTD had sought funds from the state government. The support of Caltrans was also necessary for requesting funds from the federal government.

All those institutions coalesced into a decision-making body labeled the "Board of Control." The Board of Control for the Guadalupe corridor transportation project included elected and appointed officials from the Santa Clara County Transit District, the city of San Jose, the city of Santa Clara, the Association of Bay Area Governments, the Metropolitan Transportation Commission, and Caltrans. The Board of Control provided policy direction in the process of analyzing alternatives, coordinating with local government bodies affected by the project, and helping administer the overall planning analysis.

In addition, to effectively coordinate the views of all government agencies involved in the Guadalupe corridor study, and to assist the Board of Control, a technical advisory committee was established at an early stage, in 1979. This committee, composed of representatives from the UMTA, the Federal Highway Administration, Caltrans, the Metropolitan Transportation Commission, the cities of San Jose and Santa Clara, and the SCCTD,[33] met on a monthly basis and reviewed the technical data submitted by consultants and participating agencies.

Probably one of the most significant differences in California's transit environment compared to the other case studies in this book is the financial and institutional support provided by the state legislature. The institutional climate is often not very receptive to transit investments. Although several measures had been put in place to ensure a relatively stable base of support for all local transit systems, the number of projects implemented have been few and far between, and supported by a very small number of legislators. The achievements here are mainly a reflection of the vigorous advocacy played by key legislators. Transit must compete for funds with other state programs, and most of transit funds, unlike state highway funds, are not constitutionally dedicated.[34] This situation has created a piecemeal process whereby legislative involvement has come in increments rather than through a prolonged, comprehensive action. Interestingly enough, the legislature has established some performance and productivity measures to assure that transit funds are spent in an efficient manner. For instance, local support in the form of local matching funds, minimum farebox revenues, or contributions from property taxes and bridge tolls is required. These local efforts are necessary as proof of local interest and commitment, and to limit the state's costs.

Project History

The history of the Santa Clara County (Guadalupe corridor) Light Rail System spans more that 15 years. The initial proposals for specific transportation solutions date back to 1974, when consultants to Santa Clara County began a study of the county's transportation needs with the year 2000 as the horizon.[35] This preliminary study recommended a medium-capacity transit guideway network—consisting of 140 miles of track—fed by an extensive bus collection system.

The County Transit District contracted another study in December 1975 to investigate the feasibility of a light rail or bus transit alternative in five of the highest demand corridors identified in the first study. In this study, the Guadalupe corridor was singled out as the most feasible route with the greatest potential for high ridership.[36] This study, published in August 1976, indicated that "none of the alternatives studied except for the baseline bus [would satisfy] the given constraints on capital and operating costs." Nonetheless, a light rail system was the only mode that would be capable of attracting 15 percent of the 1990 peak-hour travel—the goal of San Jose's 1980 General Plan. A starter line would cost $113 million in 1976 dollars for a total length of 12.5 miles.

The study concluded with some actions to seek early UMTA approval. Taking into account the then-recent rejection of the Denver region's request for an LRT starter line after completing studies worth millions of dollars, and the approval of the Buffalo's LRT line based on "population density, size of the downtown CBD employment, ease of automobile access, expected number of daily riders in the short-range, and the total annualized costs per passenger carried (cost-effectiveness),"[37] the study recommended that the UMTA waters be tested to avoid "the wasting of scarce funds on pointless additional studies and/or help focus the County's efforts most productively."[38]

In 1975, the Santa Clara Valley Corridor Evaluation (SCVCE) was started. By its completion in 1979, after over 200 public meetings and workshops to solicit comments,[39] the study concluded that transit could carry up to 12 percent of the work trips during peak travel periods, and that none of the transit options would recover more than 31 percent from the farebox. The study also indicated that current transit funding would allow for an approximately 700-bus system plus about ten miles of rail transit on the southern section of San Jose and an upgrade of the commuter rail system (the Southern Pacific line).

Even before completion of the draft report, the consultants' preliminary recommendations advocated construction of light rail transit (LRT) as the mode to link downtown San Jose with the southern residential areas. The predilections for an LRT system were attuned to the preferences (for a rail system) strongly voiced, from the beginning of the proposals, by some local elected officials. In 1976, the Board of Supervisors of the SCCTD was vested with decision-making powers regarding transit proposals. In addition, voters approved a one-half cent sales tax to finance the SCCTD.

The SCVCE considered nine transportation alternatives and several land-use scenarios for Santa Clara county in 1990. The report stated that the Guadalupe corridor had long been master-planned for major freeways (state Routes 85 and 87) that had never been built and that the right-of-way was then over 70 percent in public ownership. For these reasons, in the SCVCE Draft Report that was released in 1978, the consultants concluded that alternatives along the Guadalupe corridor deserved the largest consideration. The reserved right-of-way was a good advantage for a fixed-guideway system, and particularly for their recommended ten-mile light rail starter line between San Jose and the southern areas. They further recommended acquisition of the remaining right-of-way property and construction of a four-lane freeway—between I-280 and Curtner Avenue—within that right-of-way (see Figure 3.2).

Regional and local governments approved the conclusions but indicated that areas north of San Jose should also be included in the rail-line plans. Subsequent to completion of the SCVCE, in 1979, the UMTA approved plans totaling $650,000 to conduct the alternatives-analysis process to evaluate transportation alternatives in the entire corridor and the production of an environmental impact statement.[40]

In August 1981 the Alternatives Analysis was published and circulated for comments. The UMTA indicated that at the moment federal policy (Reagan had started his first presidential term eight months earlier) was to defer any new rail start, so Santa Clara County should not expect federal involvement in the project.[41] The Alternatives Analysis report stressed the importance of the area (the Silicon Valley) to the rest of the nation. The report stated that the fact that the county was the center of the U.S. electronics industry could not be overlooked. It also indicated that competition from other countries could be counteracted by providing the necessary transportation capacity to the county, which would allow an increase in the number of housing units at affordable prices.

The 1981 Alternatives Analysis and draft environmental impact statement documented the environmental impacts of 14 alternatives for transportation improvements in the Guadalupe corridor. It also documented the anticipated

Figure 3.2
Santa Clara County LRT

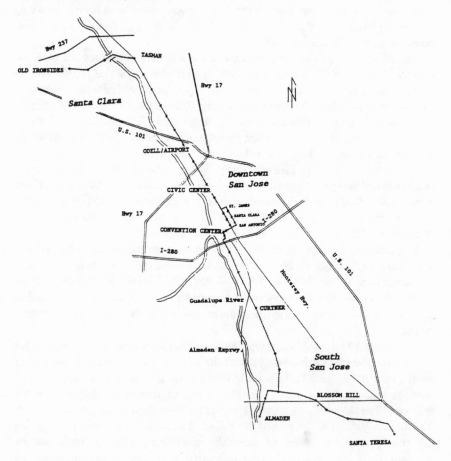

costs, impacts, and benefits of those alternatives in order to facilitate informed decision making regarding implementation of a transportation facility within the Guadalupe corridor. The statement had been prepared in accordance with both the provisions of the Council on Environmental Quality in California and the UMTA regulations.

The alternatives included: (1) no-build, (2) baseline TSM (including some highway construction), (3) busway and high-occupancy-vehicle (HOV) lanes, (4) only-LRT (including TSM improvements), (5) busway and freeway, (6) busway and expressway, (7) LRT and expressway, and (8) four alternatives related to the expansion of the commuter rail service.[42] Alternatives (2), (3), and (4) had parallel alternatives with no highway construction. Alternatives (2) to (7) also included a bicycle facility for the full length of the corridor.[43] The 14 alternatives were quickly reduced to 3, as discussions focused on alternatives (3), (4), and the locally preferred (7).

The light rail options consisted of 20 miles of new double-track line. LRT operation would require 50 vehicles, and daily mileage would amount to 9,091 miles. Table 3.2 shows the estimated capital and operating costs for the three most controversial alternatives as well as the daily patronage forecasted for all transit modes—express buses, light rail, and commuter rail—in the corridor.

In order to achieve a consensus, the board of control adopted a public participation strategy in an attempt to encourage expression of a wide variety of opinions; allow maximum dialogue among technical staff, consultants, and the general public; and permit maximum opportunity for public review of technical materials.[44] The strategy proved successful in supporting the board's preferences, and in November 1981, SCCTD and the cities of San Jose and Santa Clara selected alternative 7, the light-rail, expressway, bikeway alternative as the locally preferred alternative.[45] The SCCTD promptly applied for Section 3 federal funds to proceed with the preliminary engineering of the light rail line. The Santa Clara County Transportation Commission endorsed, by a majority vote (15 to 6), the technical recommendation and urged the approval by the Guadalupe Corridor Transportation Board of Control. The board also approved the Technical Advisory Committee's recommendation by majority vote (6 in favor, 1 against, and 1 absent).

Upon sending the report of the locally preferred alternative, the chairman of the SCCTD Board of Supervisors stated that this was a land-use and "quality of life" decision. Other reasons for the support included: (1) that if by 1990, there was a justification for expansion of the transit system, LRT would be less expensive to expand; and (2) that if there is a sudden crisis—such as an oil shortage or a strike—which required additional transit capacity, LRT would be less vulnerable and would offer the best opportunity for tackling the problem.[46] A local newspaper stated that "some form of a light-transit system would be safer, less polluting, faster and cheaper than any other solution including another highway or a special roadway for exclusive use by buses and carpools."[47] Farebox revenues were expected to cover 85 percent of operating and

Table 3.2
Capital and Operating Costs and Daily Patronage
for Selected Santa Clara County Alternatives
(Cost figures in 1980 dollars)

Alternative	Daily Patronage (all transit)	1990 Oper. & Maint. Costs ($ thousands)	Capital Costs ($ thousands)
Busway/HOV lanes	41,800	$96,400	$121,800
LRT only	44,800	93,500	208,000
LRT/Expressway	43,600	93,400	268,100

Source: U.S. Department of Transportation (1981).

maintenance costs, compared to 57 percent for buses. The 1981 report on the preferred alternative further stated that although expressway alternatives would have a reasonable chance of being funded, there would not be sufficient local, state, and federal money available to fund the large capital costs of the highway portion of a freeway-busway alternative.[48]

At that moment, the California Department of Transportation (Caltrans) supported the LRT-only alternative, and threatened to not provide the almost $1 million of state money needed for the corridor study for the LRT-expressway alternative.[49] The Caltrans staff was not convinced that light rail patronage would be about the same with or without the competing highway link. These events were denounced by the San Jose City Council as an usurpation of local authority. Eventually, other state agencies—the Business, Transportation and Housing Agency, and the California Transportation Commission—persuaded Caltrans to reverse its earlier position and deliver the study money. Still, among the general public, the proponents had their share of critics. Some people wanted a busway facility that could be upgraded to LRT when patronage warranted it; others expressed concern that funding for the LRT could be cut off by the federal government at any time; others indicated that a busway-HOV would maximize independence from bureaucracy and annual labor disputes because it would easily permit privatization.

In March 1982, the UMTA responded to the preferred-alternative report and the SCCTD request with a technical assessment of the alternative transportation investments. In this report, the UMTA indicated that land-use patterns in Santa Clara County did not support a rail alternative mainly because ridership, a major consideration for successful implementation of a light rail system, would probably be limited by "difficulties in access to the system and the lower than average potential for direct service" (i.e., passengers would need to take a bus to a station, then ride the LRT, and then again take another bus from the LRT station closest to their destination). The UMTA further indicated that the four basic arguments in support of light rail did not have a strong footing. For instance, the busway-HOV facility was put at a disadvantage by not considering the flexibility of this facility as a means of accommodating increased demand for transit. In addition, the UMTA indicated that although light rail would reduce subsidy requirements by about 5 percent, capital costs made light rail the least feasible alternative. Furthermore, in terms of cost per added transit-HOV user, the busway alternative would be more cost-effective than the light-rail alternative.[50] The interpretation of the economic efficiency data could lead to the inference that either the busway option was 43 percent more cost-effective in shifting auto users into transit and HOVs, or that the investment required for the light-rail proposal beyond that required for the busway actually decreased the economic benefits. The report concluded that the busway-HOV would be more consistent with local land-use patterns because it would remove the need for many transfer trips.

By January 1983, an impasse had developed, and the federal UMTA administrator indicated the resistance of the county in looking at buses and carpools as an alternative.[51] Later that year, in March, the SCCTD agreed to expand the analysis of the busway option. This more detailed analysis was finished in April. In June, a Santa Clara delegation presented the final EIS to high-level DOT and UMTA staff, and requested additional grants to carry out the final design of the selected alternative. Nonetheless, in July 1983, the regional UMTA administrator recommended to SCCTD that the busway-HOV alternative be withdrawn from the Final Environmental Impact Statement (FEIS) because of concerns about how its cost-effectiveness had been calculated in comparison to the rail alternative.

On August 19, 1983, the FEIS was published, including public comments on the DEIS and responses to significant environmental issues. Previous to this, the House of Representatives, through its appropriation committee, recommended to the UMTA approval of construction of the entire 20-mile Guadalupe corridor light-rail project and issuance of the necessary paperwork for Section 3 discretionary funds.

In September, the SCCTD responded to the questions raised about the cost-effectiveness of the busway alternative but did not delete this alternative from the FEIS that had been approved by the UMTA and the Federal Highway Administration (FHWA). The regional administrator, however, indicated that no funding contract would be signed until the cost-effectiveness issue was resolved. Congressional pressures on the UMTA, however, made the federal office encourage the regional office not to delay approval of the project, mainly because, in spite of everything, the LRT alternative was still a cost-effective and environmentally preferable choice. The regional office then proceeded to approve funding for right-of-way acquisition only.

Complaints by opponents of the alternative selected (that is, the LRT-expressway alternative)—such as the bias against the busway alternative and the lack of overall consideration of the effects of the LRT proposal—were abundant at this time. Nevertheless, the UMTA and the FHWA announced the decision to provide financial assistance for construction of the Guadalupe corridor project as a response to a congressional mandate. The UMTA justified the decision by indicating that the LRT offered the opportunity for private-sector participation, minority business enterprise contracting opportunities, and higher than required local matching commitment.

The full funding contract between the SCCTD and UMTA was signed on June 22, 1984. The total cost at that moment was estimated at $411 million, of which $39 million was for the budget related to the transit mall. Out of the $411 million, 36.67 percent would be covered by local funds, and 63.33 percent would be covered by the federal government (subject to availability of funds from Congress).[52] Those amounts were in current values assuming construction would be ended in 1987 and with an inflation ("escalation," according to the report) rate of 7.5 percent beginning in March 1984. Any additions or changes to the system that would increase costs would need to be covered with local funds, except in cases of extraordinary costs—namely, inflation beyond the expected rate, acts of God, eminent domain cases, costs directly caused by federal legislation, and those caused by unavailability of funds from Congress.

The SCCTD agreed to secure and provide (without further federal assistance) whatever additional resources were necessary to pay for extra amounts not covered as extraordinary and complete the project. The full funding contract also included the condition that the SCCTD not request federal operating assistance in excess of the smaller amount between either the one specified by Section 9 or the one set forth by the SCCTD in its five-year plan of March 22, 1983. Anything in excess of this would be funded from state and local sources. In its appendices, the contract specified which items of the project would be covered by local or federal sources (e.g., 45 articulated light-rail vehicles, not including spare parts, tools, training, or technical support, was stated as local activity). In another appendix, the contract with the state indicated that no more funds could be requested from state sources than those specified in 1983 ($60 million).

A few weeks after the UMTA decided to provide the funds, a group labeled "People for Efficient Transportation" filed a suit in U.S. District Court for the Northern District of California. This group alleged that there was a lack of adequate consideration of modal alternatives, among them the busway alternative, that they believed were environmentally preferable and more cost-effective than the LRT alternative. They requested an injunction against any construction or expenditures for the Guadalupe corridor transportation facility. The effect of this lawsuit was a delay in the development of the project for almost 24 months. The first ten miles of the LRT system were opened for revenue operation in May 1988.[53]

Table 3.3 shows the changes in the estimates of capital and operating costs from the 1976 study to the initial construction of the system.[54] Several reasons can be pinpointed for cost increases since the signing of the full funding contract (Table 3.4 provides a summary of them):

- Locally funded project enhancements. After the full funding contract was signed in 1984, a number of local initiatives were studied to improve the basic LRT system (e.g., transit mall extension, automatic train protection in the South Line), and other locally funded projects were mandated by the California Public Utilities Commission (such an underpass at a railroad crossing on North First Street[55]).
- Preliminary estimates. At the time of the full funding contract, estimates were based on preliminary design concepts and, as such, swings of 30 percent were anticipated; some estimates such as the vehicle costs proved very accurate, while other such as professional services were too low.
- Environmental delays. A lawsuit concerning grade separation in the South Line delayed the award of the contract to the lowest bidder; a Supplemental Environmental Impact Report (SEIR), which evaluated ten design alternatives, required a lengthy process; also the Transit District decided to delay the Final SEIR until other risks related to asbestos were studied in more detail; these events, added to the lawsuit of the group People for Efficient Transportation, delayed the beginning of the construction 24 months.
- Measure A impacts. This measure involved an increase by one-half cent in the sales tax to fund improvements in local routes, and particularly on the expressway in whose median the LRT was going to be located; after this measure was passed, LRT stations and park and ride access had to be upgraded and therefore made more complex and expensive.
- Utility escrow for private utility relocations. At the time of the full funding contract, it was assumed that private utilities would pay for any relocation of their facilities in the public right-of-way; a utility escrow was set aside, pending the final ruling of the court.
- Transit mall. Design services and construction change orders increased the cost of the transit mall by $5 million.

Administrative costs, for the final figures, were around 30 percent of the total costs, well above the usual 10 percent. SCCTD officials were not sure why that was the case, but a possible explanation was related to the many times the system had to be redesigned because of citizen opposition or lawsuits, and hence consultant fees and other administrative tasks increased substantially.

Any enhancements to the system had to be paid out of local funds since, under UMTA's mandate and the full funding contract, the original scope and budget had to be kept intact.[56] The full funding contract was signed by the UMTA after the corresponding appropriation was made by the U.S. Congress. Therefore, at the end, funds were earmarked and mandated by the U.S. Congress, not actually approved by the UMTA as a result of the process of analysis of alternatives.

Local public officials underscored the inappropriateness of the federal planning process and the annoyance that it causes in the local decision-making process, since it cannot address the needs and particularities of different local constituencies. The technical studies are necessary, they stated, but there are other issues that can easily override any conclusions from those studies. This apparent disdain at the local level for the technical components of the project

Table 3.3
Comparison of Capital Cost Estimates for Santa Clara Light Rail

Study/Year	Proposed System	Current Cap. Cost Estimate ($ millions)	Constant 1976 Cap. Cost Estimate ($ millions)
Santa Clara County Transit District Light Rail Feasibility and Alternatives Analysis (1976)	34.08-mile LRT	$268	$268
	12.25-mile LRT	113	113
Alternatives Analysis/UMTA Grant Application (1981)	20-mile LRT	180	132
Preferred Alternative Report (1981)	20-mile LRT	187	137
Guadalupe Corridor Briefing Booklet (1983)	20-mile LRT	320	179
Full Funding Contract (1984)	20-mile LRT	372	219*
	w/transit mall	411	242*
Forecast Update/Cost to Complete Estimate (1988)	20-mile LRT w/transit mall	559	305*

Sources: Santa Clara County Transit District, 198?; *Engineering News Record* (building cost index), various issues; and own calculations.
* Approximated values whereby costs have been discounted from the year 1987, as the approximate middle year of construction.

produced tensions with the federal regional office and delayed initiation of the project and prevented its approval through the formal federal procedures.

Comments on the Santa Clara Case

Public opinion indicated that highways were largely supported as the way to improve the transportation conditions in a wealthy and predominantly service-oriented area. Some political compromise was reached between freeway and transit advocates, to include alternatives that comprised LRT, expressways, and improvements in the bus system. At some point, the chairman of the Board of Control explicitly indicated that freeways had to be built to placate those who

Table 3.4
Reasons for Cost Growth in Santa Clara County's LRT, 1984-1988
(Growth of $147.5 million = $558.6 m. - $411.1 m.)

	Cost Increase ($ millions)	Percent of Total Cost Increase
Locally funded enhancements	$32.1	21.8
Preliminary estimates	62.5	42.4
Environmental delays	24.6	16.7
Measure A impacts	8.3	5.6
Utility escrow	15.0	10.2
Transit mall	5.0	3.4
Total cost increase	$147.5	100.0

Note: Unexpected inflation effects are embedded in those items that caused delays in the construction of the project (mainly environmental delays) or that presented unanticipated cost increases.

consider highways the most efficient transportation system conceivable. The pooling of several modes reduced the chances of opposition from some parties and increased the likelihood of constructing the LRT system.

However, consideration of expressways and LRT on the same corridor created some contradictions, since the former would detract riders from the latter, reducing its effectiveness.[57] The hope was that any potential decrease in transit ridership would only last until highway gridlock set in again. A 1981 technical report stated that highway construction was deemed necessary to attend to the travel needs of those who would not or could not use transit. The same report also indicated that an expressway would attract close to 3 percent of the passengers from the adjacent transit facility, but that a freeway would attract many more and its capital costs would be much higher.[58]

Initially, the LRT line was going to be located in the median strip of a highway designed for expressway standards (that is, with signaled intersections and not fully separated). Later, as a response to voter demands, when County Measure A was passed in 1984, the highway was upgraded to freeway standards, requiring full separation. The new stations on the line then had to be redesigned according to these standards. In addition, the LRT track had to follow the same profile as the freeway.

Paradoxically enough, the redesign of the expressway to freeway standards, along with the required LRT changes, was perceived by some as a major drawback for the LRT line. In an area where most people drive cars, a freeway along an LRT would not be likely to take people out of the cars. Furthermore, the redesign forced construction of overpasses that LRT patrons would have to climb up and down to get to the stations. The effect of this inconvenience would be that, once near the highway, people would rather stay on it and finish the whole trip in their car. At the other side of the line, the northern portion, another deterrent to transit use consisted of the distance—almost a quarter of a mile—an individual must walk across some landscaping strip and a parking lot to get to a building from a LRT stop. The way buildings are normally designed, because of city requirements, such generous landscaping strips are provided in between the street and parking lots. There is also an almost guaranteed free parking space for every employee. All these conditions amount to strong disincentives to abandon the private automobile and take the LRT line. Ridership figures for the year 2000 were reduced to around 6,000 from initial estimates of 20,000 to 40,000. The main reasons consultants revised the demand estimates were voter demands for the freeway standards paralleling the rail line; it was also because trains would have to traverse downtown San Jose at low speeds (10 to 15 miles per hour).[59]

The main objectives to be achieved with the LRT investment included revitalization of the downtown area, the fact that such a wealthy area did not have a "visible" transportation system, and changes in land-use patterns (toward higher densities).[60] To a large extent, this latter objective was the one that motivated the decision to select LRT, with the hope that the change in land use would create a high-density commercial corridor 20 or 30 years from now.

This vision was not in harmony with that of the higher level institutions, particularly the UMTA. Although their working relationship with the UMTA was termed good by the local people, they also felt that the UMTA was prejudiced, with an East-Coast, high-density mentality. The UMTA expressed skepticism about the outcome of rail investments in low-density corridors. Therefore, it thought that a system based on buses would be more than enough, and would be more cost-effective (i.e., buses would achieve the same goal at lower cost). Local people, on the other hand, thought that cost-effectiveness criteria were important, but that other elements also counted, such as supporting a growing and dynamic economy (with transportation enhancements and potential changes in land use that in turn would, sooner or later, reinforce the LRT project). The busway-HOV alternative was added at UMTA's request, and its technical elements were developed with considerably less in-depth analysis than the LRT alternatives.

The technical reports, therefore, reflected the enthusiasm for LRT that consultants and transit supporters had at the time of deciding which alternative to pursue. An example of this optimism relates to the estimation of operating costs. Although only raised by a few people, there were some concerns that after coming up with ways to finance the capital improvements, the county would still have to bear the large burden of paying for the operation of the whole transit system once it had been constructed. The 1981 preferred-alternative report concluded that, for the LRT system, farebox revenues would cover 85 percent of the operating costs. At the end of 1986, when bus ridership had fallen around 3 percent from the previous year, Santa Clara County Transit recovered about 11 percent of its operating costs from fares.[61] (The less optimistic SCVCE 1975 study indicated that no transit option would be able to recover more than 31 percent of its operating costs from the farebox.)

Some of the advantages of the LRT—mainly accidents, safety, and operating and maintenance costs—were based on achieving the expected ridership. In fact, the preferred-alternative report indicated that "the greater the demand there is for transit . . . the less expensive it becomes to operate light rail transit versus a busway."[62] But if certain minimum levels were not achieved, many of the conclusions of the technical study would no longer apply, particularly the adequacy of the selected alternative, since other alternatives would largely surpass the LRT option in most of the economic, financial, and cost-effectiveness factors.[63]

Finally, in the case of the Guadalupe corridor project, about 200 public meetings were held in the first stage (up to the SCVCE), and about 300 during the process of analyzing alternatives. After such an exhaustive effort, one wonders why so many design changes had to be incorporated later. This situation arose from the need to compromise many competing interests that never reach a stable position, and the political nature of the project. On October 27, 1981, the Chamber of Commerce indicated that it supported the LRT option, but expressed concern for applying sound business practices, and for loading up the project with "frills" that may be favored politically but did not have a strong impact on meeting the transportation needs in the county. Also, some institutions did not raise their concerns until the moment they had to face them, or when their complaints would prove more successful. In addition, the static nature of technical documents does not allow for changes to be made as quickly as they need to be incorporated.

All the individuals interviewed agreed that the Santa Clara County LRT project survived the many battles of the planning process because of persistence by major actors to push the LRT technology ahead.[64] Consultants played key roles in the planning and design effort, but worked all the time under the technical guidance of SCCTD staff and policy direction of the board, as transmitted by that staff. Community support was always sought, and success-fully achieved, by the broad participation program and by careful selection of components of alternatives to encompass most of the community interests.

Buffalo's Light Rail Rapid Transit

The Buffalo case illustrates issues such as changes in design elements, attempts to redirect land-use patterns, and optimistic estimates similar to the Santa Clara County case, but from the perspective of a completely different socioeconomic environment. Buffalo is a typical example of a midsize northeastern U.S. city. It is a mature, stable community characterized by relatively high (for U.S. standards) population densities, with a metropolitan population of 1.5 million in 1980 that had been declining for a decade. Ridership rates (measured by passengers per mile of service) have been above the U.S. average.

Since the end of the 1960s there had been growing interest in a fixed-guideway transit system, stimulated by the fact that winter weather in Buffalo includes sporadic periods during which automobile and bus travel is impractical (or even impossible), owing to poor visibility and accumulated snow. This interest increased at the beginning of the 1970s, as the area's manufacturing base decreased. The fixed-guideway system was seen as a way to revitalize downtown Buffalo and arrest the decline in transit use. The enhancement of economic and social conditions in the region required commercial and institutional development, but this development was thought to be possible only with significant improvements in the mass transit network.

By the end of the 1970s, Buffalo, New York State's second largest city, had lost more than 40 percent of its 1950 population. A few miles north, the city of Toronto, which had been involved in construction of an extensive transit system since the 1950s, was booming economically. With some envy for its Canadian neighbors, local officials perceived the need to revitalize Buffalo as a government, financial, and business center. A fixed-guideway transit system would be the shot in the arm to turn around the area's sagging economy.[65] The transit project would provide jobs during the construction period and for years to come through a multiplying effect and extensions of the system. Coincidentally, the federal government was looking for a place to prove the advantages of light-rail systems as an alternative form of public transit. Buffalo was one of the preferred choices. The political climate could not have been more conducive to the development of a fixed-guideway system in the Buffalo area. By the end of 1986, a 6.4 mile LRT line was finalized, but not before a rather long and tortuous process.

Institutional Environment

Several organizations were part of the transit development process in the metropolitan area. The Niagara Frontier Transportation Authority (NFTA), created in 1967 by the legislature of New York State, has been responsible for the operation of the Port of Buffalo and the Greater Buffalo and the Niagara Falls International Airports, as well as the development and implementation of a unified mass transit program and policy for the transportation district known as the Niagara Frontier Region. The Authority acquired and consolidated six of the seven municipal and private bus firms in 1975, and has provided for the operation of these bus services through a subsidiary organization, NFT Metro Systems, Inc. The NFTA is, in addition, a regular participant in any transportation planning proposals for the area.

At the state level, the Division of Community Affairs in the New York Department of State has the responsibility for coordinating and effecting budget controls for the planning functions of various state departments (including the Department of Transportation), and coordinating state planning with planning from regional agencies. The Department of Transportation is responsible for planning and developing mass transportation and aviation facilities, and administers financial assistance programs from the state and federal levels.[66] The State University of New York at Buffalo is responsible for planning educational and supporting facilities, including utilities and transportation, on its campuses and is concerned with matters outside the university, such as ingress and egress for students, faculty, and staff.

At the regional level, the Niagara Frontier Transportation Committee (NFTC) is the Metropolitan Planning Organization designated by the governor as being responsible, in cooperation with the state and the NFTA, for the federal (FHWA and UMTA) transportation planning process. The NFTC staff reviews and approves final plans for transportation systems in the study area. Assisting the NFTC technical staff is a Planning and Coordinating Committee that includes representatives of the principal technical staffs dealing with transportation in Erie and Niagara counties. The technical work is financed jointly by the New York State DOT, UMTA, FHWA, and other participating agencies.

At the local level, the counties as well as the cities of Buffalo and Niagara Falls have planning departments involved in transportation matters. From the citizen side, support for major transit improvements became strong at the beginning of the 1970s. During this period, individual citizens and citizen groups, many of whom wanted transit improvements but objected to preliminary designs involving miles of aerial structure, were especially active and able to force the redefinition of the alternatives.[67] Not Overhead Transit (NOT), an aggressive community organization against the construction of an overhead transit system, later became a staunch supporter of the light-rail proposals and secured 72,000 signatures on a petition to federal officials to release funds for the construction of an LRT line.

Project History

The initial proposals for a fixed-guideway system in Buffalo date back to 1971.[68] The UMTA-funded 1971 study recommended, among other things, construction of an 11-mile heavy rail line running from downtown Buffalo northwest to the North Campus of the University in Amherst (Figure 3.3). The initial estimates for this line amounted to $241 million, to be funded primarily by discretionary grants (with an 80% UMTA share, authorized under Section 3 of the Urban Mass Transportation Act of 1964), and by local funds (20%) administered by the metropolitan transit authority (NFTA).

In the 1971 study, a basic engineering approach to the problem was adopted. In order to minimize capital costs, the alignment was aerial, at the expense of community cohesiveness and growing concerns for environmental impacts. Owing to local opposition to the proposed system (the alignment was mostly elevated), a new study (again funded by the UMTA) was undertaken in 1972. This study resulted in the adoption of a rock-tunneled alignment through the middle corridor and cut-and-cover alignment through almost two miles of the outer corridor. Both decisions were influenced by the very strong concerns of the community and the economics involved. Balancing both long- and short-term environmental impacts against increased capital costs resulted in the only decision that could be made for rail transit at that moment. The new cost estimates rose to $476 million, mainly because of an 80 percent increase in the underground section of the line.

Owing to escalating costs (in addition to concerns about ridership figures), the UMTA proposed another study where, in addition to alternative alignments, alternative modes were compared and analyzed. The alternatives consisted of four bus-based alternatives (one of them equivalent to a "no-build" alternative), several heavy-rail alternatives (the benchmark 11-mile elevated HRT, among them), and various combinations (in terms of branches) of light-rail alternatives. (Table 3.5 summarizes the capital and operating costs of the most significant alternatives.) The final report came out in 1976 (and the final environmental study in 1977), recommending construction of a 6.4-mile light-rail rapid transit (LRRT) [69] line from downtown Buffalo to the South Campus of the State University in Buffalo (Figure 3.3). The estimated cost was $336.3 million (with operation planned for 1982). [70] Operating costs were estimated at $23.6 million in 1995, with an annual patronage of 63.6 million passengers. These figures were going to provide an operating surplus of $0.6 million by the year 1995. The capital cost estimates were prepared in 1975 by consultant engineers under contract with the NFTA. Operating costs were developed in 1975 by NFTA. [71]

When the final environmental report was generated, a decision was made to hold train consists to a maximum of four units, in an effort to keep costs to a minimum. This allowed a reduction in station length (to 300 feet), but increased operating costs slightly and reduced system capacity. Another decision made to save capital costs included simplifying the roof and wall architectural design of stations to cover only the middle half of the platform area. [72] For estimating bus operating and maintenance costs, a relationship was developed, based on then-current operating costs in Buffalo, that calculated those costs on a per mile basis, separating costs between those dependent on speed and those independent of speed. Further, it was assumed that initial 1982 operating costs would be lower than 1995 levels, by matching patronage with a linear growth between 1982 and 1995. However, the estimated reduction in costs over 1995 levels was proportioned to only 75 percent of the reduction in patronage. For years after 1995, operating and maintenance costs were assumed to remain at the 1995 level. Rail operating costs were developed for the assumed 1995 operating schedules by estimating each major component of the cost individually—labor, energy, administration, and so on—and by using employee production values

Figure 3.3
Buffalo's Rail Options

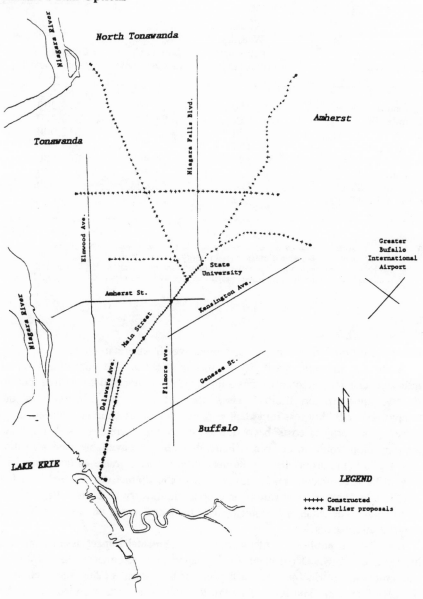

Niagara River

North Tonawanda

Niagara Falls Blvd.

Amherst

Tonawanda

Elmwood Ave.

Greater
Bufallo
International
Airport

State
University

Niagara River

Amherst St.

Kensington Ave.

Main Street

Delaware Ave.

Filmore Ave.

Genesee St.

Buffalo

N

LAKE ERIE

LEGEND

+++++ Constructed
+++++ Earlier proposals

Table 3.5
Capital and Operating Costs and Daily Patronage
for Selected Buffalo Transit Alternatives
(Cost figures in 1974 dollars)

Alternative	Average Weekday Patronage (thousands)	1995 Oper. & Maint. Costs ($ thousands)	Capital Costs ($ thousands)
Advanced Bus[a]	150	$22,300	$75,200
11-mile HRT	212	23,600	373,000
Maximum HRT (19.6 m.)	224	25,300	518,000
13-mile LRT	193	26,300	357,000
6.4-mile LRT	184	24,900	246,000
11-mile LRRT	212	23,800	371,000
6.4-mile LRRT	184	24,400	245,000
6.4-mile LRRT & Bus[b]	212	23,600	336,250

Source: U.S. Department of Transportation, 1977.
Notes: [a]The advanced alternative combined reserved bus lanes, exclusive right-of-way facilities, contraflow lanes, and traffic signal priority.
[b]This was the preferred alternative. In addition to the 6.4-mile LRRT, it included a realigned and rescheduled Metrobus system serving as feeder network for the LRRT line.

based on rail operating experience in other North American cities.[73]

As to the financial feasibility of the alternatives, the consultants report indicated that "the amount of financing appears impractical to achieve due to Federal appropriation limits." They also indicated that, "further on the unfavorable side, but less important perhaps, is that inflation is expected to increase the project costs beyond that which the current New York State appropriation would meet even if Federal funds were available, and a further increase in the appropriation in the near future must be rated as uncertain." In spite of these comments, made only for one of the alternatives, and extrapolated to others as "neutral" evaluation, the report did not try to address the issue in more detail. The financing problem, they indicated, could be eased with some reduced alternatives.[74]

Even before publication of the final environmental impact assessment, the head of the U.S. Department of Transportation announced the UMTA's "commitment in principle" to the funding of 80 percent of the construction of the LRRT system. The balance of the total $336 million was pledged by the state. By then, the entire New York State representation in the U.S. Congress was united to press for approval of the Buffalo project, and in addition community groups were putting pressure on Washington. However, the UMTA indicated that the commitment would be subject to completion of the necessary environmental and legal requirements. In addition, it stated that the federal share would not exceed $269 million (80% of the estimated total cost), and that it would make a contract with the NFTA only with the assurance that there would be enough money from other sources to cover any cost overruns. The NFTA noted that the $336 million project cost estimate included sufficient allowance for increases in labor and material costs.

The willingness of construction contractors and unions to sign a written no-strike agreement for the duration of construction (aimed at averting cost-escalating work stoppages) and the then-innovative proposal to create a downtown transit mall with the LRRT operating on the surface in an auto-free zone were two of the key elements highlighted by the UMTA as determinative for the decision to fund the project. But the question of how operating deficits and cost overruns would be met still lingered, and some wondered whether or not more thought should have been given at that moment to an overall view of the project in terms of scaling down initial proposals (i.e., basically from an 11-mile to a 6.4-mile rail network).

Construction began in April 1979 and was completed at the end of November 1986, four years behind the schedule indicated in the Final Environmental Impact Statement.[75] As the project evolved from the planning to the preliminary engineering, to the construction stage, NFTA revised its cost estimates. In November 1978, the contract between the UMTA and the NFTA was signed, indicating a total cost of $449.8 million (with $359.8 million federal share, in 1977 dollars, a sizeable increase from the $269.0 million, in 1974 dollars, estimated two years earlier). The estimate was prepared by the NFTA and four principal consultants during the preliminary engineering phase.

The Buffalo system was financed under Section 3 statutes, by which the federal government would cover 80 percent of the construction costs. This project was funded, as in the case of the Santa Clara LRT line, under the statutes of a full funding contract. Under this concept, the UMTA committed federal funds in specified incremental amounts over the life of the project, subject to availability of funds from Congress. The federal share could only be increased if certain extraordinary costs were incurred.[76] This concept, by establishing obligation ceilings and grantee responsibility for excess costs, was supposed to be an incentive for applicants to develop more accurate cost estimates (since cost overruns would need to be covered by the municipality). However, in Buffalo, the UMTA assisted in financing additional project costs not included under the provisions of the full funding contract. Table 3.6 summarizes the evolution of costs and federal contributions. In 1986 a revised cost estimate indicated that the project would cost $534.8 million. Through that date, the federal contribution had been $426.3 million.

Table 1.2 summarized the changes in capital cost estimates that occurred during 16 years of the planning and construction of Buffalo's rail system and some of the reasons for those changes. Between 1976 and 1978, underground conditions were surveyed, and detailed plans, including construction schedules and project cost updates, were developed. These plans indicated a 33.8 percent increase (in nominal values) in construction costs owing to engineering changes, delays in starting the service (inflation), increased contingencies, and higher insurance rates. Between 1978 and 1985, the 18.7 percent increase (in nominal values) was due mainly to unanticipated inflation, expenses incurred in implementing federal regulations, and changes in project scope. Table 3.7 focuses on the LRRT cost growth between 1976 and 1985, based on data reported in a 1986 General Accounting Office (GAO) study.

Almost 50 percent of the cost changes could be attributed to scope or engineering changes that had to be made along the way. When considering the utilities relocation and the "unknown," the percentage almost reaches 60 percent. Most of these changes were later approved by the UMTA—and hence covered by the 80 percent federal share—mainly because Congress appropriated funds for assisting several cities in financing the completion of their transit systems.

In explaining why the costs of starting and equipping the system were not included in any of the cost estimates, the 1986 GAO report indicates that:

> A former NFTA official [stated] that those costs were not included in the initial estimate because NFTA staff did not believe they could determine a cost for requirements that would not be known until much later. Another former NFTA official [indicated] that the costs were going to be included in the estimate for the full-funding contract, but were deleted when NFTA learned that UMTA would not accept a cost estimate over $450 million.[77]

Eventually, the UMTA awarded $6 million out of the $8 million to cover startup costs because UMTA officials thought that was the mandate of 1984 and 1985 congressional legislation (as well as the Surface Transportation Assistance Act of 1982).

Another interesting development in the planning and construction process involved a major station on the line. In 1979, the NFTA thought that the La Salle Street Station would not be necessary in light of the expected extension of the system along the Tonawandas corridor (the station was located right at the merging of the Tonawandas branch line with the original LRRT line). In 1981, the UMTA approved the NFTA's request and the La Salle Street Station was dropped from the initial plan of 14 stations, and its funds were transferred to assist in financing enhancements in the transit mall [78]. About a year later, however, the NFTA asked that the station be reinstated in the plan, and the UMTA eventually funded almost $20 million for that purpose because of congressional mandate.[79] In 1983, the enhancements in the transit mall were also funded ($14.2 million federal share of the $17.8 cost estimate) with discretionary funds because the UMTA felt the mall was a worthwhile addition to the Buffalo LRRT project.

Table 3.6
Summary of Capital Costs for Buffalo's Light Rail Rapid System
(Current values)

Grants/Cost Estimate	Approved Project Costs ($ millions)	Federal Share ($ millions)
Basic grant application (Oct. 1976, 1974 $)	$336.3	$289.0
Full funding contract (Nov. 1978, 1977 $)	449.8	359.8
Amendments to full funding contract	44.9	35.8
Total basic grant	494.7	395.7
Four supplemental grants	31.0	24.8
Total—all grants (1985 $)	525.7	420.3
Including art work and start-up costs	534.8	426.3
Cost of complete estimate (1987)	551.9	N/A

Source: U.S. General Accounting Office, 1986b; Niagara Frontier Transportation Authority, 1987.
Note: See Table 1.2 for additional information on cost changes in the Buffalo case.

Almost two years after the beginning of revenue operation, with an average weekday ridership of 28,000 passengers, the LRRT farebox recovery ratio was 27 percent compared to 40 percent for the bus system. The LRRT added almost $8.5 million to the $24.5 million operating deficit of the bus system,[80] while the annual operating cost per rider for the rail system was $1, almost 30 percent higher than the $0.77 for the bus system. (At the end of 1988, some local officials were even considering the possibility of closing down the underground section of the system, leaving only the 1.2 miles of the transit mall open.)

Comments on the Buffalo Case

In Buffalo, the initial concept of transportation improvement as a means to improve the economic conditions of a depressed area was not undermined by the unsuccessful attempt to construct a rapid transit line. The idea evolved into something close to the initial proposal: a light-rail transit line with an unconventional design—with the downtown area at grade and the outer sections underground—that would give the system some of the operating characteristics (mainly operating speed) of the defeated proposal.

As summarized in Table 3.6, an 1977 study provided a set of capital and operating costs (estimated in 1975) in terms of which none of the alternatives had a clear advantage. In fact, if some sensitivity analysis had been performed, none of the alternatives would probably have presented costs significantly

Table 3.7

Reasons for Cost Growth in Buffalo's LRRT, 1976-1985

(on an amount of $197.5 million = $534.8 m.- $336.3 m.)

Cost Growth Factor	Percent
Engineering changes	20.3
Delay in starting service	13.5
Increased contingencies and insurance rates	15.2
Utilities relocation	2.1
Unanticipated inflation	10.6
La Salle Street station	12.7
Extension of transit mall	15.2
Other (start-up activities, station artwork, minority business enterprise)	4.6
Unknown	5.8
Total	100.0

Sources: U.S. General Accounting Office, 1986b, and own calculations.

different from those of the others. Interestingly enough, the selected alternative, although it considered a rearrangement of the bus system (methodology that should have been followed with the other alternatives as well, but was not), had the same ridership than an almost twice-as-long LRRT, and similar operating costs and a mere 9 percent lower capital costs. (Because of instances like this one, the results of the 1977 alternatives analysis always left room for criticisms by the detractors of the proposals.)

During the planning process, concerns were raised about the financial feasibility of the alternatives, but no major thought was given to these concerns, except for indicating that reduced alternatives could always be implemented (without considering that the benefits of reduced alternatives would probably be much less and their effectiveness very much reduced). The NFTA responded to comments made at public hearings in July 1977 concerning operating deficits by stating that if sufficient subsidy could not be provided by all levels of government involved, service in the corridor could be reduced, or system fares raised to make up the difference. This was a very weak argument, since cutting service or raising fares usually leads to further cuts in service and probably to larger deficits. The careful examination of alternative scenarios in relation to which level of demand may turn out to be attracted to the system did not receive careful consideration. Furthermore, scaling down initial proposals should have required a whole reexamination of the project, since the same set of assumptions does not hold for two systems with different lengths, different levels of service, or different technologies.

It is also important to note that in this project, the preoccupation with cost overruns probably distracted attention from more basic design elements. For instance, in spite of the half a billion dollars invested in the project, no provision was made for conveniences for LRT drivers. Drivers have to request permission from the central control operator to leave their car and enter an open building in the central area in order to look for a restroom (buildings that, besides, may be particularly hard to find during late evening hours or weekends). Another example is the location of the crossover at the South Campus terminal station. The crossover is located before the station, and since at the crossover the speeds must be much slower, it causes delays and reduces the capacity of the line, particularly during peak periods. Finally, in order to attend to the needs of handicapped passengers, stations in the at-grade section have an elevated platform to serve the first door of the car. The LRT car has high floors, but for those doors beyond the platform area, some steps must be released for people to get on and off.[81] The whole operation requires considerable dwelling time at each of the six stops in the at-grade section, further reducing the capacity of the system.

As major obstacles to accomplishing the project within the budget initially estimated, local officials mentioned (1) uncertain funding from the federal and state governments; (2) disputes with the city over relocation of water lines, unexpected vaults, and telephone systems; and (3) inaccurate utility maps. Nevertheless, the almost 60 percent cost change owing to design elements (see Table 3.7) is a fairly large number for items whose uncertainty can be reduced with additional and careful analysis (unlike other elements such as inflation, which is beyond the control of the analysts). Some of the increase in costs were due to enhancements incorporated into the system to attract additional passengers, such as art work. Even by these accounts, however, the project cannot justify some cost increases, since several other planned amenities, such as an icerink and a laser show, have not been implemented.

Buffalo's LRRT case has become a well-publicized case of cost overruns, although once cost figures are corrected for inflation, as indicated in Figure 1.1, the overruns are not more dramatic than for other, less publicized instances. The decision to construct Buffalo's LRRT system came from many sources, but mostly it was motivated by the sagging economy in the area during the 1970s. The strong and united congressional representation, with one of its members chairman of the appropriations subcommittee of the transportation committee, helped overcome some technical hurdles and secured the necessary funding. Once again, the presence of persistent advocates for the transit system kept the project alive beyond the results of the technical analysis. Hence, the role of this analysis as the critical element in making decisions was rather curtailed.

CHARACTERIZATION OF THE DECISION-MAKING AND ANALYSIS PROCESSES IN ESTIMATING COSTS

This section summarizes the characteristics of the decision-making and analysis processes that can be drawn from the case studies. These characteristics and the issues related to them will be developed in detail in the following chapters.

The case studies clearly reflect how similar types of transit plans and proposals come about from different motivating factors. In Boston, a rapidly growing area, the main motivating factor was fear of congestion on a corridor with no fixed-guideway transit facilities, in light of a major highway reconstruction. The elected officials from that area quickly fueled the possibility of revitalizing an abandoned commuter rail network traversing their constituencies' districts. In Santa Clara County, also a growing area, the motivating factor was an attempt to gain control over land development, through redirection of urban sprawl toward higher density patterns and revitalization of the downtown area. The fact that such a vital area, in the forefront of the world's computer technology, did not have a visible transit system also stimulated those in the political arena to support construction of an LRT system. In Buffalo, a distressed area, the main motivating factor was the need to turn around a declining economy and, in that attempt, to revitalize its downtown core. The perceived competition from nearby urban areas—mainly the canadian city of Toronto—further funneled the interests for a fixed-guideway system.[82]

Once they come about, transit plans and proposals easily become an end in themselves, giving people involved very little time or willingness to reflect on their real desirability. This situation translates into an attempt to diminish the potential impacts—for instance, in terms of capital and operating costs—of the initially preferred alternative and ends up putting the technical agenda behind the political agenda, affecting how the technical study is accomplished. This characteristic is illustrated by the fact that not one of these case studies did the preconceived ideas about which project to pursue change substantially along the lengthy analysis process since the formation of the initial proposals (except for scaling down the Buffalo rail system from heavy- to light-rail standards).

The permanence of a fixed-guideway system and the life-long impact creates once constructed [83] contributed to the steadiness of support for its implementation. This type of system can help build a strong and committed constituency willing to fight for or against the system. Once this constituency is mobilized, the political stimulus becomes intense and even oppressive.[84] The political agenda then goes ahead of the analysis process, with politicians monitoring it very closely and preparing it to support its predefined desired outcomes. As indicated earlier in this chapter, the uncertainty of both cost and demand estimates at the time of project planning further allows the decision-making political agenda to take control of the process.

Cost estimates along with demand estimates, because of their uncertainty, constitute one of the workhorses of the analysis process. The output of the cost-estimation process is paramount for political acceptability of the project—in addition, of course, to its financial feasibility. Capital and operating costs must stay at reasonable levels. But an effort to keep costs down, by ignoring or scaling down some elements of the system, will most likely turn into cost overruns once the system is constructed. As the case studies illustrate, the reasons for cost growth are mainly changes in scope after taking into account the effects of inflation. Sometimes the growth in costs comes from the accidental or deliberate ignorance of the person—or institution—in charge of paying for particular items. In the case of Buffalo, the NFTA believed that a New York State law required privately owned utility companies to bear the expense of relocating their lines when their paths conflicted with proposed public improvements. The affected utility companies pursued the matter through federal and state courts, and later the state supreme court ruled that the utility companies were to be reimbursed for removal, relocation, and/or support and maintenance of their lines.[85] A similar instance occurred in the case of Santa Clara, since the transit agency had to add the costs of upgrading the trackbed of the downtown section of the LRT system (from ballast to concrete) because the city of San Jose refused to take that responsibility.

In terms of the technical process itself, the size of the projects that are the subject of this book requires a substantial amount of data, hardware (tools to process, maintain, and manipulate the data), and expertise (knowledge of accounting strategies, operations planning, and experience). For capital costs, the main task consists of figuring out precisely what items need to be included and, simultaneously, what items are the least reliable. But in all the case studies, analysts indicated that the most difficult task was the calculation of operating costs. Calculating these costs requires considering not only the operating strategies for the proposed system but also the changes that introduction of the new system will generate in the existing transportation network.

In calculating both types of costs, a major issue consists of maintaining the data and updating them as changes take place along the process. In the Boston case, the analysts attempted to tackle this issue through available computer technology, mainly microcomputers. In no case, however, was a reliable and somewhat powerful computer-based information system in place, either because the technology was not available, because it was not known at the moment, or because the specific project planning exercise was perceived as temporal, with very low chances of being replicated in a future situation.

In all the cases, the expertise needed in the technical process required hiring outside analysts—that is, people not part of the decision-makers' organization—to carry out the technical process and "advise" the decision makers. This situation generates a two-way relationship, whereby each party needs the other: the decision maker needs the analyst to perform the technical analysis to support the final decision; the analyst needs the decision maker to have projects to work on. This relationship induces a partnership whereby the analyst tries to please the client so that he or she may have a good chance of getting additional projects. The need the decision maker has for the analyst gives the latter some leverage to be more effective in trying to direct the political agenda or, at least, to not to be left behind. This situation, however, depends on the mobility of the political agenda itself and, as the case studies illustrate, hardly occurs.[86]

Another relationship emerges from the need for outside funds to construct the preconceived transit proposal. The presence of the higher institution—the federal government—and its financial powers generates the need for a planning study that "justifies" the transit proposal. In this relationship—between the funding institution and the decision maker's organization—another game takes place, with each trying to influence the other's opinion about the design and desirability of the project. Other actors, such as the analyst or the affected constituencies, will try to interfere in this relationship in an attempt to make their particular opinions heard.

In the case studies, development of the planning process (with the decision makers' continuous support for a single alternative since the conception of the preliminary ideas) seems to suggest that decision makers, although fully aware of the importance of the technical process to put the project forward, do not believe that the technical studies can influence the final decision about which transportation alternative to pursue. If not explicit, this statement is reflected by the events and by decision makers' lack of knowledge about the general technical issues, controversial values, and so forth involved in the analysis process, or their statements about the merits of their preferred alternative. Another indication is the frequent complaints about the technical process itself (in particular, about the alternatives-analysis process).

Decision makers also stated that if they had not been able to secure the funds to construct the project from the higher level institutions, the transit project would probably not have been built. This belief indicates that decision makers had a major interest in obtaining the funds needed for the construction of the particular transit project, and that they perceived the technical analysis mostly as a requirement to secure those funds. In the case studies, three main reasons were cited for the need of the analysis process: (1) to satisfy federal and state environmental laws; (2) to get the necessary funding from federal and state agencies; and (3) to assist the community in arriving at a consensus.

CONCLUSION

This chapter has included a description of the case studies along with some comments on the main issues raised in the presentation of each case study. In addition, three major set of characteristics have been identified as common themes of reference in the case studies: (1) the technical, (2) the decision related, and (3) those that affect the interaction between analysis and decision. Within the technical set, three characteristics were highlighted: (1) the sources of rises in capital and operating costs; (2) the special features of fixed-guideway systems (mainly their permanence) and the implications of these features on the development of the project and the support for it by the affected constituencies; and (3) the requirements of the technical process. Within the decision-related set, three other characteristics were identified: (1) the explicit or implicit motivations for proposing the system; (2) the local versus central government contentions about the viability of the transportation projects and the reflection of these contentions on cost estimates; and (3) the constraints and requirements on the decision-making process. Finally, as to the relationship between analysis and decision, three major characteristics were recognized: (1) the relationship between analysts and decision makers, and between funding institutions and decision makers; (2) the force of optimistic expectations on the analysis process; and (3) the different interpretations of the intent of alternatives analysis requirements, and the perception of decision makers about the role of the technical process. The next two chapters discuss at greater length the first two sets of characteristics as part of both the analysis and the decision-making processes. The third set of characteristics is developed in Chapter 6, as the two processes are brought together and the analytical framework is developed. The issue of the role of technical analysis is further discussed in Chapter 7.

These characteristics support the use of the theoretical framework highlighted at the end of Chapter 2. They illustrate the difficulties of achieving optimality from a rational perspective; they portray the different actors' attempting to gain control of the process; and they illustrate how the process unfolds as a struggle over ideas with a strategic purpose generated by the political environment surrounding the planning process. Stone refers to similar conclusions in her discussion of how problems are defined in the policy process:

> Problem definition is never simply a matter of defining goals and measuring our distance from them. It is rather the strategic representation of situations. Problem definition is a matter of representation because there is not objective description of a situation; there can only be portrayals of people's experiences and interpretations. Problem definition is strategic because groups, individuals, and government agencies deliberately and consciously design portrayals so as to promote their favored course of action. . . . Representations of a problem are therefore constructed to win the most people to one's side and the most leverage over one's opponents.[87]

The argumentative approach helps develop a framework for the cost-estimating process and identify those components that prevent the pure rationality of the process and the achievement of the intended results (the ones advanced by the normative rational framework). The argumentative approach also helps explain how decision makers' perceptions about the role of the technical process, coupled with their relationship with analysts, influences the technical process and why some deviations from the expected outcome take place.

NOTES

1. Smerk (1974), Altshuler et al. (1979), Weiner (1983), Jones (1985), Smerk (1987), Weiner (1987).

2. This was in part due to insulation of the public authority from day-to-day politics, so transit services were better tailored to revenues. Fielding (1983a).

3. Fielding (1983a). See also Pucher (1988).

4. Pickrell (1985), Fielding (1983b).

5. Hamer (1976), Altshuler et al. (1979).

6. At the federal level also, but not directly related to mass transit projects, the Federal Highway Administration is responsible for developing federal policy and procedure guidelines pertaining to highway planning and construction. It also funds the design and construction of qualified transportation projects. In addition, the Federal Aviation Administration is responsible for developing federal policy and programs pertaining to air transportation and for providing funds for airport planning and construction.

7. In 1987, Section 3 and Section 9 funds constituted 86 percent of UMTA appropriations for transit systems (equivalent to more than $2.8 billion out of a total of $3.4 billion). Section 3 appropriations amounted to $0.9 billion (27% of total UMTA grants), while Section 9 amounted to $1.9 billion (56%). Information provided by UMTA, April 1988.

8. U.S. General Accounting Office (1987), pp. 246-48.

9. Information provided by UMTA, April 1988.

10. The subway line, however, extended for a length of 11 miles from South Station and, therefore, did not reach very far along the corridor, with travel lengths of up to 37 miles.

11. The 79 towns contribute to the MBTA budget according to specific assessment procedures. These procedures try to appreciate that the 79 cities and towns of the MBTA District that benefit from the system must share some of the deficit and that a greater portion of the cost of operating the MBTA must come from those cities and towns that get a greater degree of service.

12. Each municipality has a weighted vote on the Advisory Board.

13. Massachusetts Bay Transportation Authority (1984), p. 2-1.

14. The feasibility study also included the possibility of providing commuter rail service only up to Braintree or Quincy Adams, where passengers could transfer to subway lines. These options were quickly dropped from further consideration owing to strong local opposition where these stations were located, to the point that later alternatives for the commuter rail system did not even have stops at these stations. Massachusetts Bay Transportation Authority (1984).

15. Most of the track was currently in place (85% of the 80 miles), although much of it needed to be upgraded, a new signal system installed, and a new bridge over the Neponset River be constructed. In the Middleborough line, freight service operated on

part of that trackage, while passenger service was limited to seasonal service to the Cape Cod area. On the other hand, near the center of the city, with a single track, the provision of passing tracks (to improve reliability of service) was already thought to be costly and time-consuming.

16. Massachusetts Bay Transportation Authority (1986, September).

17. At that moment, in 1985, UMTA account for "new starts" had $368 million, and $411 for "rail modernization."

18. One major item in the list of increased costs was the need to reconstruct a bridge over the Neponset river. This bridge had been burned down shortly after abandonment of the lines in 1959. Another item was land acquisition costs for station sites and rail right-of-ways.

19. The state request came about as the governor filed a bond issue providing $827 million in direct state support to the MBTA (twice as much as the $442 million two-year bond issue of 1985). Out of the $827 million, $195 million was allocated for the restoration of the commuter rail service on the South Shore. This bond issue took place as part of several large highway proposals for the Boston area. The total bond issue was close to $3.1 billion, to be supplemented by an additional $1.5 billion in federal funds. The highway projects included $3.2 billion (that later escalated to $4.3 billion) for the reconstruction of a major thoroughfare underground and the construction of a tunnel under the harbor.

20. For one of the rail alternatives, the upper value was less than 0.1 percent higher than the best estimate. When I indicated this apparent discrepancy to the analysts, they stated that it was probably due to a technical error. If it was an error, it was carried forward through the whole length of the project, since the same figures appeared in all the reports from the beginning of the study up to the one that came out in July 1988.

21. In November 1988, a nonbinding referendum held in Quincy and Braintree (the two communities closest to Boston's CBD where the commuter service was going to pass by but did not have any stations) asked people how they think their state representatives should vote in the legislature in relation to restoration of the Old Colony lines. Analysts and decision makers were glad to know that the referendum gave some support to restoration of the line (around 60% in favor and 40% against). However, they did not like the results of another vote, this time in Braintree only, about the possibility of making the Braintree station a transfer point. This vote resulted in an almost 50-50 decision, which did not clarify community support on this issue.

22. Between 1985 and 1988, the project manager (MBTA official) held around 200 meetings with the communities affected by the project. At some times, meetings were held three or four times in the three-year period. (Conversation with MBTA officials, July 1988.)

23. In several conversations with key people involved in the project, no answer was given when asked about the value of the cost-effectiveness measure, or the question was avoided altogether.

24. This issue is discussed at greater length in Chapter 5.

25. U.S. Department of Transportation, Urban Mass Transportation Administration (1981), p. 2-1.

26. Ibid., p. 2-3.

27. De Leuw, Cather and Company (1976), p. 326.

28. Santa Clara County Transit District (1981), p. 20.

29. This goal was supported in a strong belief that land-use and transportation decisions influence one another.

30. Statement by County Supervisor Rod Diridon, "Major Transit Decision Is Near," *San Jose Mercury News*, October 14, 1981, pages 1B and 2B.

31. Santa Clara County Transit District (1981), p. 26.

32. State legislation requires performance evaluations of operators and transportation planning agencies every three years.

33. Almost half of the members of this technical advisory committee belonged to SCCTD.

34. There exists, however, a .25 percent general sales tax dedicated to local mass transit, and a formula-based share of gasoline tax revenues. In fiscal year 1983-84, the state provided approximately $715 million in transit funds.

35. This was the Rapid Transit Development Project.

36. DeLeuw, Cather and Company (1976).

37. Ibid., p. 352.

38. Ibid., p. 353.

39. Joint Policy Committee of the Association of Bay Area Governments and Metropolitan Transportation Commission (1979), p. 2.

40. Jack Ybarra and Associates (1981), p. 1.

41. As indicated in the Boston case, UMTA policy at that moment was to defer federal involvement in new rail starts and extensions until economic conditions improved, except where Interstate Transfer Funds were available to fund these projects.

42. The inclusion of highway alternatives led to the appearance of the Federal Highway Administration as the overseer of the highway options. The busway-HOV alternative was included at a later stage at UMTA's request.

43. Although the bikeway was a mere $1 million investment, it was given as much space in the brochures advertising the project as the LRT and expressway investments, which amounted to more than $275 million in 1980 dollars (1981 estimates).

44. Over 300 meetings and workshops were held with community leaders and community organizations. Some of the concerns voiced in these meetings, reflecting a wide diversity of opinions, included: (1) how much each alternative would cost the taxpayers; (2) that ridership figures were too low (vocalized by the light-rail advocates) or too high; (3) that results of public opinion polls be disclosed; (4) that the decision about the light rail line had already been made and that the study was a way to justify it; (5) that the board of control was biased in favor of the LRT; (6) that highway projects should be completed; and (7) that contingency plans be developed in case funding from state and federal sources did not materialize.

45. Measure A, a nonbinding, advisory vote of confidence on the County Transit District's nearly $1 billion transportation-improvement plan for the 1981-86 period (which included the design and construction of a fixed-guideway system, either light rail or a busway), was approved by 85 percent of the voters. This vote suggested that the public was enthusiastic about mass transit.

46. Some parties, particularly LRT interest groups such as the Modern Transit Society, even claimed that the LRT system could carry 50,000 passengers per hour. Vuchic (1981), based on an analysis of several systems all over the world, estimates that capacities of LRT systems fall between 15,000 and 20,000 persons per hour (p. 577).

47. "Board Hears Praise of Light-Rail Transit," *San Jose Mercury News*, October 1, 1981, page 12B.

48. Santa Clara County Transit District (1981), p. 20.

49. The State Transportation Director was then depicted by her antihighway convictions ("More Studies, No Transit," *San Jose Mercury News*, June 25, 1980, p. 14B). In February 18, 1980, the *San Jose Mercury News* indicated that "we are sick and tired as anyone of paper exercises, but this study . . . is a necessary step if the area is going to be eligible for federal mass transit money." On December 7, 1980, the newspaper stated that "public planning agencies have an extraordinary ability to deal in esoteric terms which mean nothing to most of us, and nowhere is this more true than in our planning for public transit."

50. These data indicated that increased transit and HOV use would be gained at costs of $1.66 per new passenger for the busway alternative, and $2.37 for the light-rail alternative.

51. He further indicated that "the County's approach will not provide the technical analysis and evaluation that we think should be performed before either the light rail proposal or bus and carpool facilities are advanced into final design and construction."

52. The cost for the LRT included 31 stations and nine park-and-ride lots. The $39 million for the transit mall were going to be covered 70 percent by UMTA and 30 percent by local or county funds. The highway component of the transportation project was a four-lane freeway with an estimated cost of $106 million to be funded 41 percent by the Federal Highway Administration, 37 percent by the city of San Jose, and 22 percent by the County Transit District.

53. In fact some of the vehicles started running on December 31, 1987, to make use of harbor leasing proceeds that helped the SCCTD save $7 million dollars.

54. It is interesting to note that the 1976 estimates indicated a cost of $168 million for a 20-mile LRT, assuming constant returns to scale (i.e., assuming proportionality). Decreasing returns would probably yield values very close to the ones estimated before the 1984 full funding contract. In other words, the 1976 estimates seem to have been more accurate than subsequent estimates.

55. Public officials complained about this requirement since only a few trains per day use this railroad line.

56. A consultant firm was contracted to undertake the project management oversight (PMO) to avoid mismanagement of project funds and complete the project with the specified cap on federal funding participation. The PMO firm had also the role of providing the UMTA with reliable, objective information relative to all aspects of the engineering, design, procurement, and construction of the LRT system. The PMO firm was engaged by the UMTA.

57. Many reasons for the dwindling state support came from disagreements with the freeway option.

58. Santa Clara County Transit District (1981), pp. 79 and 81.

59. An express bypass was considered at some point at the end of 1986 but was not pursued, mainly because downtown merchants and businessmen did not like the idea.

60. Many proponents of the LRT kept arguing about the positive effects of fixed-guideway systems on density patterns in spite of repeated indications that density inducements from those types of transit facilities do not very often come about (Meyer and Gomez-Ibanez (1981), Altshuler et al. (1979), Hamer (1976). Others (e.g., Allen (1986)) indicate that rail transit has the potential for changing land uses, but there is no definitive study about both the necessary and sufficient conditions for those effects to occur.

61. Jansen (1987), p. 11.

62. Santa Clara County Transit District (1981), p. 23.

63. Furthermore, technical uncertainty was high in this case because LRT technology was relatively new at the moment of the Santa Clara County's transit studies, since LRT technology had not been tried on a full scale in any other part of the world (and particularly in North America).

64. The absence of a major supporting actor has been highlighted as the primary reason for failure to construct a similar LRT system in Denver, Colorado. In fact, the former director of the SCCTD was hired by Denver's Transit Construction Authority in 1986 to lead another attempt to put forward a fixed-guideway project in this city.

65. The project was many times justified as a matter of survival for the Buffalo area.

66. Capital funds from New York State are available to match federal funds for rapid transit development and bus system acquisition and improvement.

67. Among ways of participating, the citizen groups inundated federal agencies with letters of protest and visited the UMTA and Congress to personally register complaints.

68. Actually, a 1969 study by the New York State Office of Planning Coordination had recommended that a rapid transit line be developed to serve future development in the Buffalo-Amherst corridor.

69. Light rail rapid transit (LRRT) is a variation of the more flexible light rail transit (LRT). LRRT provides high-level platform, improving system accessibility in general and elderly and handicapped accessibility in particular. Station design allows for elimination of on-board vehicle fare collection. LRT's alignment flexibility is maintained to a large extent by operating, wherever practical, at grade.

70. The $336.3 million supposedly included $22.7 million for improvements necessary to complete an adequate feeder bus network to complement the LRRT. U.S. Department of Transportation (1977), p. 10-33.

71. Incidentally, a careful review of the reports comparing the alternatives that eventually led to the decision to construct the LRRT line reveals some discrepancies. For instance, the NFTA 1976 conclusions that came out in February of that year were supposedly based on the consultant's report that came out (later) in June. Furthermore, the February 1976 report stated conclusions not fully supported in the June report. No explanation was given by the NFTA officials about this discrepancy.

72. For the light-rail alternative, they indicated that a key point was that LRT is oriented toward a lower unit capital cost than heavy rail. Therefore, any characteristics that would prohibit low cost of an adequate LRT facility constituted a constraint.

73. Interestingly enough, ridership estimation is compared at some point with the "successful" 14.5-mile Lindenwold line in Philadelphia. They proudly stated that the patronage level for the LRRT line was estimated at over three times the patronage on the Lindenwold line. This probably should have raised concern about the estimation process rather than pride.

74. They also stated that a busway branch would offer the opportunity to request highway funds rather than transit funds, therefore making more probable the approval of financial assistance for some transit alternatives. Niagara Frontier Transportation Authority (1976, February).

75. U.S. Department of Transportation (1977), p. 4-11.

76. Extraordinary costs include inflation beyond that estimated in the contract, natural disasters, eminent domain settlements, federal laws or regulations enacted after the contract award date and that may affect the project, and unforeseen delays in the

availability of funds from Congress. Anything else was going to be the responsibility of the local institutions.

77. U.S. General Accounting Office (1986, July), p. 37.

78. These enhancements included structures for two more stations, a skywalk, and a redesigned square.

79. This measure was approved when Congress passed the Emergency Jobs Supplemental Appropriations Act of 1983.

80. Operating statistics for fiscal year 1987-88, provided by the Niagara Frontier Transportation Authority, August 1988.

81. These steps are activated at the request of passengers, who must press a button located on either side of each door.

82. In all the cases as well there was an implicit intent to put in place systems that could serve as the trunks of expanded multimodal services. This goal can be better achieved, owing to their permanence, through construction of rail networks rather than other systems.

83. This is related to what Henry (1974) calls the "irreversibility effect." This effect is an important consideration for investment decisions under conditions of uncertainty.

84. In all the cases, the survival of the proposals in spite of setbacks, and the development of constituency support, required leadership, or an individual, individuals, or coalition of individuals—probably political actors—who were willing to persist in moving the project forward. These individuals are what Bardach (1977) calls "fixers" of the implementation game. The problem, Bardach mentions, is that too few fixers are able to know where, when, how, and about what to persist effectively. The lack of a fixer seems to be one of the major reasons for setbacks in planning an LRT system in Denver, Colorado.

85. In response to the ruling, the UMTA awarded the NFTA a separate grant for utilities relocation in addition to the funds specified in the full funding contract.

86. For a fuller account of this relationship see, for instance, Szanton (1981) or Benveniste (1972).

87. Stone (1988), p. 106.

4

The Technical Process
of Estimating Costs

This chapter discusses the technical process of cost estimating within the context of analyzing and comparing transit alternatives. The main components of this process are data and methods. Data are the values for the different variables used as input to the methods; methods are the ensemble of equations used to represent the relationships among the different variables. The methods reflect the assumptions adopted to imitate as closely as possible what has happened, does happen, or will happen in the real world as it concerns the monetary disbursements needed for covering the capital and operating costs of the project. These methods may be readily available (e.g., the calculation of the present value of a stream of costs) or may need to be created by the estimator for the particular situation under analysis. For example, the calculation of the operating costs may happen to be particular to the project under study, and as such may require some empirical research and equation development.

The technical literature stresses that a good cost estimate is a necessary input to informed management decisions.[1] This literature emphasizes the importance of a sound information basis for estimating costs. This basis consists of two major elements: the quantities of the components that will constitute the transportation system, and the unit prices for those quantities. Other components that are equally important are those that affect the ultimate results of the estimating method, such as the length of construction, the inflation rate, and the financing techniques.

The planning of public transportation projects requires great skill and care in estimating—in particular capital and operating costs—because of the presence of unknowns that are difficult to foresee at the time of carrying out the planning process. The size of the project activity, the need for multiple skills, and the span of time usually required for its design and construction result in the need for precise planning, scheduling, estimating, and management. In many cases, as in the ones discussed in this book, the need for technical expertise forces the transportation operators and decision makers to contract out such studies.

Most of the literature on cost estimating focuses on processes taking place within the private sector. Within this context, a major consideration is the importance of making profits. This framework differs markedly from that for the public sector, where the objective may be to gain support for other projects or simply to generate political gains for an elected official. The case studies clearly reflected how similar types of transit plans were generated with very different objectives in the mind.

The private-sector framework helps private management understand clearly the function and meaning of cost estimating. In the public sector, however, that function is more diffuse and vague, and sometimes constitutes a way to support previous decisions rather than a way to help decision making. Furthermore, as the institutional framework of the case studies illustrated, many public-sector projects are very complex in terms of the number of actors involved or their impacts. This complexity makes it more difficult than it is in the private context to identify the decision makers or the quantities the decision should try to maximize (i.e., the goals to be achieved). (More differences between public- and private-sector projects, as they relate to the decision-making process, are discussed in Chapter 5.)

COST ESTIMATING: APPROACHES AND GENERAL ISSUES

An estimate is a judgment, opinion, or forecast of a future work or activity. A project cost estimate, therefore, is a judgment or opinion of the cost of that project; it is a forecast of what the accomplishment of the works and activities needed for carrying out that project will cost, in monetary terms.

Quantities and unit prices are the two essential ingredients of a cost estimate. The calculation of quantities is accomplished by using an estimating method, whereas the calculation of unit price to be applied to the quantities is determined by gathering and analyzing data. An estimating method is a systematic and consistent approach to predicting or estimating the cost and schedule for the execution of the works and activities needed to carry out the project. For each item, whether it be equipment, bulk materials, labor, or engineering, a method must be developed. The degree of sophistication applied to the estimating method must be balanced by the estimating process needs, and will be limited by the organizational capabilities of the institution in charge of performing the cost estimate. Cost-estimating methods can be developed in-house or be taken from similar exercises performed in the planning of other public transportation systems.

Approaches to Cost Estimating

The two general approaches to estimating either capital or operating costs are the *top-down*, or parametric approach, and the *ground-up*, or industrial-engineering approach. The parametric approach uses historical data from previous projects and extrapolates the cost of a new project based on an increase or decrease in quantity, size, weight, power level, or other factors for that new project. The industrial-engineering approach requires the estimating of man-hours and materials of each element and subelement of the project, and the pricing and accumulation of all the costs of the elements and subelements into a total cost estimate. Both methods of estimating are satisfactory for various phases of the estimating cycle. For instance, at the time of a feasibility study, an estimate based on the parametric approach may prove satisfactory; on the other hand, for a more advanced stage of the planning process, a ground-up estimate would be more appropriate. The parametric and the industrial-engineering approaches become more closely related as the estimating function deals with more specific and itemized project components.

There is no clear-cut rule as to which method of cost estimating is the best, although it would probably be possible to indicate which approach is preferable for a particular situation. The top-down parametric estimate, used alone, has limitations from the standpoint of visibility of estimate components, identification of major cost drivers, isolation of inflation effects on each cost element, and adjustment of costs to reflect subtle changes in the project scope. At the time of project planning, some of these purposes may not be deemed of major importance, and hence a top-down approach may be adequate. Furthermore, one or the other approach may better serve the purposes of the decision-making process in terms of, for instance, claiming which alternative is the best and advancing the planning stage into preliminary engineering and construction. The approach used to estimate the costs depends, then, on the intended final use of the estimate and the need for an accurate overall total versus the need for details (for instance, for control purposes). It also depends on the estimating tools available, the time available to prepare the estimate, the money available for preparing the estimate, and the amount of previous historical cost data available.[2]

In the case of Buffalo, initial (1976) studies were conducted under time constraints. The detail with which some cost estimates were carried out differed from one alternative to another (e.g., more detailed for those for which some preliminary work had been done, like the heavy-rail alternative). In fact, some estimates, in particular those of the later-selected LRRT alternative, were calculated on the basis of extrapolating cost estimates from other alternatives. Subsequent decisions, however, took the preliminary estimates for all the alternatives as having an equal footing and did not attempt to account for the higher uncertainty involved in the capital and operating cost values of the extrapolated alternatives, among them the selected LRRT system.

In the Boston case, the technical process followed an approach closer to the ground-up methodology because of federal requirements and the more advanced stage of analysis. Federal requirements try to improve the accountability of the estimates by requesting a larger specificity in the cost components. This ground-up approach, however, was rated as too demanding by the analysts in charge of applying it. They indicated that large amounts of time had to be spent gathering information and that the approach did not allow for the dynamism required by the planning process.

Very little standardization in estimating procedures has occurred to date because of the competitive and bargaining nature of the cost-estimating process itself, as well as the different requirements of the decision-making and institutional processes. In the United States, the federal government has attempted to boost the accountability of the projects that it partly funds and, in addition, has made it harder to complete the necessary requirements for approval of transit capital projects (in an effort to minimize demands on UMTA formula and discretionary funds and, indirectly, reduce the size of the federal deficit). This has increasingly moved the costing method closer to a ground-up approach. The Boston case was one of the first attempts at standardizing the cost-estimating process (among other components of the overall planning process); however the attempt did not get too far because of the difficulties of applying such an approach at the planning stage of analysis—not only because of the uncertainty about cost values but also because of the perspectives and expectations decision makers and analysts had about the technical analysis. Because of this, some elements of the estimating process closely followed the federal guidelines; other elements (or alternatives) did not. Hence, the characteristics of the planning process and the conditions surrounding it, which change from one situation to another, do not allow for easy standardization.

In any situation, the approach selected indicates some assumptions about the investment. For example, by adopting a top-down approach the estimators assume that the investment will behave similarly to previous projects upon which the values are taken (e.g., the case of Buffalo, with the extrapolation of cost values for some alternatives). In addition, different approaches support certain functions better than others. For instance, for control purposes in subsequent stages during final design and implementation, the ground-up approach has obvious advantages over the top-down approach. However, during the planning stage, this function is relegated to a second stage since it does not present a major priority for decision makers (vis-à-vis, for example, the decision to select one among several alternatives or the need to comply with a set of bureaucratic rules). In this situation, therefore, the need for a ground-up approach is largely diminished.

Furthermore, the estimation is made on certain assumptions about the scope and schedule of the project. If these assumptions are not kept—because, for instance, monitoring the implementation of the project cannot be (or is not) performed adequately—they are not likely to produce an accurate estimate. In other words, if monitoring is lousy, estimates will very likely be faulty. This type of assumption and its breakdown were present in most of the case studies. In fact, as was illustrated in the cases of Santa Clara County (underpass for railroad line, highway standards, etc.) and Buffalo (La Salle Street Station, underground utilities, etc.), the largest proportion of cost increases came from the failure to keep the assumptions made during the estimating process in the subsequent design and implementation stages.

Approaches, perspectives, assumptions, and functions are intertwined and affect how the cost-estimating process is undertaken and how we ultimately perceive the accuracy of the technical process. This intertwining suggests that depending upon which perspectives or functions are prevalent at the moment, assumptions and approaches should be adapted accordingly.

Either of the two general approaches to cost estimating can be complicated if different construction schedules are considered—that is, if the possibility of starting the alternatives at different times or in different stages is incorporated into the analysis (or if different financial mechanisms are evaluated). The possibility of phasing the transit investment is rarely considered for four main reasons: (1) it would increase considerably the number of alternatives to compare (and the computational requirements to perform in the estimating process); (2) the total costs would probably be higher as the economies of scale associated with a single large project would be lost; (3) the consideration of the project as a single package would assure, if approved, its complete construction, otherwise some parts of the project may stay unbuilt; and (4) the demands on the decision-making process and local institutions to follow the project over a much longer period of time are more compelling and require more persistence.

However, elimination of these possibilities, in a attempt to speed the process and gain approval for a total project, misses the point that by phasing the investment the annual disbursements would be lower and, although the final costs may be higher, the likelihood of getting quick approval for smaller incremental parts would be greater (as showed in the Boston case study). The incremental approach does not, by any means, assure the "tidiness" of the proposals since it may induce funding requests for segmented proposals that are inoperative by themselves and require additional segments, and the subsequent additional funds, to achieve their full potential. Therefore, segmented alternatives are worth full consideration in the analysis process, although they may not end up being the most adequate alternative from an operating strategy or financial standpoint.

Interestingly enough, as the case studies illustrate, the final decision about which system to pursue usually includes only a portion of the initially desired project. In spite of the fact that an incremental-investment approach is not usually considered in the analytic process, this approach often turns out to be the one that results from the negotiation process between the higher-level institutions and the transportation agency. For instance, in the case of Buffalo, the possibility of phasing of alternatives deserved some discussion, but it was never carried out very far. However, the alternative ultimately constructed resembled a first stage (6.4 miles) of the initial attempt to construct a larger network of 20 miles or a more limited one of 11 miles.

In some cases, the explicit indication of the phasing of the system is not possible owing to political considerations. In the case of Boston, the project called for the investigation of seven alternatives, four of them involving commuter rail. The implicitly preferred alternative included three commuter rail lines terminating in Boston's South Station, a centrally located major rail station. The federal government initially required the study of the complete alternative, and its comparison to the other alternatives, because it believed the full system would be the only one that could justify the investment.[3] As the cost of the system grew from $200 million to almost $400 million, the federal government started mentioning the possibility of phasing the investment, mainly because funds available for that particular type of projects were not in good supply at the moment. In addition, the fact that some communities were protesting commuter trains passing through their jurisdictions, changed the perceived support for the entire project and caused local transit officials and the federal government to support the scaling down of the commuter system, by starting with a reduced system (the one including the least controversial and the least expensive lines) and continuing with the other lines as knowledge of all the impacts improved. The reaction of the supporters of the restoration of commuter service was tremendous, and the governor quickly indicated that the full system would be constructed, and successfully persuaded the state legislature to approve a bond issue to pay for the local share of the total system (at the moment, almost $200 million). The draft environmental study, then, did not include the possibility of phasing the investment, although this possibility was still in the minds of the consultants and transit officials.

Cost Classifications

Since the quantities of the different items required for the construction of the transit project are one of the two major elements of a good basis for cost estimating, an adequate process must be established to account for all the cost items and to avoid any double counting. But this effort may be futile if, in both the top-down and ground-up approaches, no attempt is made to distinguish between types of costs so that the relation of what changes with what can be easily perceived and possibly account for the uncertainty of each item.

Costs can be classified according to different criteria. One of most widely used criteria consists of dividing costs depending on how directly they are attributable to the specific work activity or work output being estimated. For capital costs, we have: (1) direct costs or those associated with the materials and labor involved in the construction of the project; and (2) indirect costs, or costs of items that do not become a part of, but are necessary costs involved in, the design and construction of the project. These indirect costs comprise engineering costs, contractors' fees, field labor overhead (which includes temporary construction facilities, field supervision, construction tools, and labor payroll burden), and miscellaneous costs such as insurance, freight, and duties and taxes.[4] For operating costs, direct costs include labor—operators and maintenance crews—wages, energy—fuel and electricity—costs, maintenance parts, and ticketing and fare collection costs, and indirect costs include administration and scheduling of transportation and maintenance operations, system security, and insurance.

Other classifications are also possible. Depending on how they change along the life of the project, costs can be divided into fixed costs, or costs involved in an ongoing activity whose total cost will remain relatively constant regardless of the ridership on the transit system or the phase of the demand cycle being estimated (e.g., peak or off-peak periods); and variable costs, or costs that vary in relationship to the demand on the system. Of course, fixed costs are meaningful only if they are considered during a given period of time, since inflation and escalation will always provide a variable element to the "fixed" costs.[5]

These classifications are useful for purposes of relating capital and operating costs with other elements of the analysis, namely the demand calculation and the financial appraisal, and account for the uncertainty of estimates and improve the transparency of the cost-estimating process. On the demand side, there are elements of a project that do not change with the level of demand (at least for a wide range of demand values). For instance, the cost of stations, tracks, poles, or signalization, does not change for a range of demand values. On the other hand, the cost of rolling stock equipment and some elements included under operating costs depends on the ridership level, and as such its accuracy is affected by the accuracy of the demand estimates. Table 4.1 shows the classification of major operating costs as fixed and variable, depending on how they change with demand.

The case studies indicate that this type of cost classification is hardly used, at least with the purpose of realizing how much changes in output—demand— will affect costs. In the case studies, the accountability concern thwarted the possibilities of relating cost items to demand and, therefore, did not allow for quick sensitivity analyses based on demand.

If variable costs are directly related to demand, sensitivity analysis can be performed for different values of demand.[6] In such a case, the explicit recognition of different types of costs, in addition to improving the transparency of the process, can help cope with uncertainty and the problems of defining the scope of the project (escalation); it can also help structure the estimation process and possibly make analysts and decision makers realize how decisions based on different criteria may change with potential changes in the assumptions of the analytical study.

Table 4.1
Operating Costs Classification

Category	Type	Item
Transportation	fixed	administration and scheduling of transportation operations; ticketing and fare collection
	variable	operator wages and fringes; fuel and lube; tires and tubes
Equipment	fixed	maintenance administration for vehicles; maintenance of fare collection and counting equipment
	variable	servicing revenue vehicles; inspection, maintenance, and repairs of vehicles
Way and structures	fixed	maintenance administration for facilities; maintenance of roadway, track, and structures; maintenance of signals, communications, and control facilities; maintenance and repairs of buildings, grounds, and equipment; maintenance of passengers stations; operation and maintenance of electrical power facilities
General and administrative	fixed	systems security; injures and damages; general insurance; other general administration

Source: Ryan et al. (1986).
Note: The distinction between fixed and variable refers to which costs change with a medium change in ridership (e.g., increase or decrease of 15%).

More frequently, costs are categorized according to the other classification criterion: how directly they relate to the construction or operation of the transportation facility (direct and indirect costs). This type of classification plays a major role during final design and construction for the purpose of allocating costs to particular activities with a view toward procurement and work contracting. However, during the planning stage, the direct-indirect classification does not help reduce the uncertainty of the estimates, or elucidate the tradeoffs among transit alternatives in the light of that uncertainty. In this sense, the demand-based classification can better serve the needs of the decision-making process. Furthermore, the demand-based classification could be used to assign financial responsibility to the institutions involved in the funding of the project. By assigning items to particular institutions based on how responsive to demand the costs of those items are, a better internalization of the funding consequences of the project would be incorporated into the process. For instance, if a local institution is in charge of paying for items whose costs vary with demand, an effort would likely be made at the local level to estimate as accurately and unbiasedly as possible those costs and the demand for the system, and see what the consequences would be if the estimated demand is not realized or surpassed.

Computerized Estimation: Database Management Issues

In addition to the quantities, the other element of the cost-estimating basis is unit prices. This information is gathered through surveys, quotations, historical background, comparable systems, and the like. Together, quantities and unit prices encompass an enormous amount of information that must be organized and managed so that it can be kept up to date during the planning process. In addition, the cost-estimating process involves using this large amount of information for fairly repetitive tasks. These two characteristics make the process particularly suitable for computer-based technology. Moreover, developments in both hardware and software computer technology during the last ten years have made this technology easily available for any estimating process. In addition, automation of the cost-estimation process presents some interesting benefits in terms of speed, consistency, fewer unintended errors, neater presentation, and improved communications.

Application of computer technology involves management of information systems (MIS) and decision support systems (DSS).[7] The first field discusses the organization, processing, retrieval, and update of data needed for cost estimation. The second covers manipulation of the data for purposes of cost analysis and sensitivity analyses. In general, the management of information includes all steps from gathering the data, to analyzing it, to the application of the estimating unit data, to the generation of final cost reports. For purposes of cost estimating, the major thrust is not so much on how to organize the relevant information but rather on figuring out what it means and what relevance it has to the decision at hand. Decision support systems are MISs that also have some processing capability designed to help the decision maker use the information ("what if" analysis) to perceive the tradeoffs between different courses of action.

The automation process involves several important issues. First, cost programs must be developed or purchased. Buying a program makes it available for use sooner, enables the user to use the experience of others, and overall, costs less. On the other hand, the purchased program may not meet the needs of the estimator, and it may be difficult to verify the quality of the program. Furthermore, it may be difficult to revise.

Second, the organization managing the computer-based information system must have the technical and organizational capabilities to develop and maintain the data-collection or data-management system. Methods are ineffective in producing reliable estimates if good unit-cost data to convert quantities to costs are lacking. In addition, most cost data are dynamic and subject to almost instant obsolescence, and a data management system must keep data current. The task of the cost estimator in setting up such a system is further complicated by the massive amount of the data that must be accumulated and managed.

These issues reflect the fact that the cost-estimation process is just as critical, if not more so, than the cost estimate itself. Often a cost is quoted without qualifications. This is one reason for frequent misunderstandings and confusion concerning the costs of an activity. For instance, the Buffalo case has become known for its large cost overruns.[8] However, as noted in Chapter 3, when inflation is taken into account, the increase in initial estimated costs is not more dramatic than in other less publicized cases (see Table 1.1).[9] In Boston, the near-doubling of the initial estimates (from $200 to almost $400) was mostly due to the lack of consideration of some items in the first estimates (such as land acquisition costs and provisions for design, administration, and contingencies) and the different years of comparison (the feasibility study was based on 1984 dollars, the alternatives analysis was based on 1986 dollars [10]). After accounting for "missing" elements and inflation, the two estimates were much more similar, a fact that was unknown to some of the key detractors of the system. These arguments are examples of the consequences of the lack of qualifying cost estimates. (Of course, these situations also come about as some actors use cost figures for strategic purposes. However, this is a different issue that will be discussed in Chapters 5 and 7.)

Whenever the cost of an item is quoted, it should be accompanied by qualifying information including: (1) a full description of the item; (2) the date for the cost of item (or key milestones for an activity); and (3) how the item relates to output (demand). Depending the stage of analysis and the resources available to carrying out the cost-estimating function, the qualification could also include (4) the geographical location of the item or activity; (5) the skills and organizations assumed available to perform the work to complete the item or activity; and (6) the expected quality and service life of the output related to the item. This structure parallels the one that in construction management is called a *work element structure* (sometimes also called a work breakdown structure).[11] The structure serves, in addition, as a framework for collecting, accumulating, organizing, and computing the direct costs of a work activity or work output.

This information structure can be organized within a computer-based framework that allows for easy editing and updating when changes occur in the planning process. The implementation of database relational systems [12] further improves the possibilities of relating cost items to other variables, such as demand, that affect the quantity levels that enter the cost-estimating methods for the purposes advanced in section on cost classifications.

In the case of Boston, the amount of data involved was much larger. The spreadsheet system was built in a modular fashion and did not attempt a full relation to variables that affected the level of investment. The system did not allow for easy sensitivity analyses. This was reflected in some mistakes that appeared in the capital cost figures. For instance, the first attempt to calculate capital costs included for each alternative a low, a medium (the best estimate), and a high value for each of the cost items. For one of the alternatives, the upper bound (or high value) of one of the items (contingencies) was lower than both the lower bound and the best estimate, given an overall total for the upper bound only slightly larger than the middle value (or best estimate). This error appeared in several reports during the planning process, including the one submitted to the federal government for approval—the Draft Environmental Impact Statement.

The importance of these issues is not so much the computerization per se but what they mean in terms of organizing the technical process, allowing flexibility in the planning process, and offering a more effective interaction—however futile that may turn out to be—of the technical with the decision-making process (effective in terms of quick response to changes and requests from decision makers). The computer-based framework, by specifying which items to consider and the relationship among them and other input variables, can also help structure the thinking, learning, and argumentation processes.

Although the many particularities of any transit project do not permit easy implementation of a standard cost-estimating information system, the considerable time spent gathering cost information could be reduced with implementation of a management information system. In the United States, this "centralized" approach was supported by the UMTA but rejected by local analysts on the basis that projects are too specific to merit a unified central database. Although this topic falls outside the scope of this book, careful consideration should be made of implementing a databank that would allow transit planners to obtain unit-cost information for quickly estimating the costs of any proposal.[13] This approach would not directly and substantially reduce the cost-underestimation problem (as the case studies illustrated by showing that unit-cost information is not the major reason for cost underestimation), but it would shorten the time to perform some components of the technical process and would help carry forward some other proposals advanced in this book (e.g., sensitivity analyses, criteria argumentation).

COST ESTIMATION IN TRANSIT PROJECT PLANNING

In the process of analyzing alternatives, an important issue is the level of effort and detail that must be spent on developing cost estimates. Theoretically, the level of effort and detail invested in estimating capital and operating costs should be that necessary to ensure that the choice of alternative does not change with additional cost information. Analysis then is extended to the point that additional information eliminates the chance that the decision will be changed (i.e., the expected value of additional information is zero). In other words, since the final outcome of the alternatives-analysis process is the selection of the best alternative, the technical process should be carried out to the point that the "benefit of the marginal knowledge" is zero—that is, to the point at which knowing more about the estimates would not improve the effectiveness of the selection. This is, obviously, a theoretical reasoning, but sets the stage for more practical discussion.

In practical terms, there are two levels of estimating effort—one following the top-down approach, for typical facilities, and another, much more detailed, following the ground-up approach, for special situations.[14] The first level can be applied to those segments—hence the name *segmentation*—that consist of a typical cross section (e.g., track sections) or for a typical facility (e.g., station). Detailed unit costs are used with quantities taken from the typical segments to derive costs per linear foot for each section or per type of facility. Costs can then be computed to represent the capital cost of each identified typical section or facility, exclusive of systemwide elements and add-on items.

The special situations approach consists of those segments or structure that do not present typical characteristics (e.g., major structures or track sections on difficult terrain). Costs for these special elements are computed from the ground up, with drawings and more detailed quantities and unit costs.

Systemwide elements include those items of capital investment that cannot be defined on a segment-by-segment basis (e.g., vehicles, electrification). They must be calculated with units costs applied to systemwide quantities. Some of these systemwide elements are related to operating costs that, in turn, depend on patronage levels and, hence, on the results generated in the demand models. Add-on items consist of contingency allowances and the costs of engineering and construction management services. The costs of these items are usually calculated as percentages of the estimated baseline capital costs (depending on how detailed the calculation of these costs has been).

The estimation of operating costs is more controversial because their calculation depends to a great extent on the estimation of other similarly controversial variables: service and patronage levels. (As was mentioned before, some capital costs—for example, rolling stock equipment—also depend on patronage levels.) Furthermore, the costs should be calculated to optimize the performance of the system to provide the expected service and patronage levels. This process involves analysis of the transit network, demand estimation, and balancing of transit supply with transit demand. Once the operating statistics are obtained (vehicle-miles, vehicle-hours, peak vehicles, etc.), the pertinent cost models can be applied to account for the resources required to meet the expected demand and provide the expected level of service—hence the name *resource build-up* for this methodology. The development of these models usually requires application of some regression analysis with a calibration procedure to adapt the parameters to the particular situation of the city where the transit system is being planned. To the greatest extent possible, the calibration should be done using typical conditions (e.g., no significant changes in service levels, labor productivity, or ridership patterns). Furthermore, service characteristics should be similar to the ones proposed for the system being planned.

Summarizing, the prevalent approach to cost estimating in transit project planning is a combination of both the top-down and the ground-up approaches:

- For capital costs, the prevalent method is the segmentation approach. In this approach, all capital items are divided into segments with common characteristics (e.g., track section between stations) or particular facilities (e.g., stations), composite costs for typical cross sections are estimated within common segments and multiplied for the length of those segments, and overall costs are estimated for particular facilities. Finally, other systemwide elements and add-on items are added (e.g., contingencies, engineering and construction management costs).
- For operating and maintenance costs, the prevalent method is the resource buildup approach. This approach is usually based on past performance of similar transit systems, but at the same time includes a detailed analysis of productivity measures and service levels for the particular context of the transportation project under analysis. In a first step, based on the service levels that one wants to achieve (based, in turn, on demand and the desired capacity, comfort, and environmental impacts), quantities are calculated so that the transportation facility will provide those service levels. Then quantities are multiplied by productivity measures to obtained the quantities required to operate and maintain the system. These quantities are multiplied by the unit costs to obtain the quantity costs so that, by adding all these costs together, the final total costs are calculated.

The flow chart in Figure 4.1 summarizes the main components of the technical process in cost estimating. As the case studies illustrated, this graph represents more a normative process than a descriptive one. This is because components of the graph are sometimes missing or not fully considered: for instance, the financial context that is barely considered at the time of calculating costs or is mostly considered a posteriori—that is, after costs have already been calculated. Other difficulties that are discussed in the next section highlight the constraints of applying the normative ideal.

Notwithstanding, as was mentioned at the beginning of this chapter, two components stand up: the level of investment and the unit prices. The investment level comes from two main sources, the level of demand and the amount of resources available (i.e., financial context). The demand level, in turn, depends mainly on the socioeconomic characteristics of the area (that will give an indication of the number of rides per person) and how much the transit facility will cost the users (understanding cost in a general sense, including time and comfort costs, and vis-à-vis the "generalized" cost of competitive modes of transportation on the corridor). The demand and fare levels are important in the

Figure 4.1
Schematic Representation of Major Elements of Technical Process

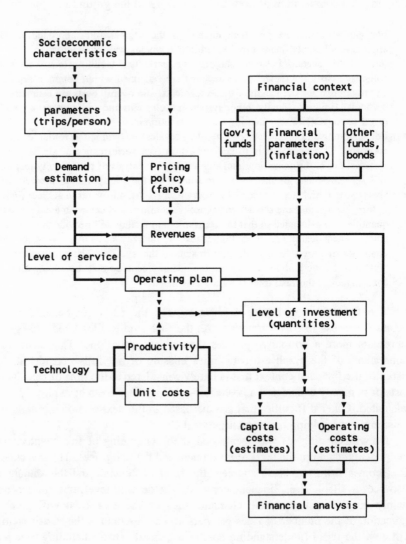

design of the operating plan and knowing the stream of revenues that the transit system will get from its users. The level of revenues is complemented by the financial context to ascertain the total level of funds available to construct and operate the transit facility or system. The financial context sets the terms of how much money will cost in the future (i.e., inflation and interest rates), how much is available from higher level institutions or other organizations, and what can be obtained by issuing bonds or other financial mechanisms.

The level of service variable serves as a cushion between the demand variable and the operating plan (and possibly investment levels for some capital items, such as number of vehicles). Several demand values would require the same level of investment, in both operating and capital terms, but would yield a different level of service for passengers. However, the level of service provided would probably affect the demand level (as fewer patrons use the system if the level of service, such as the probability of getting a seat, decreases), but this effect is hardly considered.

The operating plan and the investment level are further complemented by productivity measures for the particular technology. For each specific technology, these productivity measures, coupled with the unit prices of the different components of the transit facility, are in the final step inserted in the investment level to generate the capital and operating cost estimates. These estimates, taking into consideration the financial context and the stream of revenues, evolve into the financial analysis for each specific alternative.

PROBLEMS AND ISSUES IN THE TECHNICAL PROCESS

The previous section summarized the main components of the technical cost-estimating process. That summary may suggest that, in principle, the process is a clear sequence of steps that should lead to a final set of correct capital and operating costs of a transit project. The process, however, presents some difficulties. The next paragraphs discuss these difficulties and the issues that generate them.

The Issue of Uncertainty

The consistent underestimation of costs at the planning stage is often attributed to a lack of consideration of all elements of the project. This shortcoming relates to the inherent uncertainty in any estimating process. In project planning, several factors are highlighted as potential sources of error for estimating costs: (1) changes in the scope of the project; (2) changes in design standards; (3) incorrect unit cost or parameter assumptions in the planning estimates; (4) bad estimating analytic methods; (5) and unforeseen problems in implementing the project. Except for the application of inadequate analytic methods, all other factors are closely related to the uncertainty associated with elements in the estimating process.

Uncertainty stems from factors beyond the inherent characteristics of any estimating function, since one can never predict any event or value with absolute certainty. Moreover, it is often the case with transit projects that they take several years to be planned and completed. Hence, the prediction of capital and operating costs (and the other variables upon which costs are calculated) that will take place far in the future becomes very difficult, even with highly sophisticated technical resources, since the reliability of these estimates inevitably decreases with time (as uncertainty increases).

In addition to the impossibility of predicting the future, other reasons for the uncertainty of cost components relate to the argumentative content of the estimates (the one that allows the competition and argumentation among different perspectives and different actors). The argumentative content of a cost estimate usually centers on the levels or magnitude (scope) of resource predictions rather than on the methods or assumptions used in making the estimate (that is, the focus almost always is on factors (1) and (2), and less often on (3), (4), or (5)). That is the case because the standards and scope of the project are the elements that eventually, if the project is constructed, have the largest impact on the affected constituencies. Cost methods, unit costs, or how long it will take to construct the project, though important in defining the final cost of the project, do not ultimately influence the effects of the project once constructed, while the visibility and impact of the scope and standards of the project—including operating strategies—in attaining the specified objectives are the most important. In the case studies, all of the preferred alternatives were initially scaled down to minimum requirements (in an attempt, probably, to keep capital costs at a reasonable level). Later, as communities on the corridor requested that standards be raised, costs increased correspondingly.

Another component of the uncertainty related to the competitive nature of the cost components refers to assumptions about which institutions are in charge of covering the costs of particular elements of the proposed transit system. For instance, in the case of Buffalo or Santa Clara County, technical analysts thought that public utilities would pay for costs of relocating underground utility lines. As it later turned out, after the inevitable legal battles, the transportation agency had to pay for those costs—and, therefore, should have considered them as costs of the transportation project.

The case studies illustrate some attempts to tackle uncertainty from the technical standpoint. These attempts were, however, rather tenuous. In the case of Buffalo, a 1976 report included some sensitivity tests. One of these tests consisted of escalating costs by 1, 2, and 3 percent compounded annually between 1974 and 1995, to assume a differential with fare increases.[15] Another kind of sensitivity test involved consideration of different incremental construction schedules. In the 1976 report, conclusions were reached about operating deficits with a average fare level of $0.38. With a value of $0.37, however, some alternatives that showed operating surpluses would have yielded operating deficits. This example indicates the low level of reliability of the estimates, and the negligible attempt to account for the uncertainty of the estimates.

One possible way to reduce uncertainty is to increase the detail in the cost estimates. But this may not be possible owing to the tradeoff between resources available for the estimation process and the need to go beyond conceptual engineering. In any case, an effort can be made to improve the estimation of costs of those components that are both major items and that have significant uncertainties in their costs (e.g., segments whose right-of-way falls within highly developed areas, which may require unexpected mitigation measures and added physical amenities).

Another possibility that can help reduce errors from a procedural point of view consists of starting with preliminary estimates at the very early stages of the alternatives-analysis process and then periodically updating the costs to reflect accumulation of better information. The final cost estimates then come out of a continuous process rather than out of a final effort made at the end of the study. This approach, however, has the danger of taking the initial estimates for granted, keeping the final project evaluation with the initial values (maybe because those were the values everybody agreed on). For instance, in the case of Boston, the initial tag of $200 million was assumed from June 1984, the date the feasibility study was released, until March 1987, when capital cost estimates went up to almost $400 million (this was in 1986 dollars, however). The expectations created in the initial stages were based on the $200 million cap. When, in April 1987, the plans to scale down the project were announced, most communities in the corridor and their elected officials reacted angrily because they felt they had been cheated.

Another approach involves performing complete sensitivity analysis involving changes in the values of those variables that appear to be more susceptible to change. This process will produce upper and lower bounds for major cost components, and will allow decision makers to assess the accuracy of the cost estimates and how much they may eventually change. With sensitivity analysis performed in both quantities and unit costs, uncertainties in quantities related to possible changes in scope, design standards, and other variables, as well as those related to unit costs, may be better perceived and taken into consideration by decision makers.

The sensitivity approach is something of a departure from usual practice. Typically, most project planning cost estimates have assumed a specific scope for the project, applied the unit-cost assumptions, and used an overall contingency factor to account for uncertainties. (Often, the same contingency factor is used for all alternatives, regardless of their nature and uncertainty.) Sensitivity tests can be expanded to include changes not only in the unit cost of a particular variable but also in the analysts' or decision makers' perceptions of the future. In the case studies, the transit projects were designed assuming the economy was going to keep growing at the same pace (or close to that pace), and that this growth was going to cause an intolerable level of traffic congestion that, in time, would limit the potential growth of the area. Since these expectations were not realized, the assumptions in the study did not hold and the estimates did not materialize.

Scenario design [16] is another methodological approach that was not formally incorporated in the technical process. This approach can complement sensitivity analysis to account for changes in broader environment-related assumptions. It takes into consideration the effect of these assumptions in the value of cost variables, such as if the economy does not grow at the same pace or the price of oil decreases or inflation peaks, what would happen to construction costs, and what level of investment or transit alternative would then be more appropriate if those changes take place. This methodology parallels the framework highlighted in Chapter 2, in which consideration of an argument-oriented paradigm translates into incorporation of strategic issues, with a long-term view of the elements related to the goals the transit investment is attempting to address (e.g., downtown revitalization, land use and density guidance, economic growth, etc.).

Still another way is to use contingency factors. But these factors usually take the form of a single percentage value to be applied to the final cost figure. A more precise method consists of assigning different contingency factors to different elements of the capital or operating cost figures, depending on their reliability.[17] In the case of Boston, a 10 percent contingency was used overall for TSM elements; in the commuter rail alternatives, a 5 percent contingency was used for trackwork, 15 percent for signals and communications, and 10 percent for all other items; in the busway alternative, cross sections of the right-of-way had a 5 percent contingency while all other elements had a 10 percent contingency factor. This level of aggregation was deemed appropriate for purposes of planning. These percentages reflected the consultants' perceptions about the accuracy of the elements depending on how close to a top-down approach the estimation of particular costs was.

A final option, as suggested earlier, consists of designing a modular, transparent computer-based model with a reclassification of cost components in terms of which are certain and which are uncertain. The model better allows one to (1) see and explore the ripple effects of uncertainties and (2) make changes to key initial assumptions (e.g., via a database management system). This option—that can be used in conjunction with some of the other options indicated above—should improve communications among the actors in the process and also help perceive the likely variations in final costs.

Other Issues

An issue that creates difficulties in the technical process is knowing exactly what elements to include as components of a transit alternative, apart from the difficulty that comes from the inherent technical uncertainty. For instance, in the case of Buffalo, the capital costs did not include the additions to the bus fleet that would be needed to feed the LRRT system.[18] These costs were eventually acknowledged in response to community concerns raised at a public hearing.[19] The issue relates to what elements must be included at the time of estimating costs since every alternative must consider any additions or deletions that would take place for the adequate operation of the proposed transit system (e.g., feeder bus system for a commuter-rail alternative). However, it is no small task to figure out which changes the implementation of a new facility will bring to the whole transportation system. If riders are attracted from other transit services, those services may involve lower operating costs (or the fleet may be reduced and sold to other transit authorities); this reduction in other services would then decrease the overall cost of the project. Conversely, the new facility may need additional feeder bus lines to be able to reach the estimated demand; this need will increase capital and operating costs. In the end, the process requires consideration of the transportation system with and without the project in order to accurately estimate both capital and operating costs.[20]

Still another difficulty in the technical process is generated by the phasing issue (mentioned in the second section of this chapter). If project implementation must be carried out on an incremental basis owing to funding constraints, higher project costs will probably result because of lost economies of scale, since each systemwide contract would be signed in smaller parts and purchased and installed at separate times. Also some elements, such as yards and shops, must be constructed anyway as soon as revenue operation begins. Likewise, it may be necessary to relocate certain elements required to operate the system from the second phase into the first increment constructed. These arguments were indicated, for instance, in the case of Buffalo, where, in one of the few cases in which the phasing concept was discussed, the incremental construction of one of the alternatives (the 11-mile heavy-rail system) would have increased costs owing to the need to relocate a yard and demolish the initial structure. Interestingly, the cost of the incremental implementation was estimated a mere 2 percent higher than the full implementation.[21]

Yet another important issue is the initial lack of consideration of the financial context surrounding the transit project. This deficiency, coupled with a frequent overestimation of demand, tends to yield investment levels higher than may actually be required. But in order to keep costs low and eventually obtain approval of funds from higher level institutions, productivity measures tend to be rather optimistic, and design standards and unit prices rather low. Once the project is started, the transportation agency hopes that involved institutions will see the construction to full implementation.

In the United States, conversations with UMTA officials indicated that, from their point of view, the lack of consideration of the financial context was one major reasons for posterior financial problems and strained relations between the UMTA and the local agencies. Once the project is started, the local agencies realize they cannot afford the system, and start requesting further funds; local politicians then take the lead in requesting the additional funds needed to complete the project. In other words, UMTA officials argued that, often, the financial costs are subject to the requirements of the estimated costs rather than subjecting these costs (and hence the corresponding transit alternatives) to the constraints of the financial context.

Regardless of these perceptions, what actually happens is not so much that the financial context is not considered (all three cases illustrated how adequate financial provisions were made at the local level to meet the local share of capital costs), but rather that this consideration was not put in the context of possible increases in cost estimates. Therefore, the optimistic cost estimate was more the source of the problem than the fact that the financial context was not carefully considered.[22]

CONCLUSION

This chapter reviewed the technical process of estimating capital and operating costs for the construction of transit facilities, identifying its main components, the major approaches, and the main difficulties and issues involved in undertaking these approaches. It showed how the cost-estimating approach must be tailored to the decision environment, how cost classifications can help players understand the implications of changes in demand estimates, and how the management of cost information can help analysts organize and structure the cost-estimating process. In another section, the major components of this process were identified along with their relationships. Figure 4.1 set the path to a broader discussion of uncertainties in the cost-estimating process and the possible means of dealing with them.

Finally, this chapter illustrated that certain difficulties in the technical process leave room for deviations from the rational ideal of comprehensiveness and impartiality, although specific actions can be taken to get closer to that ideal. Chapter 5 discusses the decision-making process and elucidates other components of the overall planning process that can affect the technical process and how this process is undertaken. Nevertheless, just as the design of the technical process—in terms of which approach to follow, how to deal with uncertainty, and so on—affects the technical process itself, so too how the ultimate users of that process—the decision makers—perceive the role of the technical analysis constitutes a fundamental element in understanding and structuring that technical process. In the end, the success or failure of the cost-estimating process depends on how useful it is in the decision-making process, rather than its accuracy or technical sophistication.

NOTES

1. Clark and Lorenzoni (1985), Stewart (1982); Calder (1976).

2. Clark and Lorenzoni (1985).

3. If the system did not reach the central station, the federal government and local groups thought that not as many people would use the system, because transfers would decrease the quality of service. This decrease would reduce the cost-effectiveness of the system, and the required thresholds could not be reached.

4. Clark and Lorenzoni (1985).

5. Stewart (1982).

6. The variation in demand, in addition, could ideally be related to changes in the fare level.

7. Gorry and Scott Morton (1986), Senn (1984), Keen and Scott Morton (1978).

8. U.S. General Accounting Office (1986, July).

9. A different criticism (voice by some individuals interviewed) targets the low number of miles Buffalo's LRRT system covers considering the amount of money invested, but this is a much more subjective and controversial assessment.

10. This is an assumption of the author, since it was impossible to find a consensus about which year the cost estimates of the alternatives analysis were based on.

11. A work-element structure is developed by subdividing a process, product, project, or service into its major work elements, then breaking the major work elements into subelements, and subelements into sub-subelements, and so on. This framework assumes a hierarchical relationship among the elements: the resources or content of each work element are made up of the sum of the resources or content of elements below it. The major subdivisions can be either functional or physical elements. The second level usually consists of a combination of functional or physical elements if a product or project is being estimated (Stewart 1982).

12. Date (1986), Holsapple (1984).

13. The Highway Design and Maintenance Standards Model (HDM) is an example of a computer-based program that allows the user to calculate the costs of several road-maintenance alternatives based on some prespecified relationships and after the introduction of specific unit-cost information. This program is being used in several countries in spite of the fact that conditions vary markedly. The HDM is an effective tool in structuring the road-maintenance process. At the same time, HDM is flexible enough to allow for incorporation of different assumptions and performance of calibrations as needed. It is also a good example of a cost-estimating tool that reduces substantially the time to generate cost estimates for road-maintenance alternatives (World Bank 1988).

14. Ryan et al. (1986).

15. The only conclusion related to this sensitivity analysis was that if differential escalation of costs over revenues continued, large annual deficits would be forecast, and some administrative action would be required, such as a cutback in feeder bus service or increase in fare levels.

16. Pearman (1988), Meyer and Miller (1984).

17. Ryan et al. (1986).

18. U.S. Department of Transportation (1977), p. 4-8.

19. Ibid., p. 10-33.

20. A similar approach should be applied to ridership, since analysts must compensate ridership gains on some lines with losses on others. In other words, ridership estimation would involve calculation of overall figures with every transit alternative being considered and compare those estimates to the do-nothing alternative (i.e., the alternative with no new investment to the transportation system in place besides the standard additions being already applied to it).

21. Niagara Frontier Transportation Authority (1976, June), p. 104.

22. Nevertheless, the system seems to work well for the local interests if their purpose is to preselect a project and then build the political base necessary to persuade a higher level institution (e.g., UMTA) to pay for that project.

5

Decision Making: Perspectives, Elements, and Problems

From the previous chapter, one may think that the cost-estimating process consists of a clear set of steps that, once some technical difficulties are overcome, leads to a final, accurate cost estimate for a specific project. The reality, however, reflects a different picture, as the history of chronically underestimated capital and operating costs in large transportation projects proves.[1] Most of the studies that have attempted to explain cost underestimation have looked at this history from a technical standpoint, using statistical analyses to explain and tackle the issue. However, the case studies illustrated (and the analytical framework in Chapter 2 suggested) that a rigorous study must also encompass other components of the estimating process to find out where the "disturbances" come from. These other components include both internal and external effects within the institutional and political dimensions of the transportation planning process.

The decision-making process inherently involves organizations and individuals, whose perspectives are very different from those of the "rational" systems analyst. Allison's *Essence of Decision: Explaining the Cuban Missile Crisis* (1971) presented these perspectives by illustrating three different models to "see" a single decision process. Simon's *Administrative Behavior* (1976) related the limitations that are unavoidably present in any human-decision making process and how these limitations affect the pure rational-system perspective.

The characteristics and assumptions of the rational-system perspective include the ability to abstract problems; the certainty of solving those problems; the optimality of the results; the possibility of reducing problems to a very limited number of elements and the interactions among them; the reliance on data and models; the possibility of quantifying information; objectivity (or the assumption that the analyst is an unbiased observer outside of the system); the ignorance or avoidance of the individual (and instead averages are used to generate results); and a view of the time that is linear (with no consideration of differential time perceptions).[2] The success of this method and its paradigms in applied mathematics and modeling gradually led its extension to society and all its systems.

The rational model was discussed in Chapter 2. Application to the transportation planning process indicates that the elements of comprehensiveness and impartiality of that model have limitations within that realm. The main reason derives from particulars of the transportation planning process such as its interdisciplinary nature, the scope of its impact, and the fuzzy line between its technical and political aspects. These characteristics make the decision-making environment a complex one, where, in addition, it is hard to define who the decision makers are.

By contrast, in the private sector, application of the rational paradigm has been rather successful. But transit projects are public projects and, as such, present characteristics that differ from those in the private context. The following is a list of some differences between the public and the private context as they relate to the decision-making environment:

1. Public decision makers tend to have a relatively short time perspective delineated by political necessities, the political calendar, and the short-term budget cycle.[3]
2. There is little if any agreement on the standards and measurement of performance to appraise a public decision maker.
3. In the public arena, emphasis tends to be placed on providing equity among different constituencies to the detriment of efficiency, although both equity and efficiency can be part of a rational analysis.
4. Public decision makers tend to be more open and exposed to public scrutiny, and they must contend regularly with the press and media (and their decisions are sometimes anticipated by the press).
5. Public decision makers often seek to mediate decisions in response to a wide variety of pressures and must often put together a coalition of groups to survive; in addition, they tend to regard themselves as responsible to many superiors instead of a single higher authority.
6. Public decision making is often subject to close scrutiny by legislative oversight groups or even judicial orders, constraining executive and administrative freedom to act.
7. A variety of other factors affect and constrain decision making in the public arena, such as the difficulties of implementing change, resistance to change in large-scale bureaucracies, and the frequent imperfect control and coordination among different public institutions.[4]

Added to these characteristics are two more that make the transportation decision-making process even more complicated. The first is the ever-changing focus of the political agenda and of public priorities. The brief history of transportation planning presented in Chapter 2 shows that continuous change in focus. The second is the frequent inseparability of decisions. For instance, the decision to revitalize the downtown area and reduce congestion may be inseparable from the decision to construct some sort of transit system.

The case studies illustrate many of these issues, and a full account here would unnecessarily lengthen the scope of this chapter. A few instances should suffice to indicate how, within the transportation planning context, decision makers are affected by the characteristics of the public arena. For instance, the cases illustrate the short-term focus of some arguments targeted on cost-effectiveness selection criteria. However, in order to attract constituencies and reach an acceptable level of equity, stated objectives tended to stress longer term elements such as land-use changes or the city's future economic development. Frequent clashes resulted as the different layers of players in the decision-making process disagreed over which perspectives were the most important for selection of the preferred alternative. Shifting priorities were a consequence of those clashes (in addition to general trends in the constituencies affected by the transportation plans) and were reflected in the long time it took to fully implement the initial proposals. The visibility and scrutiny of the decision-making function were reflected at frequent turning points in the process (such as the case of phasing in Boston), as well as by emphasis on keeping the affected constituencies informed about the technical results. Finally, the permanence of initially preferred proposals—for more than 15 years, in some cases—reflected the difficulties of changing the course of action. These difficulties came from several sources including the complexity of the technical process, the time and effort required to ensure support by the constituencies, and the inseparability of decisions. In other words, initially preferred proposals did not substantially change along the planning process because, as time passes, it became more and more difficult politically and technically—and probably psychologically—to do so.

DECISION MAKING: THEORIES AND ISSUES

This section presents a review of the major theoretical elements that refer to decision-making theory as a background for the subsequent discussion of decision making in transportation planning and the presentation of the theoretical framework in Chapter 6.

Decision-Making Theories, Perspectives, and Elements

Theories of decision-making can be classified in two different groups: individual and general. At the individual (micro) level, two main streams of theory have been developed—those that try to define what the decision maker ought to do (prescriptive or normative theories), and those that try to define what they actually do in practice (descriptive theories). The former are included within the tradition of operations research methods and encompass the area of decision analysis. The latter include the areas of psychology and behavioral studies.

The distinction between prescriptive and descriptive theories becomes blurred when each proponent tries to address the concerns of the other.[5] For instance, a normative model may adequately predict what an individual decides to do if this individual follows the dictates of the model; in the opposite direction, descriptive considerations change the content of normative models. Contemporary normative models for decision making are little more than rules designed to ensure that acts will be coherent or internally consistent in the pursuit of the decision maker's goals.

At a more general (macro) level, the rational-actor model of decision making corresponds to the normative theories as it tries to prescribe the outcome of every decision-making process based on a given set of assumptions. Satisfying, organizational, and political (or personal) theories fit more within the psychological and behavioral theories (descriptive) as they try to explain decisions based on empirical experiences.

Theories of decision-making can be understood as a continuum. The rational-actor model misses some aspects, such as the political interests of the decision maker or the pressures from the organization that the decision maker is part of. By adding other "less quantifiable" elements, we can think of any decision-making process as a maximization of the stakes that the many actors involved have in it. The stakes include everything from the financial costs for some actors, to the political gains for others, and to savings in travel time for still others. The problem is not only that it is very difficult to define some of these stakes—for instance, the value of political gains—but also to identify all the actors involved.

In spite of its practical difficulties, the idea of the continuum allows us to accept that an outcome we may assess as an irrational decision is actually rational at a different point on that continuum. Allison's (1971) explanation of the same outcome from three different perspectives reflects the idea that political or organizational perspectives are not necessarily irrational but just rational from those perspectives (i.e., rationality is always present but its definition changes depending on the perspective).[6]

Acknowledgment of this continuum can help us better understand planning outcomes that evolve as a consequence of public decision-making processes. The predominant definition of rationality—the (economic) utilitarian definition—is not enough to explain particular outcomes. Utility functions do not allow for straightforward encapsulation of a multiple-perspective approach encompassing technical, organizational, and personal perspectives.[7]

The need for different perspectives also stems from the fact that different explanations—or interpretations—of a phenomenon are often possible.[8] These different explanations originate in elements such as: (1) the background of analysts and the specificity in the definition of their tasks (the personal perspective), (2) the type of organizational structure (the bureaucratic perspective), and (3) the type of environment (the sociopolitical perspective).

The background of the analysts and the specificity of their tasks relates to how they perceive their roles in the planning process and whether or not these roles are specified.[9] In the case studies, analysts, indubitably with respectable professional competence, did not perceive their tasks as purely technical but more as collaborative in the decision-making process and possibly influencing the outcome of the planning process. This element is also influenced by the definition of goals to be achieved in the decision-making process and how widely they are accepted. In the United States, some goals are not precisely defined because they are not widely recognized but rather are controversial—that is the case, for instance, with the issue of land-use effects of LRT and fixed-guideway systems. As the case studies illustrate, with different broad objectives stressed for similar projects and by different groups of actors, analysts are often left to fend for themselves and find a way to reconcile the different goals of a transit investment. The lack of specificity in goals and tasks, on one hand, does not help establish a solid, unique basis for a formal decision-making process. On the other hand, that lack of specificity may be inevitable in order to reach an outcome within a particular planning environment.

The lack of specificity in the case studies contrasts, paradoxically, with their high degree of formalization of the planning process. This situation creates strains and lowers the possibility that the formalization is widely accepted.[10] Formalization also relates to the roles of the actors in the planning process and the relationships among them. Formalization, when prescribed independently of the individuals in the decision-making structure, is an attempt to make their behavior more predictable by standardizing and regulating it, but again this situation is likely to clash with the actors' different backgrounds and styles.

Another important element of the technical-estimation process is the organizational context within which that process takes place. This context refers to the institutions in charge of carrying out the technical elements of cost estimating, those involved in deciding which alternative to pursue, and the relationships among them and with the rest of the institutions involved in the broader planning process.

Usually, the scale of the projects that are the subject of this book requires involvement of several institutions and, mainly, of consultants outside the public transit agency. In the case studies, the technical studies were done by outside consulting firms;[11] the transportation agencies supervised the consultants' work. Once the preferred alternative was selected, other institutions—engineering firms and construction companies—constructed the transit facility. Once constructed, the facility was operated by the transit agency. This process presents unavoidable discontinuities because the transit agencies do not have the capabilities to carry out the technical studies and the construction themselves. These discontinuities open up the possibility of collusion among transit agencies, decision makers, and technical consultants, stemming from the interdependence among these actors. They need each other to work on projects, to garner support for decisions, or simply to acquire technical information (e.g., analysts gather information from the transit agency they are working for to calculate productivity values and operating costs). Collusion has the potential for encouraging an actor to please the others to support his preferred outcome; it is almost always difficult, substantively and organizationally, as organizations or individuals must respond to other requirements that unavoidably influence how the work—technical analysis, decisions—is performed.[12] This element was present in the case studies, where the need to satisfy different audiences (mainly state and federal requirements) forced analysts, decision makers, and transit agencies to steer the analytical studies to fit that need.

The third major element that affects the explanation of decision outcomes is the environment within which the planning process takes place. Does it take place in a stable environment with clearly defined goals or in a dynamic one with changing priorities? The latter easily applies to the transportation planning domain, where, for the last 20 years, goals have been continuously added to transportation plans and have often become looser and wider.[13] The broadening of transportation plans has been the consequence of an environment with evolving needs, expectations, and policies (which, for instance, in the United States has been reflected in the changing emphasis of the federal government.)[14]

The instability of this environment affects the planning process in two ways: as a source of information, and as a setting for power relations, compromises, and conflicts. As for the environment as a source of information, the instability generates uncertainty in the technical process. As for power relations, the instability allows actors to act on that uncertainty in their attempts to support their views about the objectives to be achieved by the transit plans.

A Good Decision-Making Process

In light of these multiple perspectives, it becomes difficult to define what a good decision-making process ought to be. Wheeler and Janis (1980) state that a good decision-making process is one that abides by the right rules. Von Winterfeldt and Edwards (1986) argue that a common but often misused idea is that decisions, and hence rules for decision making, should be evaluated on the basis of their results. These authors further state that the quality of decisions really means the quality of the process by which they are made, and they can only be evaluated on the basis of information available before their outcome is known—in other words, the decision-making process is evaluated with foresight, not hindsight.

This approach shifts the question from the outcome to the "right" rules. The difficulty of defining the right rules, nevertheless, makes any arguments that link the outcome of a decision to its evaluation powerful and influential.[15] For decisions whose outcomes are rather certain, those arguments are straightforward; for decisions made under uncertainty, the arguments are controversial and elusive, and are difficult to apply in a generic fashion. This latter situation is the one that typifies the transportation planning process.

Five major stages of a decision-making process can be distinguished: (1) perception of problem (need), and acceptance and initiation of the decision process; (2) search for and identification of alternatives (with little evaluation done at this time); (3) evaluation of alternatives with considerable effort dedicated to searching for dependable information relevant to the decision; (4) commitment after the reexamination of all the information (and figuring out how the decision will be implemented including contingency plans in case any risks materialize); and (5) adherence to the decision (including anticipation of likely setbacks, preparation of countermeasures, and, in case a serious setback takes place, acceptance of a new challenge to go through another cycle of five stages to decide on a new course of action).[16] Within this process, decision makers, based on the costs of the alternatives, their cost-effectiveness, and other—not necessarily less important—factors, must select a course of action. In the decision-analysis tradition, the decision maker applies the theory of multi-attribute evaluation, constructs a decision tree, and, based on the probabilities that each option has, comes up with different payoffs and ends up with a best course of action.[17] This approach relates to what Pfeffer et al. (1976) call the application of *universalistic criteria*.

The universalism-particularism dimension describes the extent to which decision outcomes are affected by the social relationship between the decision maker and those affected by the decision. When agreed-upon, well-defined standards are available for evaluation, decision-making outcomes will be based on those standards and universalistic criteria will be applied. However, in the transportation planning process, where an absence of shared criteria is usually the norm—the case studies illustrated how the emphasis and objectives were different for different actors and at different times—processes of social influence will account for part of the variance in decision outcomes.

Particularistic criteria—criteria which derive from the particular perspectives or goals of the contending groups—are used more in decision making under conditions of uncertainty. In the transportation planning process, which is characterized by uncertainty about demand, costs, and goals, social influence tends to overshadow technical considerations and universalistic criteria. These conditions were clearly illustrated in the Santa Clara County and Buffalo case studies where projects were ultimately approved and carried forward not on the basis of technical studies but because of political mandates that came from the U.S. Congress.

When particularistic criteria play a role in the process, other decision-making mechanisms besides the technical process become important. These mechanisms include implicit exchanges or political logrolling (to vote for someone's project because he or she will vote for yours in reciprocity), familiarity with and likeness for someone else's project, and informal communication. Whether the process operates through any of these mechanisms, influence will be greater the more uncertain the decision situation is (and, hence, less likely to have objective information to anchor one's judgments). Uncertainty decreases the extent to which universalistic standards can be applied. Nevertheless, the visibility of the allocation process, the information generated—however uncertain—and the outcomes will tend to ensure that some universalistic criteria are employed. Organizations, then, are likely to employ both universalistic and particularistic criteria in their decision-making processes.

This dichotomy about how different criteria are applied in decision making highlights the difficulties of defining the right rules of the process—aside from following a set of stages, which may be hard to achieve, anyway, when some particularistic mechanisms play the major role. In Chapter 2, it was argued that good decisions are those that are made on the basis of the right information and in a democratic fashion. Since decisions are made on the basis of explicit or implicit criteria, how these criteria are defined and developed ultimately affects the information basis and the "democratization" of the decision. The definition of evaluation criteria then becomes crucial in light of the uncertainty of elements in the technical process. If the outcome of the decision was predetermined, owing to general consensus, pressures, or undemocratic practices, a good process may be precluded.

DECISION-MAKING IN TRANSPORTATION PLANNING

The case studies illustrate the many institutions that are usually involved in planning and implementing any fixed-guideway transit system. These institutions can be categorized according to the roles they play in the process: (1) providers of capital and operating funds or subsidies (e.g., federal and state governments); (2) certifiers of the process and project approval (e.g., the UMTA or state agencies); (3) issuers of regulations or guidelines (e.g., Congress and U.S. DOT); (4) providers of technical support and disseminators of information (e.g., the UMTA or state agencies); (5) budget allocators (e.g., federal and state budget offices); (6) implementors (e.g., state and local departments of public works or departments of transportation; transit authorities with their managers, technical staff, labor force and unions; and manufacturers of transit technologies); (7) analysts (e.g., consulting agencies and specific departments in transit agencies); (8) political lobbyists and other influencing actors (at all the levels of government, such as interest groups, citizen groups, transit unions, etc.); and (9) the business community.[18]

Before the best alternative is selected for implementation, several other decision processes take place that may affect the choice. These decision processes include: (1) which alternatives to consider, (2) which agency or agencies will supervise the project, (3) which organizations will undertake the analysis project and which institutions will pay for it, (4) who will be formally involved in commenting the analysis study, (5) which methods will be followed in the study, and (6) which criteria will be used as the basis for evaluating the competing alternatives. Except for the latter, which may be established by some statutory guidelines, institutions at the local (regional) level usually have the widest choice in these matters, subject to the constraints generated by actors at other levels (e.g., the funding institutions) and the resources available.

Figure 5.1 summarizes the major elements of current planning processes in terms of the decision-making process and the interaction of the institutions involved. Initial proposals are generated as a reaction to a perceived need for a transportation improvement. For instance, in Boston, the Old Colony project had existed as a plan since abandonment of the rail line in 1959. Only in 1984, when congestion levels on the corridor were assessed as unbearable, and the day the largest reconstruction effort in the state of Massachusetts [19] was approaching, did the state government activate the project and start the necessary feasibility and environmental studies. The need was then expressed as a way to reduce congestion on the major highways in the corridor, although later it was perceived that automobile volume would not be reduced on those major highways but rather on the local streets parallel to those highways. The perceived transportation need was also a consequence of the state's political need to gain support for the major reconstruction project. In exchange for rehabilitation of the Old Colony line, politicians from the fastest growing region of Massachusetts and their constituencies were expected to support the state's major engineering undertaking to date.

Once the need is established, the preliminary alternatives are defined. There always exists an initial preference for certain types of technologies, and the alternatives that include those technologies are put in front and may even give the name to any posterior analytical studies (e.g., in Boston, the "Old Colony Railroad" Rehabilitation Project). These initial preferences already place some alternatives at a disadvantage. In the meantime, constituency development is started by generators of the need (who are the only ones at the moment who have a stake in the project). Parallel to these events, some preliminary estimates of capital and operating costs are produced, based on feasibility studies or indications from interested parties (e.g., from providers of particular technologies). These preliminary estimates easily become hard currency, even if the studies they are based on clearly state that they are only approximations and that many items are not accounted for. For example, in the case of Boston, the feasibility study indicated the limitation of the $200 million estimate for the full alternative. For almost three years, however, this figure was the only one mentioned by all the involved institutions.

Based on the preliminary cost estimates, a need is perceived for additional funds. These funds must be provided by higher level institutions that require adherence to specific rules for approval. The need is often acknowledged not so

Figure 5.1
Schematic Representation of Institutional and Decision-Making Processes

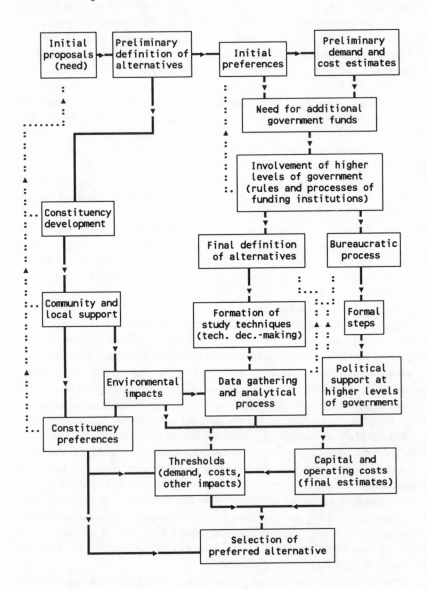

much because of the transportation project itself but rather because of the opportunity to bring "high-level" (e.g., federal) dollars to the area. This factor overrides others in the case of distressed areas, as in Buffalo. In other situations, the real lack of funds for the project is the main element. The decision to try to obtain the funds and follow the rules of the higher level institution is not an obvious one, because the whole process from planning to final implementation becomes much longer and, ultimately, affects the overall costs of the project. Owing to inflation, there are more opportunities for legal battles and changes in scope, and lost revenues. But the impossibility of collecting the necessary funds at the local level, or the need of not missing the opportunity to obtain "cheap" funds—that is, funds that cost less to the local taxpayer since they are partly covered by a higher level institution—eventually persuades the decision makers to pursue the required bureaucratic process.

Once the local group makes the decision to pursue the process, these high-level institutions become another important actor in the overall planning process. The definition of the alternatives must be agreed upon with them, although implicitly the initially preferred alternatives keep their preeminence in the planning study. Additionally, agreements upon study techniques and schedule for delivery of specific elements in the final analytical report must also be reached.

The formal steps of the analysis process take place simultaneously with the building of local and community support for the project. Some opposition probably arises, and for that technical documentation must be quickly prepared. This forces analysts to work at a fast pace, trying against all odds not to fall behind the political environment. When opposition surfaces, the decision makers usually indicate that the studies are still inconclusive and that further analysis must be undertaken to address all concerns. Consensus building is a major effort at this stage, since continuous support from the funding institutions largely depends on perceived support from the community. While the analytical study takes place, the decision makers must also spend time at other levels of government (parallel to those of the funding institutions), gaining additional political support for the project. If a major representative from the region has some leverage in the committees or agencies in charge of allocating funds, it is more probable that the funds will be approved. For instance, in the case of Buffalo, the area's representative in Congress was a member of the Public-Works Committee, the group that allocates federal funds for urban-development infrastructure projects. His presence on the committee helped funnel federal funds toward Buffalo's LRRT line.

In the meantime, the analysis process continues. Data, particularly those related to capital and operating costs, are gathered, and methods (models) are applied to generate the demand, revenue, and cost figures. In addition, environmental studies are undertaken to quantify and qualify the effects the transit project will produce in the corridor. Local concerns must now be addressed and new cost figures must be calculated, since the initial preferences did not consider the seemingly endless wants of the affected communities. The case studies clearly illustrate this issue, as elements such as station upgrading, double tracking, landscaping, and additional parking spaces had to be added. These types of changes in project scope escalate capital and operating costs. They will not be the last, since during preliminary engineering new additions will be necessary as geological conditions are surveyed, operational strategies are refined, and new demands are likely to be made from the communities.

But costs cannot be allowed to escalate without also considering the requirements of the funding institutions, particularly threshold values that must not be surpassed to obtain the approval for the funds. This is now a give-and-take process between the analysts and the decision makers; otherwise, the analysis process may end up suggesting an alternative different from the initially preferred—the one that has already taken so much effort, politically and emotionally, to gain support from the constituencies. The situation calls for a good dose of optimism when calculating the technical figures, particularly those related to demand and cost estimates, so as to put the initially preferred alternative in an advantaged position.

Decisions of high-level institutions about whether or not to fund a project are usually based on some cost-effectiveness measure. In the United States, the UMTA uses two major performance measures to screen alternatives: (1) the estimated number of riders in the corridor (a minimum is necessary to proceed with a proposal), and (2) the cost per added rider (this cost must not be higher than a specified threshold).

Table 5.1 shows the total annualized cost per rider for the transit projects discussed in Chapter 3. The total annualized cost was calculated adding the estimated annual operating cost to the annualized capital cost (assuming a 30-year life with an interest rate of 10%). The cost-effectiveness measure was calculated by dividing the total annualized cost by the ridership estimates or the number of rail boardings (in the case of actual figures). This cost-effectiveness measure differs from the one suggested by the UMTA in two elements: (1) the numerator considers neither the time savings for existing riders nor the local contribution to the project, and (2) ridership refers to total ridership and rail boardings rather than net new riders (i.e., net of those that would take place in the base TSM alternative). The first element tends to yield values that are higher for the measure included in Table 5.1; the second tends to yield values that are lower. Nevertheless, the figure illustrates how the cost-effectiveness measure increases dramatically from initial proposals to later reports. In the case of Boston, the high value of the cost-effectiveness measure is probably another, unspoken reason for the major difficulties the project has had in obtaining federal funds (and definitely one major reason for the increase in the local share above the statutory one).[20]

The cost-effectiveness performance is not the only cost-related criterion considered in the decision. The studies usually advocate capital-intensive projects, such as LRT systems, on the basis that these systems yield higher benefits owing to their lower operating costs. The belief is that normalized

Table 5.1
Costs, Annual Ridership, and Cost-Effectiveness Index
(Various years and transit systems)

Transit Proposal	Capital Costs Estimates ($ thousands)	Operating Costs Estimates ($ thousands)	Annual Ridership Estimates (thousands)	Annualization Factor (life = 30 yrs.)	Cost- Eff. Index (curr.)	Cost- Eff. Index (1987)
Buffalo (76)	$336,000	$24,400[a]	33,580	0.1061	1.8	3.8
Buffalo (78)	449,800	24,400[a]	23,725	0.1061	3.0	6.4
Buffalo (87)[b]	551,800	11,555	8,400	0.1061	8.3	8.3
Santa Clara (81)	180,044	8,786	13,080	0.1061	2.1	2.6
Santa Clara (84a)[c]	372,000[d]	8,786[e]	6,000	0.1061	8.0	8.2
Santa Clara (84b)[c]	411,000	8,786[e]	6,000	0.1061	8.7	8.9
Santa Clara (87)	559,000	8,786	6,000	0.1061	11.3	11.3
Boston (feasib. 84)	181,200[f]	16,250	2,505	0.1061	14.2	14.9
Boston (87)	360,975	17,885	3,936	0.1061	14.3	14.4

Notes: The years after the name of the case study refer to the year of publication of the technical report. See documentation in Bibliography.
a   Buffalo 76 and 78 operating costs include the costs associated with the extensions to the bus system that would be necessary to serve the LRRT stations.
b   Buffalo 87 are actual figures.
c   Santa Clara 84 ridership is a revised estimate (from a 1987 report).
d   Santa Clara 84a capital costs are those for the project without the transit mall.
e   Santa Clara 84 and 87 operating costs are assumed similar to those in the 1981 report.
f   Boston 84 capital costs do not include land acquisition costs, engineering, administration and contingency costs.

values of operating costs (i.e., operating costs per passenger, passenger-mile, revenue-vehicle, revenue-vehicle-mile, etc.) are much lower for capital-intensive systems. As a consequence of the lower normalized operating costs, total (normalized) annual costs (i.e., operating costs and annualized capital costs) are likely to be lower for capital-intensive projects. This belief generates some rather optimistic expectations about the performance of the system. Tables 5.2 to 5.5 illustrate this situation for the case studies. The systems planned usually are presented with operating statistics where normalized costs are expected to be lower that those of other systems. Actually, an interesting situation takes place. On the one hand, operating costs per revenue-vehicle tend to be close to the maximum figure for existing systems while operating costs per revenue-

Table 5.2
Comparative Statistics from Several Commuter Rail Systems in the United States
(Fiscal year ending between 01/01/83 and 12/31/83)

Commuter Rail Systems	Total Revenue Vehicles	Tot. Oper. Expenses ($ thousands)	Vehicle Revenue Miles
Pittsburgh PAT	12	$1,924.1	290,444
Detroit SEMTA	35	2,846.2	157,872
Chicago RTA	1,023	194,738.6	19,447,773
Newark NJT Corp.	1,206	131,460.0	27,526,438
Boston MBTA	259	44,882.6	7,202,999
Philadelphia SEPTA	726	63,079.3	15,458,068
Boston Old Colony Project (87)	90	17,885.5	3,866,449

Source: U.S. Department of Transportation, Annual Operating Statistics, Section 15, 1984.

Table 5.3
Comparative Statistics from Several Light Rail Systems in the United States
(Fiscal year ending between 01/01/83 and 12/31/83)

Light Rail Systems	Total Revenue Vehicles	Tot. Oper. Expenses ($ thousands)	Vehicle Revenue Miles	Passenger Miles
San Diego Trolley	24	$4,200.6	1,587,443	35,124,848
Newark NJT Corp.	26	3,074.3	576,314	6,269,587
New Orleans RTA	35	4,323.5	609,754	16,768,515
Cleveland RTA	48	7,103.1	1,054,202	37,155,164
Pittsburgh PAT	87	15,358.6	1,088,214	18,534,793
San Francisco MUNI	140	29,815.0	4,001,576	140,340,497
Boston MBTA	229	17,564.3	1,544,505	30,384,581
Philadelphia SEPTA	313	37,960.3	5,559,584	108,088,997
Buffalo LRRT(76)	47	4,620.0	6,250,000	88,320,000
Buffalo LRRT (87)	27	11,555.0	N/A	N/A
Santa Clara County LRT (86)	50	8,786.0	2,727,300	N/A

Source: U.S. Department of Transportation, Annual Operating Statistics, Section 15, 1984.
Note: N/A = not available.

Table 5.4
Comparative Indicators from Several Commuter
Rail Systems in the United States
(Fiscal year ending between 01/01/83 and 12/31/83)

Commuter Rail Systems	Operating Costs = => Per Revenue Vehicle ($ thousands)	Per Revenue Vehicle Mile ($)
Pittsburgh PAT	$160.3	$6.62
Detroit SEMTA	81.3	18.03
Chicago RTA	190.4	10.01
Newark NJT Corp.	109.0	4.78
Boston MBTA	173.3	6.23
Philadelphia SEPTA	86.9	4.08
Average	133.5	8.29
St. Dev.	42.9	4.74
Minimum	81.3	4.08
Maximum	190.4	18.03
Boston Old Colony Project (87)	198.7	4.63
Boston Old Colony Project (adjusted)	186.7	4.35

Sources: U.S. Department of Transportation, *ibid.* (1984), and own calculations.

vehicle-mile tend to be lower than the minimum figure for existing systems. This situation seems to suggest that operating costs tend to be underestimated and the estimated number of vehicles for operating the system tends to be underestimated as well (which reduces the amount to be spent on capital costs).

Furthermore, since passenger demand is usually overestimated, operating statistics based on demand estimates put capital-intensive systems at an advantage. However, if the estimated demand is not realized, those operating-performance indicators do not hold true. Thus, another important element on the basis of which decisions are made tends to be unrealistic. Nevertheless, these performance indicators constitute an additional powerful argument to favor particular technologies and put the project forward.

In conclusion, this section has illustrated how the need to justify the project on the basis of particular criteria mobilizes the decision-making and analysis processes in an attempt to prove the worthiness of the alternative that, from the outset, has received the strongest preference. Once the performance thresholds (in terms of cost-effectiveness measures, for example) comply with specific criteria, the alternative can pass the test of the high-level institution and the final

Table 5.5
Comparative Indicators from Several Light Rail Systems in the United States
(Fiscal year ending between 01/01/83 and 12/31/83)

Operating Costs = => Light Rail Systems	Per Revenue Vehicle ($ thousands)	Cost Per Passenger Mile	Per Revenue Vehicle Mile
San Diego Trolley	$175.0	$0.12	$2.65
Newark NJT Corp.	118.2	0.49	5.33
New Orleans RTA	123.5	0.26	7.09
Cleveland RTA	148.0	0.19	6.74
Pittsburgh PAT	176.5	0.83	14.11
San Francisco MUNI	213.0	0.21	7.45
Boston MBTA	76.7	0.58	11.37
Philadelphia SEPTA	121.3	0.35	6.83
Average	144.0	0.38	7.70
St. Dev.	40.2	0.22	3.31
Minimum	76.7	0.12	2.65
Maximum	213.0	0.83	14.11
Buffalo LRRT (76)	98.3	0.05	0.74
Buffalo LRRT (76, adj.)	164.4	0.08	1.24
Buffalo LRRT (87)	428.0	N/A	N/A
Santa Clara LRT (86)	175.7	N/A	3.22
Santa Clara LRT (86, adj.)	169.0	N/A	3.10

Sources: U.S. Department of Transportation, *ibid.* (1984), and own calculations.
Note: N/A = not available.

decision will be the selection of the preferred alternative. An agreement must then be reached with the funding institution to proceed into preliminary engineering and on which percentage of the final capital costs will be covered by that institution.

DIFFICULTIES AND ISSUES

This section discusses those difficulties and issues that influence how the decision-making process is undertaken. They aid in understanding some features of the process discussed in the previous section. These difficulties and issues have implications for how we must view the decision-making process and how we can devise ways to improve it (as will be discussed in Chapter 6). Three major elements are included: the types of problems, the nature of information, and the organizational issues.

Types of Problems

The literature on decision making highlights the differences between types of problems and the different responses they require from decision makers. Ungson et al. (1981) discuss the issue of well-structured versus ill-structured problems and indicate that certain types of problems can be described as ill-structured owing to (1) the ambiguity and incompleteness of the problem-related information, (2) the extent to which those problems are continually defined and redefined, (3) the lack of a clear program for the desired outcomes, (4) the possibility of influences from many actors or institutions, and (5) the extended period in which the decision is made.

The cost-estimating process in transportation planning conforms largely to these characteristics. The case studies clearly illustrate that (1) it is hard to gather all the information necessary (at least at the planning stage) for all the possible alternatives; (2) the scope of transit projects, affecting at the same time several communities and both horizontal and vertical government layers, calls for a constant redefinition of the design characteristics of the alternatives; (3) the existence of many interested parties with a stake in the outcome fosters development of formal and informal influences and pressures; and (4) the development of a transit project, from its conception to final approval and implementation, may take more than a decade.[21]

The ill-structured nature of the planning process—and of its estimating component—is compounded by the public nature of its context. Decisions in public agencies are, in that regard, much more complex than in private organizations.[22] This is the case because public agencies must weigh the decision in terms of public or community values, while private organizations take into consideration only (or largely) those consequences that affect the organization.

Also, the decision maker in the public sector cannot simplify the hypothetical conditions assumed to calculate the estimates, no matter how much this difficulty complicates the selection of the optimal alternative, and cannot disregard conditioning facts or consequences simply because they fall outside the scope of a particular project or decision maker's interests.[23] For instance, economic conditions or citizens' complains cannot be isolated from the process of planning and selecting an optimal transit alternative. Further complications are introduced if more than one individual is involved, for their stakes and decisions must be included when reaching a decision. For instance, the case studies illustrate the give-and-take nature of the funding process, whereby decisions were reached after an iterative process among the actors involved. This does not mean that a final—mutually agreeable—decision is always possible, but that the process is complicated by the existence of several individuals with a stake in the outcome.

Decisions are also largely influenced by the decision makers' perceptions of the problem and the impact of the decisions on constituencies. In addition, decision makers develop impressions from their experiences and use them whenever applicable. It is in this context that decision makers may obscure the other alternatives because they already have a solution in mind, as was largely the situation in the case studies in this book.

When the decision has already been made, independently of the analysts' work on the problem, a common and legitimate purpose of the analysis process is to justify the decision. However, this situation places a constraint on the analyst, who should ensure that the analysis is honestly reported and that elements which argue against the decision are not distorted or suppressed. This is hardly ever an easy situation.

Decision Making and Information

In the light of the conditions indicated in the previous section, decision makers receive considerable information about the state of the world in addition to the purely technical one. This situation has led to development of analytical decision aids as a way of easing the decision-making process, with a tendency to focus on building models based on theories of rational choices. Inevitably, simplification becomes necessary, and some sources of information receive more attention than others, depending on the requirements for making the decision and the demands of the organizational or bureaucratic structure.[24] The cost-effectiveness criterion meets these needs with its simplicity. Yet, it is possible that the information the decision needs does not constitute the most convenient criterion.[25] This difficulty arises, as discussed in this book, when a single attribute or dimension tends to dominate, but uncertainty—and the ill-structured nature of the problem—makes the choice difficult.

It is unavoidable to see the relevance of information as the links between the different steps of the planning process; indeed, it is one of its most powerful components. The difficulties of the decision-making process and how they are addressed influence the decision maker's attitudes toward information. In turn, information eases or intensifies those difficulties, closing a circle which can easily become a vicious one. Two main factors can make information highly unreliable: (1) the failure to recognize its relevance to the decision-making process, and (2) the distorted nature of its generation. Both factors were present in the case studies as (1) decision makers and analysts mostly viewed the planning process as a requirement to satisfy the bureaucratic structure, and (2) the studies consistently underestimated the costs involved.

Adams and Swanson (1976) discuss the issue of accuracy in the operations-management estimating process (e.g., the critical path method) and indicate that uncontrollable factors (e.g., political delays, strikes) have a much smaller impact on accuracy than is generally believed. They indicate that accuracy is positively related to the amount of information. Furthermore, this amount is related to what they called decision-maker talent and perception of the importance of accurate estimates. (These last two factors are, in turn, positively related to each other.) The authors conclude that formal feedback to inform the estimator about the accuracy of his estimates should be beneficial and that rewards can also help.

The importance of the estimate as perceived by the decision makers should determine their motivation and the amount of effort they are willing to spend in the search for accuracy. This perception is almost certain to be affected by conditions in the decision environment, such as the resources available to carry out the technical process, the possibility of being overburdened with information, or the chance that information may become dysfunctional to the decision objectives (e.g., reach a compromise among several constituencies). These conditions sometimes lead to even increase uncertainty, and consequently increase the likelihood of generating inaccurate estimates.

Organizational Issues

Some organizational issues refer to the layout of the institutional framework, the responsibilities of each institution, and the consequent demands upon those institutions. In Boston, a metropolitan agency reporting to the state legislature and the state Department of Transportation was in charge of leading the planning process while the federal government could possibly contribute funds to the construction of the selected alternative; in Buffalo, the involvement of the state was somewhat lower than in Boston (although, at the congressional level, the state representatives made a difference) and the federal government provided the largest percentage of funds for the construction of the LRRT system; in Santa Clara County, the involvement of the state was even lower (to the point of opposing the local initiatives) and the federal government again covered most of the capital costs associated with the construction of the LRT line.

As was mentioned before, these differing responsibilities create some difficulties in the technical process, for the process must meet the requirements of the different audiences. But organizational requirements also create difficulties in the decision-making process. For instance, as the institutions have responsibilities over several geographical jurisdictions, the decision makers may have to provide some jurisdictional equity when constructing the transit facility, as in the case of Boston, where plans were geared toward areas that lacked the transportation infrastructure existing in other parts of the metropolitan area. These organizational requirements, however, do not necessarily translate into selection of the most cost-effective alternative, nor do they easily allow design of alternatives involving incremental construction, which would permit more flexibility in allocating funds to cover capital costs.

Another organizational issue pertains to the role of institutions in charge of carrying out the technical elements of cost estimating, and the relationship among them and with the rest of the institutions in the broader planning process. Usually, this scale of project requires involvement of several institutions and, mainly, of consultants outside the transit agency. In the case of Boston, the technical studies were done by an outside consulting firm coordinating the efforts of several others consulting firms, each one in charge of a different technical element. The transportation agency supervised the consulting firm's work. After construction of the project by contracting with other companies, the transit agency will be in charge of operating the new facility.

The number of institutions involved creates some discontinuity in the cost-estimating process. This discontinuity, however, is unavoidable as some institutions—for example, the transit agencies—do not have the capability of carrying out the studies themselves. Each one needs the other. For instance, the consultant must get information from the transit agency to calculate some productivity values and particularly operating costs.

Other Issues

Another issue in the decision-making process is the extent to which decision makers fully consider the consequences of their decisions. Some authors have examined specific ways in which the high-level subsidies for transport projects (and transit operation) have distorted decision making, reduced efficiency, and increased costs.[26] These authors state that, in the United States, with its large federal subsidies, state and local decision makers consider only the small portion of costs that they have to bear and thus tend to underestimate the full costs of transit projects. Subsidies also create an incentive to construct new systems, the benefits of which fall far short of total costs yet exceed local costs. Pucher (1988) asserts that countries where both decision making and financing are decentralized to the local of provincial level or government display considerably higher productivity and lower unit costs than countries where the central government plays the dominant role. For large transit projects, however, full decentralization may not be possible because regional or local institutions may lack the funds to construct those projects even if they are truly necessary. Some approach to internalization of costs in the decision is recommended to force decision makers to balance the consequences of their decisions and to promote sensitivity to the different needs and conditions of each area.

A final issue is that the project-planning process often goes from design to cost; in other words, first one decides what is wanted—for example, an LRT system—and then one calculates how much it will cost to construct what is wanted, trying to find the lowest cost for the alternative selected. An alternative approach is *design-to-cost*; in other words, to select that project that best fits the resources available. Both approaches require a form of cost estimating; neither prevents underestimation. However, the emphasis changes. The latter approach is more difficult than the simple process of defining an alternative and estimating its cost because it requires an iterative process of defining-estimating-redefining-reestimating, and so on until the alternative can be accomplished with the funds allocated. It is also more difficult because the amount of resources available is seldom known in advance. On the positive side, a design-to-cost approach helps internalize costs in the decision-making process, since from the outset decision makers are aware of the level of resources available.

CONCLUSION

This chapter has covered the issues of cost estimating related to the decision-making process. After a brief discussion of decision-making theory and presentation of characteristics that apply to the decision-making process in transportation planning, this chapter presented the decision-making context and how it can affect the cost-estimating process.

The importance of the decision criteria used to rate the alternatives, the need to acknowledge multiple perspectives involved in the process, and the difficulties that surround decision makers' responsibilities illustrated the issues that frame the prevailing decision-making process. The way information is perceived by decision makers affects its use and how much effort is put into making it as accurate as possible. This creates a reinforcing circle, where the difficulties decision makers find in the process are affected by their attitudes toward information from the technical analysis, attitudes that in themselves affect how the difficulties are overcome.

The next section puts these elements together and those discussed in Chapter 4 to generate a framework for the analysis of the cost-estimating process in transportation planning, and to suggest some specific ways that address the difficulties and issues that prevent achievement of a better decision-making process.

NOTES

1. Table 1.1 presented some instances. See also Merewitz (1972), Charles River Associates (1983), and Pickrell (1989) and (1992).
2. Linstone (1984), pp. 7-24.
3. The length of service for politically appointed public decision makers is often relatively short.
4. Kelman (1987), Scott (1981), Lipsky (1980). There are still other characteristics that were not listed here because they do not directly relate to the issues discussed in this thesis. Some of these additional characteristics are: (1) decision makers do not usually have the imperative to train a successor (because of political reasons that affect both the incumbent and the successor); (2) the public decision maker must act with constraints on

personnel mobility and changes, since civil service, union contract provisions, and other regulations complicate the recruitment, hiring, transfer and layoff or discharge of personnel to achieve the decision maker's objectives; these constraints, in addition, tend to create conflicts between civil service officials and political appointees; and (3) decision makers have insufficient power and authority over autonomous units.

5. Von Winterfeldt and Edwards (1986).

6. Simon (1976) suggests a similar theoretical construction as an alternative to avoid the complexities of defining rationality as "to use the term 'rational' in conjunction with appropriate adverbs." Then we can have a decision that is "objectively" rational, or "subjectively" rational, or "organizationally" rational, or "personally" rational (pp. 76-77).

7. Linstone (1984).

8. Scott (1981), Allison (1971).

9. Drake (1973) provides a fuller discussion of this element in the context of several transportation planning exercises in the United States.

10. This is compared to the less formalized nature of similar processes in other countries. In these countries, the low level of formalization allows for the process to be better adapted to the conditions of each particular project.

11. In the case of Boston, there existed a "parent" consulting firm coordinating the efforts of several others consulting firms, each in charge of a different technical element.

12. The discontinuity also affects the internalization of responsibilities of each actor, since each can easily put the blame on the institution or individual in charge of another part of the process. The increasing importance of legal liabilities to technical studies may enhance internalization of responsibilities (Innes 1988). This approach, however, may prove inefficient as lawsuits lengthen planning studies and increase initial estimates of capital and operating costs, as the case studies illustrate. It remains to be seen if this approach can work as an efficient and effective work as a deterrent to avoid bias in the technical results.

13. Altshuler et al. (1979).

14. Weiner (1983, 1987).

15. The comments gathered from the interviews and the literature related to cost underestimation support this argument, since the evaluation of transit projects is usually based on a comparison of estimates with actual outcomes rather than on the process that led to the final decision.

16. Wheeler and Janis (1980).

17. Keeney and Raiffa (1976).

18. Hamer (1976).

19. This refers to the reconstruction under ground of a major elevated highway crossing the center of the city (the Central Artery). The project was slated for construction in 1990 and was going to disrupt the whole transportation network. Particularly from the south, alternatives were needed to provide access to Boston's central business district.

20. UMTA regulations set a maximum (conservative) value of $10 for the cost-effectiveness measure (that, as has been said, is calculated in a manner different from the one shown in Table 5.1).

21. For instance, Buffalo's LRRT took 16 years from initial plans to final construction. Santa Clara County's LRT took about the same time. Boston's initial proposals for rehabilitation of the commuter rail line already started in the mid-1970s,

although the formal proposals were not submitted to the state legislature until 1984.

22. Simon (1976), p. 69.

23. This is in contrast to a purely scientific problem whereby the analyst or decision maker can chose to study only those consequences of the system he or she wishes to be concerned with.

24. Mintzberg et al. (1976). These authors stress the importance of paying attention to how individuals process information in organizational contexts, with particular emphasis on how their reactions to demands imposed by the organizational structure.

25. Ungson et al. (1981) indicate that the payback model in capital budgeting decisions has been used extensively in spite of availability of better models. This is the case, they argue, because the time required to achieve a satisfactory return on investment may indeed relate more to a decision-maker's short-term "cognitive storage" than criteria such as the present value of future income.

26. For instance, Pucher (1988), Pickrell (1985), Pucher et al. (1983), Altshuler et al. (1979), and Hamer (1976).

6

Putting the Pieces Together:
A Framework for Cost Estimating

THE INTERACTION BETWEEN THE TECHNICAL AND THE DECISION-MAKING PROCESSES

The discussion of the decision-making process supports the thesis that, unlike other aspects of human activity, such as scientific experiments, technical analysis in transportation planning does not and cannot take place in isolation and is very much influenced by the decision-making process. Furthermore, the context within which the analysis takes place (and capital and operating costs are estimated)—institutional or organizational setting, decision criteria, and so on—affects the credibility, accuracy, and usefulness of that analysis (and of those estimates) in the planning and development stages of the project.

The assertion that the technical and decision-making processes are not isolated but rather are interconnected was strongly supported by the interviews with both analysts and decision makers in the cases presented in Chapter 3. Individuals at all levels indicated how both processes feed each other, so that each can "learn" from the other. It is this learning that detaches those processes from a purely rational interpretation.

Four major dimensions can be singled out as influencing the interaction between the technical and decision-making processes: (1) the inherent limitations of the technical analysis, (2) the unstructured nature of the decision problem, (3) the organizational setting, and (4) the type of environment for the transportation planning process.

1. In the technical process, there exist limitations on how much can be accomplished and at which level of detail, owing to both time and budget constraints. At the stage of analyzing alternatives, many elements cannot be known with complete certainty

(e.g., the underground conditions in the corridor, or the percentage of funds to be received from high-level institutions). The lack of certainty clears the way for ambiguity in both the design of the proposals and the objectives to be achieved. Ambiguity allows the different actors, and particularly decision makers, to portray their proposals as plausible means of achieving specified objectives. Study constraints and uncertainty also force the analysis to become more of a feasibility study (the worthwhile quality of any project among a set of projects, following a satisfying approach) rather than an optimization exercise (the selection of the best facility in terms of mode and size).

2. In the technical process, the estimation of capital and operating costs involves myriad cost elements, some of which almost everything is known about (e.g., the number of miles of track that must be provided between two particular points) while others are open to design alternatives (e.g., the kind of station to be constructed at a particular point). In addition, some of them depend on other variables—namely the daily demand in the corridor—and therefore their design must be accommodated to the estimated values for those variables. Owing to these variables, the process of estimating capital and operating costs is a rather structured process (the techniques and steps are usually fairly specific and agreed upon) crowded with unstructured elements. Analysts must address these elements by linking up with the decision-making process, which in principle channels the opinion of outside interested parties into the technical process. This link is delineated both formally through statutory regulations and informally through the stakes decision makers have in the process (e.g., reelection, yielding to pressures from interested parties, personal satisfaction).

3. Both technical analysts and decision makers belong to organizations. The organizational structure of the technical analysis can affect the final outcome of the cost-estimation process—and that of the planning process, in general. How the analysis fits the goals of the analysts' and decision makers' organizations, and the incentives present to influence their behavior, animates the presentation of the final results with their potential biases.

4. Lastly, the type of environment within which the planning process exists affects where the emphasis is put in the analysis process. For instance, increasing attention to environmental impacts in the United States has taken away resources from other elements of the technical process, particularly cost estimation, and channeled them into analysis of environmental concerns or the conduct of community hearings. To compound this situation, fewer resources must confront the additional requirements put on the cost-estimation process generated by this increasing attention to environmental impacts. And, how higher levels of government perceive their responsibilities in planning and funding public transportation projects further influences how the process is undertaken and for which reasons. For instance, the federal process, with its emphasis on cost-effectiveness measures, is often seen by applicants as a bureaucratic hurdle to securing federal funding, not as a real opportunity to make the best decision.

These four dimensions are influenced by a similar number of actors: interest groups (encompassing a broad range, from those that provide technical data to lobbying organizations), analysts, decision makers, and funding institutions. Figure 6.1 is a schematic representation of these actors. The broken line

Figure 6.1
Actors in the Planning Process

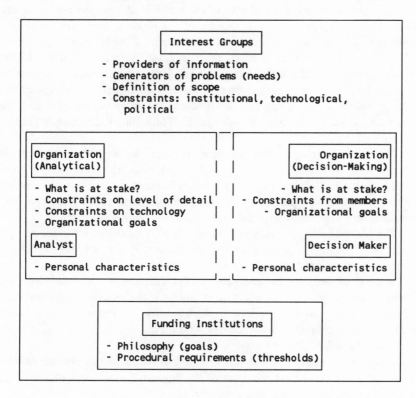

separating analysts from decision makers (and the organizations they are part of) indicates that the separation is not clear-cut; rather, communication takes place (and should always exist) between both. In fact, in some situations, the organization is the same, with open communication between analysts and decision makers. (For instance, in the case of Buffalo, the technical analysis for the calculation of the operating costs was done in-house by members of the decision-makers' organization—the Niagara Frontier Transportation Authority).

The interest groups provide information for the process. This information is in the form of problems (or needs, needs being the perception of the problem by the different interested actors), resources (data to model solutions to meet the needs), and constraints. Constraints come in the form of institutional constraints (legal), political constraints (some proposals may not entail the necessary political appeal to ensure their implementation or may disproportionally and negatively affect some sectors of the population), or technological constraints (certain technologies cannot be applied to a particular corridor at reasonable cost owing to topographical conditions).

How the needs are defined affects the scope of the project and who will ultimately be affected and have a stake in the process. For instance, if the problem is regarded as congestion on a particular road and the need is perceived solely as relief of that congestion, the (geographic) scope is limited to the vicinity of the road. If the problem is defined as the need to relieve congestion on a road in order to construct another major road in another section of the metropolitan area (as in the case of Boston), the scope is enlarged and the interested parties will include a broader range of individuals, community groups, and institutions.

The interest groups influence three parties: the analysts, the decision makers, and the staff of the funding institutions, who, in turn, perceive those interest groups in different ways. In the end, what each party tries to do is affect the vision of the other parties on the transportation problem so that a common ground is laid to proceed with the construction—or no-construction.

The analyst belongs to an organization. This organization, a consultant firm or a transit operator, constrains how the analyst acts by forcing him to perform in certain ways if he wants to stay in the organization.[1] Constraints also exist on the level of detail of the analytical study. This amount of detail depends, among other things, on how much is at stake for the analyst, the uncertainty associated with particular variables, the pressure generated by community concerns, and, indirectly, what the decision maker is asking for and how he perceives the technical process.

The decision maker also belongs to an organization. His or her beliefs tend to support the status or enhancement of the organization through strategic and political gains, and at the same time achieve personal advancement. The members of the organization (as well as individuals outside the organization) also play their game and therefore constrain the maneuverability of the decision maker. In addition, the explicit and implicit organizational goals hover over the decision maker as he or she makes a decision about a particular project.

Analysts and decision makers have in addition some personal characteristics that affect their behavior and the relationships between them. Behavior very much depends on how the analyst and the decision maker perceive what is at stake by following one or another course of action. For instance, the cognitive style of decision makers can vary from highly analytic to strongly heuristic. The former looks more at quantitative information while the latter is interested in broad concepts and makes decisions based more on intuition. Consequently, the decision maker's influence on and/or trust in the analysis process varies.

Finally, the staff of the funding institutions, also immersed in the environment, have a philosophy or culture that favors one or another type of reasoning as to how the technical analysis should be done, and the types of projects that should be undertaken and for which reasons. To accomplish these goals, the staff at these institutions establish some requirements for the technical process, as well as thresholds that must be passed to prove the worth of the transit alternative so that that alternative can be developed as specified in the bureaucratic process toward final implementation.

Based on these four actors and the four dimensions that influence interaction between the technical and decision-making processes, four main elements constitute the proposed analytical framework. First, as it relates to the environment and the limitations of the technical analysis, the uncertainty associated with the components of the environment, the analytical and decision-making organizations, and the funding institutions affects the different steps and results of the process. Second, as it relates to the analyst and the unstructured nature of the elements included in the transit facility — and of the goals to be addressed by that facility — the planning process is affected by technical problems (data collection, limits on analytical techniques, etc.) and the boundaries of the project (scale frames and scope of the project). Third, as it relates to decisions made during the technical process and the organizational setting, the final results (to be announced after the technical process is completed) are likely balanced against what is at stake and the incentives analysts and decision makers have to favor or discredit a particular course of action. Finally, as it relates to the relationship of both analysts and decision makers to the funding institutions and the characteristics of the environment, the decision criteria influence which variables and arguments are put forward and which have more possibilities of being tools for hedging against uncertainty. The next section develops the four components of the analytical framework at length.

DERIVATION OF ANALYTICAL FRAMEWORK

Perspectives on Uncertainty

Uncertainty can be defined as the attribute associated with something (e.g., the number of transit vehicles) that is subject to chance or change because its definition cannot be known in advance. Cost estimates are calculated based on either historical records or engineering estimation techniques. Each element has an associated level of uncertainty. The overall uncertainty of capital and operating costs comes from the uncertainty associated with each of the elements that influence the final calculation of those costs.

In Chapter 4, the presentation of the technical cost-estimation process— summarized in Figure 4.1—illustrates how final capital costs depend on the level of demand whose value has associated a considerable level of uncertainty, and that, in turn, depends on other uncertain values such as the socioeconomic characteristics of the region, technological advances, or even the tastes of the population. In the case of operating costs, demand also affects the uncertainty of the final figures, and so do productivity levels and the general behavior of the economy in the future in terms of inflation, interest rates and so on.

There are several ways to categorize uncertainty.[2] For purposes of the cost-estimation process, uncertainty can be divided into three categories, according to the degree of avoidability of the uncertainty associated with a particular variable or component:

- *Inevitable (or unavoidable) uncertainty* relates to those variables, such as travel parameters (e.g., trips per capita) and, consequently, demand, or inflation, for which we cannot in advance know everything with complete certainty. There is nothing much the analyst can do about reducing this uncertainty except for acknowledging it and approaching it from a multiple-scenario perspective within which several plausible futures and different assumptions for each of these futures are developed.[3]

- *Actionable uncertainty* relates to those variables for which we can, to some extent, improve the uncertainty of some of their components by "affording ground for an action." For instance, we could ideally set, regardless of demand, a price level to achieve some level of revenue. Or we could establish an operating plan for the proposed transit alternatives such that operating costs are kept to a certain level (within a more limited range of the uncertainty inevitably associated with these costs) and regardless of demand.

- *Avoidable uncertainty* relates to variables for which we can avoid the uncertainty related to the elements that influence that variable. For this last category we can distinguish between *nonanalytic* (or negotiated) and *analytic* uncertainty. The former relates to variables such as government and other funds for which we could, from the outset, know through negotiations or contracts what percentage of the capital and/or operating costs the transit operator would be able to secure. The latter relates to variables such as productivity or unit costs for which we can, by collecting additional information, reduce uncertainty to an acceptable level. The tradeoff between how much time, effort, or resources (including political leverage) we can spent on reducing the uncertainty versus what we perceive we can gain from that reduction determines how much the avoidable type of uncertainty would be reduced.

The classification illustrates that additional information can reduce uncertainty, but not impose certainty. Moreover, how much the analyst can spend on acquiring additional information is always limited. Also, decision makers may prefer to maintain uncertainty to some level—of the actionable or nonanalytic types, in particular—for the ambiguity created by the existence of uncertainty can give them the political leverage needed to reach compromise and negotiate with the different interested parties.[4]

The classification further suggests that policies that aim to establish narrow criteria—that is, criteria that focus on a small and very specific predefined set of variables and their values—for the purpose of accepting or rejecting projects may not be advisable. On one hand, narrow criteria can help reduce uncertainty as to what conditions a project must satisfy to gain final approval. On the other, if criteria are very narrow, problems may likely arise in terms of achieving cooperation and compromise, encompassing a variety of concerns, and avoiding biases. For instance, the surge of environmental issues in transportation planning has increased the uncertainty and ambiguity of the process, but on the other hand, it has provided an opportunity that allows dialogue with and the building of constituencies, bringing together people with different wishes and political interests. A criterion for evaluation purposes based on cost-effectiveness measures cannot easily incorporate these issues and would reduce the possibilities of a productive dialogue.[5] This suggestion does not provide a clear indication of which criteria should be used and when those criteria are sufficiently wide to prevent bias and encompass the variety of concerns. Nevertheless, it does imply that the planning process will have to put more emphasis on the basis upon which each individual project is evaluated rather than establish, from the outset, a common yardstick for all them.

The Planning Environment (Technical Issues)

The technical process has other determinants, besides the inherent uncertainty of the variables, that create difficulties in accurately estimating the capital and operating costs of a transit facility. Two of these are the effects of the perspectives of the actors involved and the effects of information gathering and manipulation activities. (Chapter 4 highlighted and discussed other difficulties and issues related to the attempt, within the analysis process, of achieving more accurate cost estimates.)

The first determinant affects coordination between what the technical process is trying to address and the broader social and political environment. For instance, the decision maker must pay attention to other perspectives in addition to viewing the rational-technical process, such as the sociopolitical environment and the organizational conditions. The pace of these broader processes—how fast events related to these processes occur—likely differs from that of the technical process. If the technical process falls behind the broader processes, it will become sidetracked and will be used only as a justification for decisions made largely outside the technical sphere.

The second determinant involves a methodological question. Costing methodology is simple but lengthy, particularly for operating costs. Changes may require looking back at a whole series of operating strategies, productivity assumptions, and unit-cost measures. If, for whatever reason, the cost of the project changes along the way, the technical process may be unable to incorporate those changes and become outdated. This problem arises as conflict between the frequently static nature of the technical process and the dynamism of the environment surrounding it. When that happens, the length of the process and the resources already spent create a drag (for political and emotional reasons) that easily prevents efforts to reconsider major components of the analytical study.

Time and Scale Frames (Project Scope)

Analysts, decision makers, and funding institutions have different time frames, scale frames, and overall perspectives. As to time frames, some focus on the short term; for example, the benefits in the first five years after construction of the facility are very limited and the operating costs very high, hence the system is not good. Others focus on the long term; for example, the benefits of a project accrue as changes in land use improve the conditions of the city core, revitalizing it and restoring its centrality. As to scale frames, some focus on small-scale effects (e.g., the system will improve my trip time downtown), while others focus on a larger scale (e.g., the system will bring people from outside counties into downtown). As to overall perspectives, the high-level institutions may contend that their role is more to balance the national budget and transit projects do not fall within those concerns, since those kind of projects are geared to addressing local problems. The regional institutions may contend that cities are strong elements of the national economy and therefore the high-level institutions should contribute to construction of large projects that can help improve environmental conditions and reduce energy consumption. And local governments may contend that by themselves they are unable to undertake such large investments although they must provide for the needs of its citizens (and in addition bring jobs and high-level funds, if possible).

These different frames of reference affect the technical analysis because the inevitable large number of interested parties makes it harder for that analysis to address all the issues raised, and because decision makers need to account for all the concerns. The case studies clearly indicate how changes in the final costs are, in a sizeable percentage, a result of additions to or changes in the design of the systems. In some cases, important components of capital costs were taken out and put back in during the process (e.g., the La Salle Station in Buffalo). As the process unfolds, community groups perceive the project with a different interest while analysts and/or decision makers must twist their assumptions to sort out or fit the demands of most parties (community and funding institutions).

These different perspectives have led to consideration of a broad set of variables. In the United States, a large proportion of the study resources must be dedicated to environmental issues, and not so much on costs. For instance, in the case of Boston, 19 reports were published, with only 2 directly related to capital and operating costs. Costs are, however, an important element for funding institutions and eventually are a major concern after the system is constructed. Once the system is in place, the affected parties can get used to noise or vibration (up to a certain limits) but not to taxes and cost overruns or operating deficits.

Information Systems

The technical process requires large amounts of cost data. Some data can be found cheaply and quickly, and with low uncertainty (e.g., the cost of a light-rail vehicle), while other data are hard to find, and even if found have a high level of uncertainty associated (e.g., underground conditions). Furthermore, once data are organized and stored, the dynamism of the process requires an adequate information process to allow easy maintenance and updating of the data.

The dynamism of the information is hardly recognized, and makes it harder to address the concerns raised in the previous section about changes in the scope of the process, and limits the potential use of information not only as a decision-support tool but also as a negotiation-argumentation instrument to promote a dialogue among those with conflicting views. In the case studies, information had a limited role; it constituted mainly a tool for accountability (data bank); its design responded simply to the need to take advantage of economies for handling mathematical operations (routines).

One of the major reasons for that limited role of information was the perception that data lack generality, being created and manipulated for a particular case and that it does not deserve to be expanded for a role broader than accountability. This view prevents implementation of more powerful, flexible, and dynamic information systems. Moreover, the cost of establishing and maintaining large data banks is perceived as too expensive in the light of its subsequent low use in the planning process.

These perceptions largely originate in a rationalist view of the process. Recognition of the limits of this perspective would help to acknowledge that, as Klosterman (1987) indicates, the information can become "a focus for political dispute, negotiation and bargaining as participants in the modelling process resolve fundamentally political questions of identifying the most appropriate data, assumptions, and results." This approach, however, must avoid endless discussion over minor elements of the technical process, and instead foster discussion of assumptions, methods, and facts that underlie conflicting perspectives on the transit project.

A Decision Model for Cost Underestimation

The past two sections discussed those components of the framework upon which analysts or the decision makers can act from a technical perspective (e.g., by reducing uncertainty or developing an information system). In this section, the behavior of analysts or decision makers—as they ponder what to do in the light of their personal goals, the probabilities of achieving them, and their stake in the process—is explicitly incorporated. Using decision analysis tools and developing a decision model for cost underestimation, this section explains the interrelationships among the different decisions that can be made about the study and how probable underestimation can be.

The choice of analysis method (not which alternative to pursue, but how to carry out the technical analysis and which costs to announce) can be thought of as the following: A decision maker wishes to get a particular transit project approved for particular reasons. To do that he hires a consultant or analyst who specializes in that kind of project and particularly in calculating costs. Because he wishes to avoid the emotional and monetary costs of carrying out and submitting a study that will not be approved, the decision maker tells the analyst to inform him of the progress of his findings before making an announcement of the technical study. The consultant's previous experience indicates that his prediction is correct a given percent of the times for those cases when the project is constructed.

There are four major components in this cost-estimation process: (1) how much the consultant *believes* the facility is going to cost after performing the technical calculations (the consultant's best guess); (2) how much the consultant or decision maker *says* the facility is going to cost (regardless of what the consultant believes it is going to cost); (3) how likely it is that the facility will be constructed; and (4) how much the facility ends up costing.

Those four components are interrelated. How likely it is that the facility will be constructed depends on how much the facility is expected to cost. We can assume that the likelihood of construction depends solely on specific criteria—for example, a cost-effectiveness index—established by the funding institution. Approval of the project, however, is not deterministic but, rather, probabilistic for, although the project may or may not meet those criteria, construction is not automatically accepted or rejected but, rather, depends on many other factors, particularly how close the project falls to meet those criteria.[6]

The final cost of the facility does not depend on what the consultant says the facility is going to cost; it depends on the initial design and other factors such as community concerns, legal disputes, and construction management expertise. What the consultant says does not alter the cost probabilities of the facility, but they are correlated because the consultant is knowledgeable (the consultant's accuracy for the particular type of facility). The correlation between these two probabilities—the consultant's accuracy and the final costs of the facility—allows one to calculate the conditional probabilities of how much the project ends up costing, given the consultant's estimates based on his or her record of accuracy.

Finally, the consultant is influenced in what he or she says the facility is going to cost by his or her preferences (expected utility) for likely consequences of that report, as well as a personal desire to forecast accurately. The expected utility depends, for instance, on how likely it is that the facility will be constructed or on how much is at stake by not being accurate and how the consultant or decision maker feels about the consequences of disclosing one cost or another. Incorporating expected utilities into the model adds another component, for by investigating the effect of penalizing or rewarding one of the actions—for example, underestimation—we can perceive the possibility of influencing the consultant's or decision maker's decisions about what cost to disclose.

Although the model does not incorporate actual utility values, the case studies clearly support the assumptions taken in the development of the model. First, most of the actors involved in the analytical process strongly favored construction of the preferred alternative versus no construction, and felt that if funds were not ensured the project would have never been constructed. Second, the length of the process and the perseverance of the interested parties supported utilities that are higher for those outcomes that resulted, *ceteris paribus*, in the construction of the project. Third, the fact that changes that ultimately affected the accuracy of the estimates were mostly changes related to the scope of the project, indicating that analysts usually do their best to calculate the right costs and would always prefer to be right than underestimate or overestimate. Finally, combining the last two points, the actors should usually prefer to be on target (be accurate) and, in addition, see the project constructed.[7]

With these relationships and assumptions, the model incorporates the consultant's analytical capacity—that is, how good the estimates are—coupled with the possibility of biasing the results—not necessarily by selecting the wrong costs or manipulating the results but by selecting optimistic values or minimum standards—so that the transportation facility gets approved and constructed. The model gives us an indication of how often and under what conditions the consultant or decision maker may bias the results by publishing a cost under or above the one actually estimated.

With the description of the components, we can now formally develop the decision steps and decision model from the perspective of the consultant and decision maker:[8]

1. Initially there is an unconditional probability for a given type of project (e.g., an LRT line at grade). The cost of this type of project has some probability distribution, which we assume to be discrete and symmetrical with a low, a medium, and a high value.[9] These probabilities are called $P(A)$, $P(B)$, and $P(C)$, or the probability of a low-cost, medium-cost, and high-cost, respectively. For instance, unconditional (prior) probabilities for a given project could be 50 percent for a middle value, with 25 percent for a low and a high value. In other words:

$$P(A) = 25\%   P(B) = 50\%   P(C) = 25\%$$

2. The consultant has a record of accuracy associated with similar types of projects. This accuracy comes not only from the consultant's analytical capabilities but also from how much time and money are spent on calculating costs and generating more detailed analyses of costs (reducing *analytical* uncertainty) by gathering additional information on unit costs, quantities, and productivities. These are conditional probabilities, such as

$P(\alpha/A)$ or probability that the consultant estimates that the cost is A, given that the cost is actually A. If the consultant is correct 80 percent of the times, this probability—$P(\alpha/A)$—will be 80 percent. For instance, the accuracy of the consultant could be as follows:

Correct:	$P(\alpha/A) = P(\beta/B) = P(\tau/C) = 80\%$	
Underestimate:	$P(\alpha/B) = P(\alpha/C) = P(\beta/C) = 10\%$	
Overestimate:	$P(\beta/A) = P(\tau/A) = P(\tau/B) = 10\%$	

3. We must also assume some probabilities for the construction of the project, depending on how much the project is expected to cost. These are therefore conditional probabilities (e.g., probability of the project being constructed given that the (disclosed) expected cost is low). For instance, a whole set of probabilities of construction would be:

$P(yes/A) = 100\%$	$P(yes/B) = 50\%$	$P(yes/C) = 25\%$
$P(no/A) = 0\%$	$P(no/B) = 50\%$	$P(no/C) = 75\%$

4. Finally, each outcome from the decision tree, in terms of the construction or no-construction of the facility and the accurate or inaccurate estimation of the costs, has an associated utility for the consultant and/or decision maker. These utilities can be derived by pairwise comparison of every two outcomes, the ranking of the outcomes, and the calculation of a consistency index to check that the pairwise comparisons do not contradict each other.[10] Each set of rankings and expected utilities indicate a hypothesis about the wishes of the consultant and/or decision maker or the rewards and penalties that each outcome would cause the consultant and/or decision maker (e.g., if underestimation is penalized with fewer funds for the project, outcomes that involved underestimation would have a much lower utility). For instance, Table 6.1 shows the utilities in the case that the highest utilities are perceived when the project gets built and the estimates are accurate, while the lowest utilities are perceived when the project does not get built (with lowest utility when cost is expected low, and highest when cost is expected high). In between, utilities are higher when the project gets built but overestimation occurs, and lower when the project gets built and underestimation occurs. Utilities have been valued between 1.0 and 0.0 without loss of generality.

For a probabilistic interpretation of the utility values, we must refer to the concept of certainty equivalent.[11] A certainty equivalent of a probabilistic outcome is the utility at which the decision maker is indifferent between that probabilistic outcome and that utility for a certain outcome. In this chapter, this certainty equivalent could be calculated by first specifying the most and the least preferred alternatives (and assigning utilities of 1 and 0, respectively) and then

Table 6.1
Table of Utilities: Case 1

Outcome	Ranking	Utility
Expected A, gets built, and costs A (AGA)	1	1.00
Expected B, gets built, and costs B (BGB)	2	0.95
Expected C, gets built, and costs C (CGC)	2	0.95
Expected B, gets built, and costs A (BGA)	4	0.90
Expected C, gets built, and costs A (CGA)	5	0.85
Expected C, gets built, and costs B (CGB)	6	0.80
Expected A, gets built, and costs B (AGB)	7	0.70
Expected B, gets built, and costs C (BGC)	8	0.65
Expected A, gets built, and costs C (AGC)	9	0.50
Expected C, and does not get built (CnG)	10	0.40
Expected B, and does not get built (BnG)	11	0.25
Expected A, and does not get built (AnG)	12	0.00

Note: A is the low cost, B the medium cost, and C the high
cost. Outcomes AGA, BGB, and CGC indicate accurate
estimates; outcomes BGA, CGA, and CGB indicate
overestimation; and outcomes AGB, BGC, and AGC
indicate underestimation.

asking the analyst or decision maker at which point he or she would feel indifferent between a particular outcome (say CGA) and a lottery with probability p at best outcome (i.e., AGA) versus probability $1-p$ at worst outcome (i.e., AnG). In the case shown in Table 6.1, the analyst feels indifferent between outcome CGA and a 85 percent probability of AGA and a 15 percent (i.e., one minus 85%) of AnG.[12]

On the basis of the four sets of information (unconditional probability for a given type of project, consultant's conditional probabilities, conditional probabilities for the construction of the facility, and analyst's or decision maker's set of utilities) we can now generate a decision tree and compute other conditional probabilities. To begin with, we need to know what the probabilities are that the project costs an amount—for example, low—given that the consultant has said that the project will cost another amount—medium. In other words, we are looking for $P(A/\alpha)$. To calculate these values, we can apply Bayes theorem. This theorem indicates that:

$$P(X/Y) = \frac{P\ (X\ \&\ Y) \quad \text{<-- joint probability}}{P(Y) \qquad\qquad \text{<-- unconditional probability}}$$

Therefore, in our case,

$$P(A/\alpha) = \frac{P\ (A\ \&\ \alpha)}{P(\alpha)}$$

We must then calculate the joint probabilities, and from them the unconditional probabilities. This is an example:

Prior probabilities		Consultant's accuracy			Joint probabilities	
	/	α	80%	-->	A & α	20.0%
A 25% -	β	10%	-->	A & β	2.5%
/ \	τ	10%	-->	A & τ	2.5%
/						
/ /	α	10%	-->	B & α	5.0%
--- B 50% -	β	80%	-->	B & β	40.0%
\ \	τ	10%	-->	B & τ	5.0%
\						
\ /	α	10%	-->	C & α	2.5%
C 25% -	β	10%	-->	C & β	2.5%
\	τ	80%	-->	C & τ	20.0%

Then, the unconditional probabilities are:

$P(\alpha) = 27.5\%$ $P(\beta) = 45.0\%$ $P(\tau) = 27.5\%$

And the conditional probabilities will be:

$P(A/\alpha) = 72.7\%$ $P(A/\beta) = 5.6\%$ $P(A/\tau) = 9.1\%$
$P(B/\alpha) = 18.2\%$ $P(B/\beta) = 88.9\%$ $P(B/\tau) = 18.2\%$
$P(C/\alpha) = 9.1\%$ $P(C/\beta) = 5.6\%$ $P(C/\tau) = 72.7\%$

Based on these values and the expected utilities for each outcome, we can develop the full decision tree. This is shown in Table 6.2. The numbers in bold face next to what the consultant says the project will cost—A, B, and C—are the expected utilities of each decision. Based on these utilities the consultant or decision maker will announce one or another cost, resulting in the underestimation, accurate calculation, or overestimation of the cost values.

In this particular example, the consultant or decision maker will select option A as the cost to be announced all the time, since that option is the one that yields the highest expected utility in all the three branches of the decision tree. By changing the initial conditions and assumptions, we can now investigate what this decision model tells us about the underestimation of costs.

We can establish a baseline case with the assumption that the consultant is accurate all the time and that the project is always constructed (regardless of its expected costs), and that the prior probabilities and utility distribution are the one assumed in the previous example. In this situation, the results will never be biased and the consultant will always announce the costs that he has calculated through the technical process.

In addition, the total combined utility is the highest, around 0.96. This overall utility is obtained by multiplying the unconditional probabilities of what the consultant has estimated the project is going to cost by the utility of each selected outcome in each branch of the decision tree. In other words, overall utility equals:

$$P(\alpha) * \text{max.util.}[(\underline{A}, \underline{B}, \underline{C}) \text{ in } \alpha \text{ branch}] +$$
$$+ P(\beta) * \text{max.util.}[(\underline{A}, \underline{B}, \underline{C}) \text{ in } \beta \text{ branch}] +$$
$$+ P(\tau) * \text{max.util.}[(\underline{A}, \underline{B}, \underline{C}) \text{ in } \tau \text{ branch}]$$

When all the possible outcomes report a utility of 1.0, the probability of construction is 100 percent regardless of estimated costs, and the consultant is accurate all the time, the overall utility would yield a value of 1.0. Deviations from that situation, because outcome utilities are lower than 1.0, or because the probability of construction is lower than 100 percent for some of the costs, or because the consultant is not accurate all the time, would yield overall utilities lower than 1.0. Therefore, this overall utility gives an indication of how far we are from an ideal situation where utilities have maximum values and probabilities for construction and accuracy are 100 percent.

By changing the initial values for the consultant's accuracy and the probability of construction, but keeping the same utility distribution, we can obtain the results shown in Table 6.3. These results indicate that when the consultant's accuracy increases there is, in general, a tendency to select the estimated costs—that is, not to generate any bias. When the differences in construction probabilities among the three outcomes are low, however, there is a tendency to overestimate costs—for instance, the case where the three construction probabilities are 50 percent. This is mainly because, for the particular set of utilities selected for this example overestimation reports higher utility than underestimation. (This is a questionable alternative but falls on the conservative side and supports the main conclusions.)

In addition, the model indicates that when the construction probabilities are sufficiently reduced for expensive projects, underestimation is the most likely outcome. For instance, the case where the probability of construction is 40 percent for option A and zero percent for the other two costs, there is a tendency to overestimate. However, when the probability increases to 80 percent for option A but stays at zero percent for the B and C, there is a tendency to underestimate.

Table 6.2
Model Structure and Output: Case 1

What Cons. Thinks It Will Cost	What Consult. Says It Costs	Will It Be Constructed?		How Much It Ends Up Costing		Outcome	Utility
				/A	72.7%	AGA	1.00
		Yes	100%	-B	18.2%	AGB	0.70
		/		\C	9.1%	AGC	0.50
	A 0.90	\No	0%	-	100.0%	AnG	0.00
	/						
	/			/A	72.7%	BGA	0.90
	/	Yes	50%	-B	18.2%	BGB	0.95
	/	/		\C	9.1%	BGC	0.65
α 27.5%	?---B 0.57	\No	50%	-	100.0%	BnG	0.25
	\						
	\			/A	72.7%	CGA	0.85
	\	Yes	25%	-B	18.2%	CGB	0.80
	\	/		\C	9.1%	CGC	0.95
	C 0.51	\No	75%	-	100.0%	CnG	0.40
				/A	5.6%	AGA	1.00
		Yes	100%	-B	88.9%	AGB	0.70
		/		\C	5.6%	AGC	0.50
	A 0.71	\No	0%	-	100.0%	AnG	0.00
	/						
	/			/A	5.6%	BGA	0.90
	/	Yes	50%	-B	88.9%	BGB	0.95
	/	/		\C	5.6%	BGC	0.65
β 45.0%	?---B 0.59	\No	50%	-	100.0%	BnG	0.25
	\						
	\			/A	5.6%	CGA	0.85
	\	Yes	25%	-B	88.9%	CGB	0.80
	\	/		\C	5.6%	CGC	0.95
	C 0.50	\No	75%	-	100.0%	CnG	0.40
				/A	9.1%	AGA	1.00
		Yes	100%	-B	18.2%	AGB	0.70
		/		\C	72.7%	AGC	0.50
	A 0.58	\No	0%	-	100.0%	AnG	0.00
	/						
	/			/A	9.1%	BGA	0.90
	/	Yes	50%	-B	18.2%	BGB	0.95
	/	/		\C	72.7%	BGC	0.65
τ 27.5%	?---B 0.49	\No	50%	-	100.0%	BnG	0.25
	\						
	\			/A	9.1%	CGA	0.85
	\	Yes	25%	-B	18.2%	CGB	0.80
	\	/		\C	72.7%	CGC	0.95
	C 0.53	\No	75%	-	100.0%	CnG	0.40

Table 6.3
Model Results: Case 1

Consultant's Accuracy	Probability of Construction			Cost Selected			Overall Utility
	A	B	C	α	β	τ	
100%	100%	100%	100%	A	B	C	0.96
80%	"	"	"	A	B	C	0.92
45%	'	'	'	B	B	C	0.87
33%	'	'	'	B	B	B	0.86*
100%	100%	90%	70%	A	B	C	0.89
80%	'	'	'	A	B	C	0.84
45%	'	'	'	B	B	B	0.80
33%	'	'	'	B	B	B	0.80
100%	100%`	67%	33%	A	B	C	0.75
80%	'	'	'	A	A	A	0.73
45%	'	'	'	A	A	A	0.73
33%	'	'	'	A	A	A	0.73
100%	67%	50%	40%	A	B	C	0.62
80%	'	'	'	A	B	C	0.60
45%	'	'	'	C	C	C	0.58
33%	'	'	'	C	C	C	0.58
100%	50%	50%	50%	C	C	C	0.63
80%	'	'	'	C	C	C	0.63
45%	'	'	'	C	C	C	0.63
33%	'	'	'	C	C	C	0.63
100%	80%	0%	0%	A	A	A	0.58
80%	'	'	'	A	A	A	0.58
45%	'	'	'	A	A	A	0.58
33%	'	'	'	A	A	A	0.58
100%	40%	0%	0%	A	C	C	0.40
80%	'	'	'	C	C	C	0.40
45%	'	'	'	C	C	C	0.40
33%	'	'	'	C	C	C	0.40

*This percentage would correspond to the accuracy that would be obtained by random choice.

For a given accuracy level, it can be shown that underestimation begins as soon as there is a sufficiently large differential between the probabilities of construction between the lowest and the medium and highest cost values. For instance, for 100 percent consultant accuracy, when the probability of construction for option A is 100 percent, underestimation will take place if the probability of construction for options B or C is lower than 64 percent. When the probability of construction for the lowest cost decreases, the differential at which underestimation begins augments, indicating that if construction is less likely, the willingness to underestimate—for the set of utilities assumed in this case—is reduced.

We can now assume a different set of expected utilities. For instance, we can assume that utility is still high if estimates are correct, but low if they are overestimated. The consultant may feel bad to be above the mark, lowering the possibilities of getting funds for the project. If underestimation is small, then utility is fairly high and lower the larger the underestimation is. The consultant may feel bad to underestimate by a wide margin. Utilities for no-construction are higher than in the previous case when the consultant selects the high or medium values. He or she may feel that with high or medium costs, no construction is expected and therefore he is not so disappointed if the project is not constructed. The utility is zero when the consultant selects the lowest cost and the facility is not constructed. Table 6.4 shows this set of utilities.

Table 6.4
Table of Utilities: Case 2

Outcome	Ranking	Utility
AGA	1	1.00
BGB	2	0.95
CGC	4	0.90
BGA	9	0.30
CGA	11	0.10
CGB	7	0.40
AGB	2	0.95
BGC	5	0.80
AGC	7	0.40
CnG	6	0.50
BnG	9	0.30
AnG	12	0.00

With this new utility distribution (and assuming the same prior probabilities), the results are the ones shown in Table 6.5.

The results indicate that, once again, when consultant accuracy increases the tendency is toward less bias of costs. But now when accuracy decreases there exists a stronger tendency to underestimate, compared to the previous example (since overestimation does not report high utilities anymore). When the probabilities of construction are high for the lower costs (i.e., close to the

Table 6.5
Model Results: Case 2

Consultant's Accuracy	Probability of Construction			Cost Selected			Overall Utility
	A	B	C	α	β	τ	
100%	100%	100%	100%	A	A	C	0.95
80%	"	"	"	A	A	B	0.89
45%	'	'	'	A	A	A	0.83
33%	'	'	'	A	A	A	0.83
100%	100%	90%	70%	A	A	C	0.92
80%	'	'	'	A	A	B	0.87
45%	'	'	'	A	A	A	0.83
33%	'	'	'	A	A	A	0.83
100%	100%`	67%	33%	A	A	C	0.88
80%	'	'	'	A	A	B	0.84
45%	'	'	'	A	A	A	0.83
33%	'	'	'	A	A	A	0.83
100%	67%	50%	40%	A	A	C	0.65
80%	'	'	'	A	A	C	0.61
45%	'	'	'	A	A	B	0.56
33%	'	'	'	A	A	A	0.55
100%	50%	50%	50%	A	B	C	0.61
80%	'	'	'	A	B	C	0.57
45%	'	'	'	B	B	B	0.53
33%	'	'	'	B	B	B	0.53
100%	53%	0%	0%	A	A	C	0.51
80%	'	'	'	C	C	C	0.50
45%	'	'	'	C	C	C	0.50
33%	'	'	'	C	C	C	0.50
100%	49%	0%	0%	C	C	C	0.50
80%	'	'	'	C	C	C	0.50
45%	'	'	'	C	C	C	0.50
33%	'	'	'	C	C	C	0.50

100% certainty), the consultant will again tend to underestimate costs. On the other hand, when the probabilities are very small for the higher costs but high for the low costs (e.g., the case of 53% for option A, and zero percent for options B and C), the consultant will tend to overestimate costs in spite of the probability differential because he or she does not feel so disappointed when construction does not take place owing to the announcement of high costs. For the set of utilities of this case, the differential at which underestimation begins decreases with the decrease in the probability of construction for the lowest cost. Finally, when the construction probabilities are similar for all the costs, the consultant will tend to bias the cost estimates less often (i.e., the cases where the probabilities are 67%, 50%, and 40% for options A, B, and C, respectively, or 50% for the three costs).

Still assuming another set of utilities, we can run another simulation considering that utility is highest (1.0) whenever the consultant is accurate, two-thirds (0.67) whenever he overestimates the cost, one-third in the case of underestimation, and zero if the project is not constructed (see Table 6.6). With these utilities, the results of the model are shown in Table 6.7.

In this situation, where underestimation is heavily penalized while accuracy is rewarded, and the consultant or the decision maker gets no utility from the cancellation of the project, there is a tendency to underestimate the costs when there is a sufficiently large differential between the probabilities of construction for the medium- and high-cost alternatives compared to the low-cost alternative (see, for instance, the case where probabilities are 50% for option A, and zero percent for the other two costs). On the other hand, when the probabilities are similar across the different options, the consultant will tend to be accurate, and less so—with a tendency to underestimate—when his or her overall accuracy decreases. Consultant accuracy, once again, tends to favor unbiasing the results.

Table 6.6
Table of Utilities: Case 3

Outcome	Ranking	Utility
AGA	1	1.00
BGB	1	1.00
CGC	1	1.00
BGA	4	0.67
CGA	4	0.67
CGB	4	0.67
AGB	7	0.33
BGC	7	0.33
AGC	7	0.33
CnG	10	0.00
BnG	10	0.00
AnG	10	0.00

Table 6.7
Model Results: Case 3

Consultant's Accuracy	Probability of Construction			Cost Selected			Overall Utility
	A	B	C	α	β	τ	
100%	100%	100%	100%	A	B	C	1.00
80%	"	"	"	B	B	C	0.90
45%	'	'	'	B	B	B	0.78
33%	'	'	'	B	C	B	0.75
100%	100%	90%	70%	A	B	C	0.88
80%	'	'	'	A	B	C	0.78
45%	'	'	'	B	B	B	0.68
33%	'	'	'	B	A	B	0.68
100%	100%	67%	33%	A	B	C	0.67
80%	'	'	'	A	B	B	0.62
45%	'	'	'	B	B	B	0.53
33%	'	'	'	B	A	B	0.50
100%	67%	50%	40%	A	B	C	0.52
80%	'	'	'	A	B	A	0.46
45%	'	'	'	A	B	C	0.38
33%	'	'	'	B	A	B	0.38
100%	50%	50%	50%	A	B	A	0.50
80%	'	'	'	A	A	A	0.45
45%	'	'	'	A	A	A	0.39
33%	'	'	'	A	A	A	0.38
100%	100%	0%	0%	A	A	A	0.50
80%	'	'	'	A	A	A	0.50
45%	'	'	'	A	A	A	0.50
33%	'	'	'	A	A	A	0.50
100%	50%	0%	0%	A	A	A	0.25
80%	'	'	'	A	A	A	0.25
45%	'	'	'	A	A	A	0.25
33%	'	'	'	A	A	A	0.25

1. The concern for securing the construction of the facility raises the possibility that the results will be biased. If higher cost estimates reduce the likelihood of the transit facility being built, then the consultant will tend to shift estimates to be biased low (assuming the bias is not detectable as "deliberate").

2. If the project is constructed regardless of how much the consultant says it is going to cost (the funding institution assures the project will be constructed, or earmarked funds are created for the construction of the facility), underestimation is unlikely.
3. Underestimation will more likely take place when there is a sufficiently large differential between the probability of construction for the lowest cost and the medium and high costs. This differential tends to increase or decrease (hence, underestimation will be less or more likely)—as shown in the first two cases—depending on the probability of construction for the lowest cost and how the consultant or decision maker feels about the benefits of underestimation (as reflected in the assumed set of utilities).
4. The higher the consultant's accuracy, the more likely he or she will announce the actual estimates, and the lower the tendency to bias the results.
5. How the consultant or decision maker perceives the utility of the consequences of underestimation, overestimation, and the no-construction of the facility largely affects the likelihood of biasing the results. By penalizing underestimation and rewarding accuracy, the consultant will tend to select the estimated costs, and not to bias the results.

One conclusion illustrates that when the consultant reduces the uncertainty of the cost estimates (when the consultant's accuracy is close to 100%), underestimation is less likely. An explanation for this is that, when accuracy is high, the consultant has less tendency to bias the results because his or her utility normally decreases when the disclosed costs are well off the final construction costs. Another conclusion is that if the decision to build the facility is certain from the outset, underestimation is less likely. Of course, avoiding the bias of the disclosed costs may likely not be the only purpose of the funding institution as this institution makes a decision about the construction of the facility.

The model further exemplifies how uncertainty allows ambiguity and the possibility of biasing the results, and how the technical analysis can be distorted by the interests that play a part in the decision-making process. Furthermore, the incentives from the funding institutions can play a major role in adjusting the behavior of the analyst or decision maker to proceed with more unbiased procedures.

Decision Criteria

The funding institutions must make decisions about which project to fund, and they have other competing interests influencing them. To make their decisions, these institutions must develop mechanisms for evaluating each project against proposals for other transit projects. The many components and variables of large transit projects make this an intricate and laborious task. Therefore, in order to address the complexities of the process, the funding institutions establish thresholds and criteria that a project must meet or comply with to go forward in the process and eventually receive funds for construction.[13]

Criteria are a way to establish one perception of the problem. As soon as two parties do not agree on the criteria, however, conflicts arise as well as the possibility of behaving contrary to the desired outcome, unless the right incentives are established. A narrowly defined set of criteria—based on a limited number of valuative variables—can reduce the complexity of the process and create a way to evaluate projects that in principle have no single basis for comparison (e.g., comparing a light-rail project in one town with a busway in another town). On the other hand, narrow criteria may be counterproductive in that they can distort the decision process depending on the environment and the uncertainty associated with the variables in the process.[14]

The tendency to come out with aggregate measures (e.g., aggregate performance indicators) can be valuable in narrowing down the number of alternatives, but not work as a single decision rule to decide the merits of a selected alternative. Aggregate values disregard welfare and political concerns that are likely to ultimately have an overriding role in the decision-making process. In fact, if aggregate values do not conform to local preferences, they may be manipulated to reflect such preferences, thus reducing the validity of the technical process.[15]

As was mentioned in Chapter 5, when uncertainty (lack of consensus about purposes and the means of achieving them) is high, the ability of applying standard (universalistic) criteria is difficult.[16] By contrast, the absence of specific criteria would likely favor processes of political and social influence, bringing the planning process completely outside the technical sphere.

The different perspectives on the construction of the transit facility (time and scale frames) generate different preferred criteria at different decision-making levels. The funding institutions may be interested in cost-effectiveness criteria, while the local decision makers may be concerned about expanding service to achieve particular transportation goals in other parts of the region or to attract votes from other sectors of the population. The mismatch among the preferred criteria at these different decision-making levels opens up possibilities for distrust, biasing, and distortion of technical analysis.[17]

PRESENTATION OF ANALYTICAL FRAMEWORK

Figure 6.2 is a schematic representation of the analytical framework. The figure highlights the components that affect the interaction between the technical and decision-making processes. These components should be viewed in the context summarized in Figure 6.1.

Figure 6.2
Schematic Representation of Analytical Framework

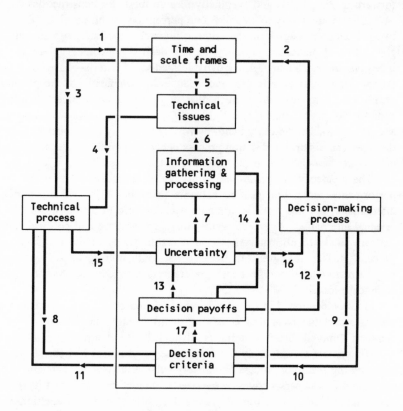

The technical process initially generates, to respond to a perceived need, estimates that reflect some preliminary ideas about the scope and timing of the project (1). Simultaneously, the decision-making process, reacting to signals or pressures from the environment, generates its own ideas about the scope and timing of the project (2). The conflict induces some reevaluation of the technical analysis (3).

The technical process is also influenced by the technical issues (4) presented in Chapter 4. Some of these issues are generated by the conflicts explained in the previous paragraph (5); others, by the information gathering and processing activities (6), which in turn are influenced by the uncertainty associated with any of the elements indicated in Figure 4.1 (7).

Simultaneously with these flows, some criteria are generated for the purpose of selecting the optimal alternative (8). These criteria are evaluated in the decision-making process (9) and sent back to the technical process if perceived not satisfactory (in terms of their values or the concerns they addressed) (10 and 11).

From another side, and concurrent with the events described in the last two paragraphs, some expectations are built as to the optimal project (based or not on the initial estimates generated by the technical process, and affected by other factors, such as the probabilities of getting additional funding). These expectations create some decision payoffs from the decision-making process where some actors may not want to miss the opportunity of getting the project ahead (12). These decision payoffs are also affected by the decision criteria (17) and the incentives or disincentives that may accompanied those criteria. The payoffs evolve in an (accidental or intentional) optimism that permeates the technical process through how the uncertainty associated with the elements of the technical analysis is treated (13) and how information is collected and gathered (14).

Finally, the technical process operates on uncertainty (15) by decreasing its level if need is perceived and funds are available. Uncertainty is also appreciated in the decision-making process (16) where further reevaluation of the technical analysis may be requested. (If a complete reevaluation is deemed adequate in the decision-making process, the level of uncertainty may increase rather than decrease from previous technical exercises.)

PRESCRIPTION AND OPERATIONAL EXTENSION

The framework advanced in Figure 6.2 helps better understand the dynamics of the planning process and the possible underestimation of costs, and illustrates the different perspectives that can be taken to analyze a decision-making process. It also shows the interaction among the different components of the technical and decision-making processes and allows development of prescriptive ideas and operational measures with a potential for improving both processes. The operational measures are designed to confront the issues and difficulties highlighted in the analytical framework, taking into consideration the different decision perspectives.

Decision makers respond to uncertainty by promoting those elements of the technical process that better support their preconceived ideas about the project. In face of uncertainty and their attempt to address the requests and needs of myriad interest groups, decision makers tend to force (deliberately or not) the technical process to emphasize the issues and establish the values that better confirm their personal goals. Sensitivity analyses, carried out to a full extent, should help avoid the difficulties generated by the inherent uncertainty of the planning process.[18]

Sensitivity analyses must encompass not only the simple change in some of the values of the input variables, but also changes in the basic assumptions (in terms, for instance, of ridership, financial conditions, or potential funding sources), and changes in the design of the facility. The stronger development of sensitivity analyses would also help address the conflicts that arose from the different scale and time frames of the participants in the process.

Sensitivity analyses can be further expanded through construction of alternative scenarios. The technical process can be strengthened if consideration is given to the possibility that some of the assumptions do not turn out to be as initially thought, such as the fact that utility companies may or may not pay for relocation costs or the communities affected by the transit facility may or may not want fancy landscaping. This approach, however, will be acceptable only if modeling methods are simple, flexible, and clear enough so that the technical process does not grow unmanageable and so that the participants can easily perceive the tradeoffs among different variables and alternatives. The development of scenarios would foster public debate over data and would provide a solid process to decide how to handle ambiguity and uncertainty.

The decision model developed earlier in this chapter supports the idea that additional information leads to less biased results, based on the assumption that additional information always increases the accuracy of the results (what is certainly likely in the process of estimating capital and operating costs). Sensitivity analyses and additional information can be coupled in the design of computer-based information systems supporting the negotiating-argumentative role of the technical process. These information systems must contain quick and robust maintenance and update procedures as well as structured strategies for undertaking sensitivity analyses. In addition, computer-based information systems must be carefully implemented to avoid the common pitfall that they end up blurring rather than clarifying the planning process.[19] The systems must be transparent and the assumptions clearly stated so that the participants can perceive the tradeoffs between the different inputs and the results of sensitivity analysis.

The fact that several audiences look at the project (and the technical process associated with it) in different ways and with different interests creates mismatches that eventually distort the very meaning of the technical analysis (and the confidence the interested parties have in it). On one account, overly specific decision criteria cannot address the concerns of the several audiences (e.g., the federal government focusing on cost-effectiveness measures, and the state government focusing on environmental and land-use issues) and promote lack of trust, lengthen the process, and bias the technical analysis. A broader set of criteria, coupled with more open discussion and negotiation of which criteria must be ultimately applied, can help achieve a substantial compromise among the different parties and avoid distortions in the technical process.

Such an approach, accompanied by adequate and necessary visibility of its development, will shift the focus of social-influence processes—institutional and political—to a decision among competing criteria, rather than among competing candidates or proposals. This means that attention will be directed not only toward which transit project is the preferred one but also toward the particular criteria to evaluate the several alternatives under consideration. In this way, the use of criteria—for example, a cost-effectiveness criterion—that does not meet the needs of particular interest groups—local decision makers—would be reduced. In addition, the local context, largely ignored in averaging methods and so crucial in planning processes at the local level, would receive more consideration.

Implementation of such an approach means assigning a critical value to the acknowledgment, from the outset of the technical process, of which consequences from an alternative or action should be included in the list of benefits and costs to be used for judging technical, economic, or social feasibility. Essentially, this involves a judgment about whose point of view should be taken, and in turn about which costs and benefits should be considered internal to the project and which external. Importantly, as the group of individuals with a stake in the process changes, a shift in point of view may occur and the final decision may change accordingly.

On another account, as indicated in the decision model, there is much room left to establish the right incentives so that the planning process is less distorted, rather than just instating a fixed set of guidelines that must be followed. For instance, the decision model evidences that when no constraints are put on the probability of getting funds for the construction of the transit facility, the likelihood of biased results decreases. Conversely, if such certainty is not implemented (for obvious reasons, such as appearing too complacent in providing funds), another possibility is to create incentives that discourage biasing the results via premiums when the final figures turn out to be close to the estimated ones.

Still another alternative is an approach currently promoted in several agencies of the U.S. government (although mostly for construction, not for planning).[20] This approach, labeled value engineering, consists of creating a parallel process of technical review by an independent party not directly involved in the project. Through brainstorming and feedback, new ideas and comments on how each alternative is to achieve the specified goals may help actors realize potential flaws and ways to perform better in the construction stage. In addition, the institutions involved in the construction of a facility have the incentive to perform better owing to peer review pressures. However, at the planning stage, this approach may promote feelings of interference in the local decision-making process. This is what happened, for instance, in the Santa Clara case when officials from the California Department of Transportation indicated their belief that the process was being biased and the local institutions complained about interference in local matters.

Another component of the technical process with some potential for improvements is that of cost classifications. The purpose of these classifications is twofold: first, they can help better perceive the tradeoffs among alternatives as changes on some items (e.g., demand) affect variable costs; and second, they can serve to design a funding process that better internalizes costs to the local decision-making process by tying outside funding sources to particular project items. For instance, the most uncertain items could be borne by local institutions while the most definite ones (or those that do not vary much with demand, for instance) would be borne by higher level institutions. Linking the funding sources from higher levels of government to more reliable items internalizes at the correct (local) level those items that can be more influenced and affected by the local decision process.

One may argue that such an approach may induce undue conservatism, since local decision makers would avoid getting involved in costly transit projects regardless of their potential economic benefits for the locality or for the society as a whole. Although it is hard to generalize, this does not have to be the case since the most uncertain items—those that would be borne at the local level—may not necessarily be a large proportion of the total cost. Rolling stock, station and right-of-way landscaping, street reconstruction, utility relocation, and engineering studies do not account for more than one-third of the total capital costs.[21] Nevertheless, this approach may also force consideration of less ambitious design standards that stay closer to local possibilities. Operating costs, which according to this approach would be borne largely if not entirely at the local level, would make a harder case for this approach, since local funds are usually tight and frequently require transfer of funds from higher levels of government.

Other possibilities can also help internalize costs to the decision-making process. As was mentioned in Chapter 5, the project-planning process often goes from design to cost; in other words, first a decision is made about what is wanted—for example, an LRT system—and then the capital and operating costs are calculated. An alternative approach is design-to-cost; in other words, first a decision is made about the level of resources available for a particular type of project and then a selection is made about that project that best fits those resources. Although the design-to-cost approach does not prevent underestimation, it does make decision makers aware of the resources available and the limitations imposed; it also promotes discussion and negotiations among the interested parties by forcing an iterative process of defining-estimating-redefining-reestimating that emphasizes, from the outset, the level of resources available.[22]

Overall, this combination of ideas suggests an approach to tackle the uncertainty of some elements (mainly the elements that compose the technical data and methods) and, at the same time, opens the discussion of the assumptions and definitions of other elements of the transit planning process (mainly the goals to be achieved with the transit project and the criteria to be used to judge the merits of each alternative).

NOTES

1. Although this situation has not been present in any of the case studies, there have been other instances where analysts had to abandon the organization owing to disagreement regarding how the technical analysis was being undertaken. (See, for instance, the situation cited in Wachs (1985b), p. 248.)

2. There is a common distinction between descriptive and measurement uncertainty, the former being that related to which elements should be included, the latter related to how to measure the selected elements. Mahmassani (1984) categorizes uncertainty in five groups: (1) the unknown, (2) the occurrence of exogenous events, (3) the randomness in values of impacts, (4) the vagueness in definition of criteria, and (5) the uncertainty of which criteria and tradeoffs we are going to use to decide among alternatives. Christensen (1985) classifies uncertainty in four groups depending on how much the actors in the planning process agree on the means (technology) or ends (goals) for a particular project. Friend and Hickling (1988) prefer to categorize uncertainty by those areas upon which the response that can be taken varies: uncertainties about the working environment, uncertainties about the guiding values, and uncertainties about related decisions. The classification presented here draws largely upon a combination of those suggested by Mahmassani (levels of uncertainty) and Friend and Hickling (possibilities of response).

3. See Pearman (1988) for a description of methods of scenario construction suitable for transportation planning applications.

4. For a more detailed discussion of the role of ambiguity in policy analysis, see Stone (1988), pp. 123-26.

5. In the case studies, participants complained about the federal emphasis on cost-effectiveness criteria, indicating that those criteria reflect a narrow focus—some said "East Coast mentality"—which cannot incorporate concerns that vary widely from one region of the country to another.

6. This assumption resembles the U.S. context where, although criteria have been established for approving or rejecting transit projects, the possibilities of getting the approval is much broader than those established by the criteria and depend on many political, institutional, and economic factors. Some probabilities can then be assigned to each expected cost. In other contexts, formal criteria may not exist, but one can assume that implicitly costs or some cost-related thresholds have an effect on the decisions of the higher level institution.

7. What is more difficult to know is how much these utilities vary from one set of conditions to another. However, this does not affect the conclusions of the model if changes in the initial conditions—with different sets of utility values—yield similar (and consistent) conclusions.

8. By taking the analyst's or decision maker's perspective, we can assume that the consultant and the decision maker are working to plan the facility whereby the consultant makes the calculations and together the consultant and the decision maker announced how much the facility will cost. The role of the decision maker is important since he or she would probably be the actor with the greatest interest in construction of the facility.

9. The approach can easily be expanded to include many more values, or a continuous probability distribution. These extensions are not necessary for the purposes of the exercise developed here.

10. Saaty (1980) explains a methodology to rank alternatives based on pairwise comparisons. The methodology is based on the perceptions of the decision maker (or group of decision makers), and hence incorporates more than just quantitative values (in fact, judgments can be verbally expressed). Through the use of eigenvalues—that is, the solutions to a particular type of matrices such as $A\ w = n\ w$, where A is the relative weights obtained through pairwise comparison and w is the vector of individual weights—we can rank activities and determine their relative weights.

11. Keeney and Raiffa (1976), chapters 4 and 5.

12. Actually, this is a case of a two-attribute utility function. The two attributes are accuracy (discrete with three values: accurate, over, or under) and building the facility (discrete with two values: is/is not built). The two attributes are not independent since how the decision maker or analyst feels about accuracy depends on construction of the facility and the final cost of the facility, which is correlated to his or her accuracy. Conversely, the analyst's utility from the construction of the facility depends on his or her accuracy in predicting the final cost. Based on these concepts, the utility can be probabilistically interpreted as the point at which the analyst or decision maker feels indifferent between a particular outcome and the lottery with p of getting the best outcome versus $1-p$ chances of getting the worst outcome. In this section, by considering three cases (the last one, assuming independence between the two attributes), results should be general enough to reach convincing conclusions and test the validity of the model.

13. The UMTA approach basically uses two cost-effectiveness indices to evaluate the relative merit of a proposal against other proposals. These indices are determined in the alternatives-analysis process. One of the two indices accounts for the level of local effort in contributing to capital funding. The indices depend upon differences in costs, travel impacts, and financing between the proposed investments and the TSM alternative (which must always be included in any alternatives analysis). A penalty is introduced if a more cost-effective alternative is discovered, and comes in the form of a composite index between the selected alternative and the more cost-effective alternative "discovered." What initial alternatives are considered and shown in the EIS, therefore, may influence how the UMTA rates the alternative selected by the local decision makers.

14. Criteria selection was discussed earlier within the context of the uncertainty associated with the components of the planning process.

15. The UMTA's rating system tries to reflect the benefits of each project and avoid any bias toward a particular type of project or geographical area. That system—with strong emphasis on cost-effectiveness criteria—however, has been controversial because it does not allow enough possibilities for obtaining funds for a project in a particular area when they are requested for reasons different from the estimated cost-effectiveness of that project. (That was the case, to a great extent, with Buffalo's LRRT.)

16. Pfeffer et al. (1976).

17. A middle ground between narrow criteria and no criteria at all is more closely followed outside the United States—for instance, in European cities, where no specific criteria exist before the planning process is undertaken. Initial discussions take place and are formalized in program contracts, where the conditions to be achieved with the transit project are laid down. This approach is a way to reach a compromise between the advantages and disadvantages of the two extreme approaches for evaluating projects—that is, narrow criteria and no criteria at all. Nevertheless, cost considerations also play an important role as incentives are established to encourage attainment of particular cost-

effectiveness objectives in the construction and operation of the selected alternative. Nellis (1989) discusses at great length the issues involved in the design of program contracts and their limitations in improving the performance of public enterprises.

18. In the United States, this approach has been advocated by the UMTA as indicated in the Alternatives Analysis Guidelines. Nevertheless, the extent of these sensitivity analyses is very limited, and still faces resistance from the local planning institutions owing, among other things, to the perceived large computational requirements of sensitivity analyses. There exists, therefore, ample room for improvement.

19. Klosterman (1987).

20. U.S. General Accounting Office (1984, November). In 1989, for an LRT system in Houston, Texas, a peer review process was set to investigate the technical recommendations of the selected LRT alternative (selection accomplished through the UMTA-established alternatives-analysis process). The review panel, composed of several experts in the field, looked at both the technical and political aspects of ridership and cost estimates since the decision makers were concerned about potential cost overruns or demand underestimation. Michael Meyer termed this process "value planning." (Communication with Michael Meyer, August 15, 1989.)

21. Transportation Research Board (1978), pp. 49-51.

22. In this approach, the higher level institution would start by defining the transportation needs for the area in response to a perceived need, and continue by allocating funds (based on their own set of estimates) to the local institution, disbursing them, and letting the local decision makers make use of those funds for construction of the locally preferred alternative. In other words, the funding institution would very much stay out of the local decision-making process as it relates to selection of the transit alternative. Faced with a given amount of external funds, local decision makers would have to internalize the true costs of their preferred alternative and not underestimate the costs.

7

Conclusions

SUMMARY OF FINDINGS

The previous three chapters presented a detailed discussion of the technical process, the decision-making process, and their interaction, as they relate to the estimation of capital and operating costs of transit projects. The discussion led to the following major general conclusions:

As to the technical process:

- The prevalent approach to estimating capital and operating costs during the planning stage, the buildup approach, tries to combine characteristics of both the top-down and ground-up methods in an attempt to address the difficulties of achieving a complete and precise cost-estimating process and the constraints generated by time and budget limitations and those that come from the sociopolitical environment in which the planning process takes place.

- Full accuracy can never be achieved because of the inherent uncertainty associated with some elements of the technical process—uncertainty that cannot be fully avoided by gathering additional information, controlling the variable, or reaching a negotiated compromise with the institution or institutions that control the values of variables.

- Classifications of capital and operating costs, according to their uncertainty and interdependence (e.g., their relation to the demand variable) or how directly they are related to the transportation project (e.g., construction or operating versus administrative costs), are seldom applied as tools for better planning, control of uncertainty, and/or delineation of funding responsibilities.

- Sensitivity analyses have hardly been incorporated to cost-estimating procedures. The large number of items normally present in cost estimating has prevented application of sensitivity tests. Reducing the number of items and increasing the scope of sensitivity analysis would better serve the needs of a dynamic technical analysis and the uncertainty associated with it.

- Computer-based information tools have not been applied to their full extent because of the perception that calculating costs for a project is too specific and has almost no replicability in other projects. Furthermore, computer-based information systems have usually been used to improve the efficiency of cost calculations rather than to effectively support decisions and/or serve as analysis tools in the negotiating process.

As to the decision-making process:

- The institutional and political pressures on the planning process largely affect how decision makers perceive information and how much attention they give to it (a more detailed discussion is developed in the next section). The case studies clearly illustrate the strong pressures on the technical process, motivated to a great extent by the need to justify previously taken decisions.
- Difficulties in the decision-making process (that can simultaneously be viewed as challenges) mostly stem from characteristics of the transportation planning process: its ill-structured nature, the uncertainty of its elements, the many interested parties involved in it, the length of the process, and the unavoidable disjointed organizational setup. To address these difficulties, approaches have tended to confine the process through implementation of standard technical methods and measures. Yet, it is likely that the type of information decision makers must focus on does not fit within the confines of standard methods and measures.
- Information is not equally relevant to all layers of the decision-making process, and it may not be accessible to people at all levels at the same time. In principle, the authorization for a new transit system should be sought after the final evaluation and selection of a complete alternative. However, the case studies illustrate that local decision makers seek authorization while the decision process is taking place, either at the outset or during development of the technical analysis.[1] For actors at higher levels in the authorization hierarchy, time is typically limited and decisions must be made in light of other strategic decisions and overall resource constraints. Moreover, outside political forces are often brought to bear on the decision at the point of authorization, not before. All this compounds to varying degrees of in-depth knowledge about the alternatives among the authorizers and other interested parties, which developers of the solution (analysts and local decision makers) probably have. The final authorization is then given by people who often do not fully comprehend the proposals presented to them, and "the comparative ignorance of the [authorizer] is coupled with the inherent bias of the sponsor" [2] (the local decision maker).

And as to the interaction between the technical and decision-making processes:

- The general framework described in Chapter 6 identified four major actors in the planning, and particularly the cost-estimating process: interest groups (in a broad sense, encompassing lobbying organizations and community groups), analysts, decision makers, and funding institutions. These actors confront the particular transit project with viewpoints that normally differ in scope and time frame. These differences create a situation whereby the decision maker must respond to conflicting audiences. In an attempt to respond to each of those divergent audiences, the decision maker tries to influence the technical process, steering the technical results toward an end not necessarily dictated by a purely rational method.

- Moreover, in spite of the rational nature of the estimating function itself, the cost-estimating process does not fully consider the effects of capital and operating costs in a broad context (e.g., financial consequences, contingency elements, local capacity), owing to influences and coercions resulting from the decision-making process, thus creating tensions between funding institutions and local decision makers that do not contribute to the improved accuracy of cost estimates.

- Changes in the technical analysis, particularly those that eventually generate increases in estimated capital and operating costs, come about mostly as a result of the long time it takes to implement the selected alternative and from changes in the design of its elements. To a lesser extent but also important, increases come from construction or relocation costs initially assumed to be in the hands of institutions outside the responsibility for funding and implementing the transit project.

- The expectations created by the decision-making process from initial project proposals (to perceived needs) and their consequent preliminary technical analyses, what is at stake (for decision makers and analysts) in announcing the results of the technical analysis, and the narrowness of cost-effectiveness criteria for funding a project are factors that introduce unrealistic elements to the design of the transit facility and/or the deliberate or accidental biasing of results.

- The objective of analyzing alternatives should be, in principle, to assist choice, as opposed to making a choice. However, that process is often perceived as the mechanism for making choices and ends up getting distorted as an attempt is made to justify previously selected choices or to delay the process so that the previously chosen alternative has a greater chance of being adopted (or not adopted).

These conclusions highlight the interrelationships between different elements of the technical and decision-making processes. They pave the way to a discussion of the role of technical analysis in decision making and to a further review of the debate about rationality in planning initiated in Chapter 2. These two topics are covered in the next two sections, respectively.

ANALYSIS AND DECISION: TOWARD STRENGTHENING THE ROLE OF ANALYSIS

The Current Role of Technical Analysis: Issues and Constraints

The case studies illustrate that technical analysis has a role in decision making—as an exercise in bureaucratic paperwork and political tactics—and that that role is not the supposedly intended one: the assistance to the decision-making process. The role is distorted because of how the analysis process ends up being structured. Such a process tends to be reactive, not being started until a preferred alternative has already been decided upon. Other alternatives may not be considered, may be given only limited attention, or may be "straw" alternatives tossed in only to meet the requirements of funding institutions.

Furthermore, as the instances investigated in this book have illustrated, so much time and so many resources are committed to development of an analysis supporting the alternative selected as preferable from the outset that, as time passes, it becomes harder and harder financially and politically to give serious consideration to major revisions or new options. The relevance of the long and tedious documents about the project then diminishes, and the technical analysis ends up being simply a paperwork exercise, a hurdle that consumes resources and adds time to the project development process.[3] The escalation in resources and time reinforces both itself and the futility of the technical analysis. This analysis then seldom serves as the basis for responsible, fully informed decision making.[4]

However, the technical analysis still serves another role, and in this role it serves well. The technical analysis structures the process, indicating what elements to include, what to discuss, what to look at, what to confront, thus focusing the terms of discourse and shaping the planning debate.[5] This role is an important one, but its usefulness is largely curtailed when it fails to achieve the other major intended objective of the technical process—namely, effective support of the decision-making function.

The case studies and the discussion of the analytical framework illustrate the decision-related characteristics of the urban transportation planning process, among them the ill-structured nature of its elements (as is typical in sociotechnical systems), the significant value content of its decisions, and the significant human aspects (societal or individual). Together, these characteristics nurture the strategic quality of transportation decisions. Furthermore, for the type of transit projects discussed in this book, there exist not one but several decision processes. These decision processes act on the technical process (and eventually the technical process on them) in order to help those involved reach a compromise on a common set of assumptions, data, methods, and results (and put particular ideas forward).

It is important to acknowledge that, in light of uncertainty, information is always interpretive, and "interpretations can be more powerful than facts[6]." Moreover, inevitably in transportation planning politics acts as a catalyst for activity in an effort to control interpretations. Furthermore, information is never complete, never fully and equally available to all participants in the planning process, and may be even deliberately withheld. The "strategic manipulation of information" [7] must always be considered in any attempt to analyze or carry out the technical process in transportation planning.

The interpretive nature of the transportation planning process has led some authors to conclude that technical analyses are ultimately a middle ground to satisfy several decision-making processes (or institutional actors), and are used to produce arguments for each institutional participant to push selectively for those components that better support their positions.[8] Others prefer to state that transportation studies are an expression of power relations between the different layers in the decision-making process.[9] Nevertheless, as discussed in the introductory section of Chapter 2, transportation studies reflect the technical, bureaucratic, and political doctrines that are dominant at particular moments, giving preference to certain types of reasoning and indicators at those moments.

The framework presented in this book suggests that the preferences are influenced by five major factors in the connection between technical analysis and decision making: (1) uncertainty, (2) time and scale frames, (3) information needs and flows, (4) decision payoffs, and (5) decision criteria. Decision makers use uncertainty to broaden the support for particular preferences, in an attempt to advance their personal or political goals. By making use of uncertainty, they can force the technical analysis to support their preferences. The technical analysis, in addition, owing to myriad interests at work, must address a variety of time and scale frames. Some of these frames will likely be in conflict; the shifts in emphases, responding to the preponderance of particular ideas at particular moments in the development process, ultimately generate outcomes that have a small chance of being close to initial plans. These small chances are further reduced by the length of time it takes to develop the projects and the hurdles likely to be put up by other institutions. The reduced chances nourish the decision maker's disdain toward the technical process, which then becomes a paperwork exercise, not a decision-assistance tool.

In relation to the scope of the project, the attempt to achieve broad goals with the transit project, beyond the pure transportation-related goals, further endangers the assistance role of technical analysis, for this analysis is surpassed by a sociopolitical agenda including broader goals. These broader goals may not easily translate to the transportation study (in terms of benefits, for example), and hence there is a good possibility that the technical analysis will become distorted. Furthermore, the criteria established for approval of the preferred alternative forces the technical analysts (with the decision maker's authority) to generate rather optimistic outcomes that, again, may have little chance of being replicated when implemented. Finally, how decision makers perceive the chances of accomplishing their intended goals—generated by myriad competing interests acting on the decision makers—also affects the chances of biasing the technical process, reducing its effectiveness.

Very often, while the technical analysis focuses on the costs and benefits of transit alternatives to society as a whole, decision makers rarely find the net social benefit criterion, which is basic to the technical analysis, relevant to their often more limited objectives. If the costs of a decision are (or can be) spread over a large number of people while the benefits are concentrated on a narrow constituency, whose support the decision maker seeks, that decision maker will have an incentive to conceal the costs and force the technical analysis to reflect his or her preferences, even if actual costs are in excess of benefits. In such situations, an unbiased technical analysis may give results that decision makers (or elected officials acting on them) are hardly interested in knowing.

Toward Strengthening the Role of Technical Analysis

With these issues and constraints as a background, the crucial question becomes whether it is possible to link directly technical analysis to decision making, and if it is what can be done to accomplish that purpose. Ideally, the theory should highlight the kind of information that is useful to decision makers and under what circumstances, and give an answer to questions of how and when technical analysis can assist decision makers in shaping their perceptions or decisions.[10] In this book, some elements in the direction of that theory have been identified. These should lead to a more effective role for the analysis process in decision making. Subsequent to that role, it is expected that some of the reasons for underestimation of costs will subside and the chance of generating results closer to expectations will improve.

The operational extensions discussed in Chapter 6 attempt to make decision makers, and those affecting decision makers, aware of the implications of their decisions concerning the capital and operating costs of transit alternatives. By more fully internalizing the analysis process and its results, decision makers should be able to strive for the best, least unbiased results, and request this effort from the technical analyst, within the project's time and budget constraints. This does not mean that full accuracy—in particular, for capital and operating costs—will be achieved, but that analyses will be carried out in a more conscious and objective fashion. The actions in that direction can be summarized as follows:

- Require sensitivity analyses of simultaneous sets of variables to help show the relationships between alternatives and the robustness of results. These analyses will acknowledge of the uncertainty associated with each variable and the nature of the data, including key interdependencies.
- Complement sensitivity analyses with development of scenarios. These scenarios would, first, note potential changes and trends in the broader environment and, second, analyze how these changes or trends will affect the values that enter the cost-estimating process. Furthermore, scenario writing can acknowledge different, conflicting viewpoints and allow reflection of that confrontation in the technical process, thus avoiding a process that reflects the decision maker's viewpoint only.
- Require development of cost classifications, at least between one-time and recurrent costs and between demand-responsive and nonresponsive costs. These classifications would focus discussion among different levels of government on which items each is responsible for, and at the same time would induce and help decision makers to perceive what could happen if certain expectations (mainly demand) are not met.
- Make better use of emerging computer-based information systems and technology to speed the process (not only of generating prompt results along with potential political developments but also redoing analyses whenever new or actual data become available), to share information with past and present project development exercises, and to keep track of changes in and sources of cost-related items. By speeding the process, chances are increased that the technical analysis will respond

in good manner to the requirements of the decision-making process and the dynamism of the political agenda will increase. To be fully effective and accepted, however, these information systems must be carefully designed bearing in mind the elements of the framework developed in Chapter 6 (uncertainty, scope and time scales, decision criteria). This means systems that are transparent and simple, and upon which assumptions can be built and sensitivity analyses easily performed.

- Make the cost model or approach, either formal or informal, as explicit and clear as possible. Particular approaches may blur rather than clarify the process, although selection of an obscure approach may be done deliberately for other purposes. Analysts should strive for transparency as a major characteristic of the cost-estimating approach and its structure should provide incentives to do so.

- Complement this explicitness with a process that puts some pressure on the analyst through argumentation. For example, an approach similar to value engineering, whereby an independent review of the project is undertaken outside the decision-making sphere to evaluate and assess the technical results (e.g., the cost estimates). Such an approach, to be endorsed by all or most of the actors involved, must consider all the constraints and opportunities related to local conditions (to avoid, for instance, having a narrow review rejected at the local level).

- The approach must reflect the decision at stake and carry a flexible technical process that can respond to the dynamism of the institutional environment. A sophisticated analysis process is probably uncalled for if the decision environment is highly tempestuous and aggressive; an initial simplified analysis can help decision makers establish the framework for posterior detailed analyses within a more controlled environment. Furthermore, in light of the satisfying side of decision making and the fact that qualitative analysis is central to assessing proposals, in some situations it is advisable to follow a design-to-cost approach whereby resources available are first identified, then the value of the proposals is established (value in a general sense as the overall value the project would bring about), and then iterative tests are performed to see if the expected costs and benefits are acceptable. In this approach, the decision problem, through successive iterations, is simplified to make it more manageable and to avoid the general weakness of a purely cost-benefit approach, which requires knowledge of and accuracy about issues and variables which are unknown, ill defined, and uncertain, particularly for innovative transit systems. In other situations, an approach that combines maximizing with satisfying may be adequate, whereby for some variables and criteria the analysis is performed to optimum values, while for others, satisfactory performance is enough for the decision at hand.[11]

- Though some standardization may be necessary or beneficial, narrow criteria should be avoided as the basis for funding a transit alternative. For instance, standard procedures can be designed in such a way that alternative evaluation criteria are considered in the process. Some components of the technical process are relevant at certain decision-making levels but are in conflict with components relevant at a different decision-making level. The most conspicuous example is that of evaluation criteria and effectiveness thresholds that must be passed to move the project forward. Emphasis on narrow criteria simplifies the evaluation process but may induce distortions in the overall planning process. By shifting the focus of discussion to alternatives and evaluation criteria, interested parties will become aware of the components of the technical analysis and realize the tradeoffs between variables.

This focus allows interested parties to participate actively in project development—to propose alternatives, suggest possible impacts, and otherwise have a say in the outcome of the studies—and is crucial to the success of a revised, more effective, transportation planning effort.[12]

- Though some screening mechanism may always be necessary for the higher level institution, this mechanism can be set up in phases, starting with broad criteria in the initial stage (criteria that include the merits of each alternative on the basis of the seriousness of the problem and the objectives pursued by the ultimate beneficiaries). The criteria would be narrowed to more specific ones as the last stages of the process are reached (and as the number of alternatives becomes smaller, including those worthwhile for the local decision-making process). At these later stages, the criteria should nevertheless encompass performance measures related to the broad merits established in the initial stages of the planning process. The higher level institution needs then to choose among competing projects and competing criteria, and select the ones that deserve further consideration and, eventually, funding (and to which extent), based on the institution's goals for urban transportation and the prevalent political agenda. This process gains in flexibility but needs to be combined with the other suggested actions (e.g., sensitivity analyses, performance incentives).

- As a consequence of the previous point, the specific methodological and valuative approaches of the analysis process can hardly be standardized.[13] There may exist, however, some benefits in standardizing some components as a mechanism to improve the quality of the process and/or its manageability, or reduce the costs of carrying it out. Nevertheless, these conveniences must be weighed against the dynamism of the planning process. This process requires innovation for, depending on which criteria are deemed more appropriate, the kind of analysis may change. For instance, if the overriding purpose of one transit project is to improve air quality, the information and technical methodologies of the analysis process would likely differ from a situation where the major concern is to reduce congestion. Moreover, innovation can help simplify the technical process in some situations, and reduce the time to complete it.

- Establish incentives so that the planning process becomes less distorted. For instance, reward good performance on the basis of the criteria selected (for instance, reduction in the carbon monoxide level in the corridor). These rewards would, for instance, increase the funding level depending on how the final project accomplishes the preestablished criterion thresholds (for instance, a 10 percent reduction in the CO level would increase funding for transit vehicles by 10 percent). This approach should encourage, first, establishment of reasonable criteria and, second, attempts to achieve the goals intended with the transit alternative.

- Establish incentives relating the level of influence in the local decision-making process to funding of particular components of the project. To the largest extent possible, those components primarily related to local decisions should be borne by the local institutions. This mechanism will internalize at the correct, local level those items that can be more influenced and affected by the local decision process.

Overall, these actions will strengthen the technical analysis and its relationship to the decision-making process, since decision makers would have to identify their perceptions about the transportation problem early in the process so as to acknowledge them in the analysis process. Those actions also increase communications among the actors, since they must discuss the content and purpose of the technical analysis and agree on the decision criteria. In this vein, the technical analysis will become the central argumentative element of the process, rather than merely a bureaucratic hurdle.

Conclusions

These strategies take into consideration the observation that decision makers mostly see the technical analysis as a response to largely useless higher-level requirements. This perspective distorts the technical process although it serves well the purpose of putting ideas and actions forward. The different actors involved have different time and scale frames, and different objectives for the transit project. The clash in objectives cannot be solved if the analysis process is confined to its current narrow limits. For the process to be more effective, it must allow for negotiation not only as to the goals but also in how to undertake the analysis (e.g., evaluation criteria).

Communications between the technical and decision-making processes increases the possibility of a biased estimate. On the other hand, that communication is needed as the only way for the technical analysis to acknowledge the many issues involved in the transportation planning process and incorporate them in the technical evaluation. Without that communication, a larger discrepancy between estimates and actual values probably occurs. The communication serves to reduce uncertainty, particularly *actionable* uncertainty. It also serves as a learning tool for the interested parties in the planning process.[14] How much learning can take place, however, is not trivial. Some sophisticated techniques may prevent any learning; in addition, learning may be in the opposite direction, since distortion is always possible (e.g., people may think that one alternative is better than another, based on distorted or biased information).

Technical studies could set a basis for litigation, encouraging analysts and decision makers to avoid excessive distortions of the process. Litigation, however, is a poor function for a transportation study. The alternative is to open the analysis process to scenario writing and design, sensitivity analysis, and discussion of evaluation criteria. This approach can, if nothing else, be "an important tool for communication," [15] and can help generate a "learning" environment. Adequate articulation of such a framework would allow the synergy of the technical (positivist) approach and the social-argumentative approach.

The purpose of the technical analysis is not to achieve the truth (that may be the correct purpose under very particular situations), but rather to inform the interested parties about the consequences of alternative actions and, ultimately, help them reach a consensus about the alternative to pursue. However, since the technical process falls into the hands of some actors and not of others, and since knowledge of elements in the process is never complete, it also serves the strategic purposes of particular actors. That is why, by recognizing the framework presented in this book, those involved can establish mechanisms to improve how the technical process is undertaken to avoid distortions and biases. In this vein, particular mechanisms such as those presented in the preceding section can contribute to achieving a consensus and effectively serve the decision-making process by providing warnings and incentives.

LOOKING AHEAD

By looking at the different steps of both the technical and decision-making processes, this book has attempted to help readers realize the difficulties, constraints, and issues involved in the cost-estimating function. The espoused process-oriented, multiple-perspective approach helped identify the different components of the decision-making process and their connection with the technical process. It also helped perceive the stakes involved and the various decision-making processes that take place in transit project planning. The approach also helped explain the relevance of technical analysis and its role as a means for meeting organizational requirements or justifying previously made decisions.

By taking such an approach, however, the research did not focus on elements of the estimating function and on achieving specific conclusions about particular elements in that process. Furthermore, some specific components of the analytical framework—such as the decision model developed in Chapter 6—could not be tested, although their validity was strongly supported by evidence in the case studies. The number of cases researched here was also limited. This did not allow elaboration of some other elements such as how sensitivity analysis should be carried out, which kind of organizational setup best supports particular decision-making environments, or which specific cost models are suitable for certain institutional environments and decision makers.

By focusing on these elements, further insights could be gained on how the analysis process can be closer to a normative ideal (as it relates not only to the rational paradigm but also to the social-argumentative one). Some areas that deserve further research are the following:

1. Approaches to sensitivity analysis and scenario writing; alternative techniques and their characteristics; and how they should be implemented to make them useful to decision makers. This research would not simply focus on the rational techniques for sensitivity analyses and scenario writing but also on how their use can be tailored to the decision-making process so that the results are effective for decision makers to perceive the tradeoffs between uncertainty and outcomes.
2. Kinds of explicit or implicit decision criteria being used to select transit alternatives.

This research would analyze the issues related to decision criteria and would identify and compare the appropriateness of particular different types of criteria in terms of their equity (across alternatives) and efficiency (allocating specific costs and benefits to different alternatives) characteristics, and their technical requirements (or how hard it is to calculate a particular type of criteria).

3. Organizational issues. This research would delve into the types of organizational frameworks that sustain a stronger or weaker role for technical analysis. In light of the unavoidable discontinuities of the transportation planning process, this research would test an alternative hypothesis about the organizational settings that minimize the negative effects of those discontinuities.

4. Incentives to the achievement of a normative ideal, along the lines advanced in this book. Further research should be undertaken on incentives that can be incorporated into criteria or institutional processes to (1) make interested actors (e.g., decision makers) internalize the outcomes of their actions and (2) reduce distortions in the planning process.

5. The impact of transit construction on local economies. The cases illustrated that transit proposals often come about from the perception that only fixed-guideway systems can help revitalize central areas or redirect urban growth (influencing land use patterns). But this perception is far from conclusive. At most, theories seem to support the idea that transit facilities are necessary but not sufficient to generate those impacts. There is a need to nail down the factors, particularly institutional, that help achieve the goals that so often are assigned to transportation projects of the kind investigated in this book.

6. Comparative operating costs. As illustrated in some of these case studies, local decision makers often claim that rail operating costs are lower than bus operating costs. This assertion is key in the attempt to raise constituency support for rail-based alternatives. Transit systems in place, however, do not definitively back this claim, in part because ridership falls below expectations. Further research should be done on this topic, with the aim of better relating operating costs to particular transit systems and to ridership figures.

7. The role of computer-based information and, in more general terms, the impact of how the information is presented to decision makers. It is often hypothesized that computer-experienced decision makers would be more suspicious or less confident of computer-derived information than would the nonexperienced. Researcher could look at the implications (advantages and disadvantages) inherent in alternative methods of presenting information and the effect they have on decision makers' choices (e.g., the possible biases that computerized information may introduce into the selection process).

NOTES

1. In fact, in the United States, owing to past experience, new transit plans are started by testing the waters of the federal government in order to come up with some idea of the initial probability of attracting federal funds.

2. Mintzberg et al. (1976), pp. 259-61.

3. Such a process would favor those projects in regions where decision makers are more persevering or have higher influence or more leverage at the federal level. However, it would not comply with the definition of a correct planning process as indicated in Chapter 2.

4. De Neufville (1987) identifies three types of explanations for apparent failure to apply data or studies in policy making: (1) the "partisan" view argues that data and studies are, at most, used to support decisions previously made; (2) the "two worlds" argument states that data and studies are often irrelevant because the analyst and the decision maker operate with divergent assumptions, problem formulations, variables, and time schedules, resulting in studies that appear too late and often focus on variables not relevant to decision makers; and (3) the "enlightenment" argument contends that data and studies are influential, but they should be viewed only as background and not as having a primary impact on particular decisions (p. 86). These three types of explanations were present in the cases investigated in this book.

5. Innes (1988) refers to data for problem framing (p. 278).

6. Stone (1988), p. 6.

7. Ibid., p. 21.

8. Johnston et al. (1988), Deiter (1985), Dorschner (1985), Hamer (1976).

9. Whitt and Yago (1985), Offner et al. (1982), Whitt (1982).

10. De Neufville (1987), p. 86.

11. Mintzberg et al. (1976).

12. In this direction, De Neufville (1987) states: "The positivist view of knowledge on planning practice has encouraged planners to try to be value neutral, to focus on measurable issues and general principles, and see the production of information as distinct from the political process. A phenomenological conception of knowledge, on the other hand, focuses on unique and particular situations, and on the everyday world; it emphasizes the subjective meaning of the problems to the actors, it assumes knowledge is constructed in a community rather than having an independent existence, and it accepts that information is shaped by preconceptions. . . . Knowledge developed interactively with knowledge users becomes influential in decisions."

13. Procedural guidelines, however, may be necessary to indicate the steps that must be followed to request funds for a project, including the minimum amount of information that must be reported for the higher level institution to initiate its own valuative process.

14. Innes (1988).

15. Pearman (1988), p. 83.

8

Recapitulation: Some Views with Hindsight

A manifest dissatisfaction with the results of technical analyses in transportation planning, and the burden that deliberate or accidental technical errors may add to national and local economies, led to my investigating the reasons for the underestimation of capital and operating costs from a process (behavioral) perspective and to identifying the components of a framework that shows the interaction among the elements that shape those technical analyses and the decisions that accompany their results.

Since data and methods cannot usually be adapted to the complexity and dynamism of some public policy issues, the underestimation issue has been looked at with a broader approach than would be dictated by a quantitative one (for instance, a statistical approach). The social-argumentative approach looks at the process as a tool for both argumentation and structuring the dialogue. It highlighted the difficulties imbedded in several components (such as the decision criteria, the management of information, the perspectives on the problem, and the poor definition of some of its elements), and led to suggested actions to address those difficulties.

The effective consideration of the normative basis stated in Chapter 2 implies the opportunity to make informed decisions. The strengthening of quantitative techniques is a necessary step in this direction. However, this strengthening must always be accompanied by the recognition of its limitations and the acknowledgment of its potential roles. Difficulties seldom lie with the quantitative elements in the strict sense. The design on paper of an efficient system does not necessarily help overcome the resistance offered by, for instance, institutional restrictions or a host of economic and political interests that inhibit an unbiased and impartial analysis of options. The reason for this stems mainly from the fact that who benefits from and who pays for the construction of a transit facility may require far more attention than the question of which alternative is more efficient or which generates the greater net of benefits over costs (e.g., has the best cost-effectiveness index, however this index in defined). That is why the framework proposed in this book underscores the need for changes in method and attitude, arising from the inability of the more quantitative and conventional methodologies to handle the sociopolitical, institutional, and personal problems that stir substantial involvement by public interests. And that is why the framework also emphasizes consideration of how the analysis can be constrained by the institutions and individuals affected by its implementation.

This does not mean to discredit the development and improvement of technical methods and approaches. Technical analyses are a fundamental tool in assisting and shaping decisions. Nevertheless, decision makers and analysts alike must appreciate the limitations of technical analyses and acknowledge what to expect from them. In particular situations, what to expect from technical analyses should be rather modest, and that may dictate the use of particular methodological approaches (in terms of complexity, flexibility, etc.). As Quade (1989) also states, technical analyses can help (1) reduce the complexity of problems to manageable proportions; (2) eliminate from consideration the demonstrably inferior alternatives; (3) find one alternative that all interested parties can accept even though they are not fully satisfied; (4) widen the area of informed judgment; and (5) yield insights, particularly with regard to the dominance and sensitivity of the parameters.

In order to achieve those roles, technical analyses must be understood as an argumentative and structuring component—which emphasizes the process rather than the product—within the overall planning exercise. Furthermore, in order to reduce the possible distortion of its results and increase its assistance role, the stakes of the actors involved must be somewhat internalized into the process. When analysis emphasizes the product and the actors' stakes are barely internalized, the technical analysis often becomes an end in itself and tends to be used for unintended purposes (like the support of previously made decisions). The case studies clearly illustrate how participants can become bogged down in technical quibbles to make the results fit the guidelines of the funding institution and meet universalistic criteria in an attempt to make the initially preferred project appear worthwhile to the funding institution.

What are the main implications of the proposed framework and the suggested actions for the case studies? In general terms, (1) sensitivity analyses should have shown that some alternatives were not discernable from others; (2) incentives should have prevented excessive distortion of demand and cost estimates; (3) discussion of evaluation criteria at the beginning of the technical process should have produced a less beleaguered process; and (4) some systems may not have been built (although this would have been unlikely in the case studies discussed in this book because of strong political motivations prevalent during their development) or at least should have been built to less ambitious design standards.

In addition, the whole planning process should have taken less time, since resolution of technical and methodological disagreements at the outset would have cleared the way to a more speedy process at the end, avoiding the threat of stalemate, endless discussions about specific figures, and decisions drastically made outside the technical arena. Advancing the discussion of the most controversial points (including evaluation criteria) at the beginning should likely reduce the time to complete the studies and implement the selected alternative. This is because, though additional time would need to be spent at the beginning, at the end the process would run smoothly and with less tendency to bias the results and produce undue tensions among the interested actors.

The adequacy of methods to the decision environment (i.e., level of sophistication, cost classifications) and the use of flexible database management systems would further allow an iterative process whereby assumptions can be tested and tradeoffs easily perceived. Analysts should then be able to respond faster to shifts in the political arena and increase their chances of shaping that arena instead of being overpowered by it. These aspects underscore the value of quantitative analysis and the value of flexibility.

In response to a local initiative, the process should start with a discussion of the goals, the range of possible options, and the criteria for selecting the best alternative. The local participants would tend to portray the alternatives as the best for meeting particular goals (and may tend to select those goals and criteria for which those alternatives are best). The higher level institution, with its own set of concerns or objectives, may or may not concur with the local level in its perception of the problem, the goals, or the evaluation criteria. If it does not, the proposal would be rejected. If it does, the proposal can go forward and new discussions would start on working out the technical details, identifying particular alternatives, and setting the specific criteria to evaluate them. This would mean that project construction would be granted at this moment, subject to limited funds to be disbursed based on which goals are important for the higher-level institution (and possibly pressures from the political side) and perhaps earmarked for particular items in the project proposal. The agreement would involve incentives for good performance—in terms, for instance, of reaching the expected demand and keeping costs within small variations of the estimated ones. Similarly, performance indicator bands should signal to the higher level institution the reasonability of the results of the technical analysis, and peer pressure can be introduced by calling on expert advice of independent parties.

In Buffalo, a concern about economic development (and comparisons with the city of Toronto) forced presentation of the alternatives with rather low capital and operating costs and with a radically unconventional design. A more open discussion of decision criteria might have indicated that construction of the rail transit system might not have been the most adequate means to bring economic development to the region and that a different, less ambitious and more flexible set of design standards would have been preferable, with more emphasis on the achievement of economic development goals. Sensitivity analyses should have shown that the preferred alternative was not necessarily the best performing one, according to several criteria, as well as exposed the potential variations in its costs and the burden to the local economy if some of the assumptions changed. Performance incentives should have increased interest in knowing more about the utility networks along the transit corridor and the potential costs to relocate them.

In Santa Clara, the concern was congestion as well as rehabilitation of the downtown area, with the aim of changing land-use patterns toward higher residential densities. Community participation was extensive but the technical analysis could not follow it, or did not try to. There was a latent dichotomy and competition between freeway and transit advocates, and within the latter group, between bus and rail supporters. Had the analysis considered these arguments, more insights should have been gained into ridership estimates and the implications of these estimates on the rest of the variables. Moreover, evaluation criteria would have played a predominant role. The in-depth discussion of assumptions, goals, and criteria from the outset would probably have led to development of a transparent technical process and would have reduced the possibility of deliberate or accidental distortions.

In Boston, the local interests emphasized congestion and environmental concerns, within the constraints of existing transit technologies. The proposed actions would have diminished the apparent juggling with cost-effectiveness measures and would have reduced the mutual distrust among neighborhood groups and local institutions, as well as the strains between the state and federal governments. The technical process would have been improved with the discussion of criteria and a more open questioning of assumptions and tradeoffs (e.g., phasing of alternatives, changes in ridership) with communities and the federal government. The mistrust—largely created because of emphasis on cost-effectiveness criteria—prevented a complementary relationship between the local decision makers and the higher level institution.

How can the higher level institution compare alternatives that come from different places if criteria among them are different? For instance, consider how different were Buffalo's system emphasizing economic development, Santa Clara's land-use changes, and Boston's traffic congestion. Criteria would follow a pyramid pattern whereby, initially, for purposes of coalition building, a set of broad indicators would be used and, further along the process, these criteria would become more specific, though incorporating (through performance measures) the concerns expressed by the local interests at the outset. The higher level institution would then have to compare competing projects and competing criteria with its own agenda of goals and political constraints, and decide which projects to fund and to what extent.

In this approach, furthermore, decision makers at the different levels would base their decisions on a broad set of indicators and tradeoffs, not necessarily more information. Moreover, the approach takes into account that decisions do not always fit the homogeneous decision makers' model, since often the individuals for whom a study is done are no more that key participants in a decision-making process; it can enhance the possibilities of a productive dialogue that uses the technical analysis to bring others to discuss their points of view and reach a consensus.

In addition, the assistance role of the technical analysis can be better achieved if decision makers perceive the need to get involved in its development and outcomes. That perception can be heightened with the right incentives, internalization of some of the outcomes, and the correct structuring of the process to better serve—not necessarily reflect—the needs of the decision-making function. But how can the decision makers be induced to pay greater attention to the technical process?. If the process focuses more on decision criteria, decision tradeoffs, and decision payoffs (incentives), they will likely intensify their interest in the implications of their decisions as their own role in the development of the technical process becomes more fundamental.

Some of these conclusions may seem obvious. It is, however, surprising to find how unlikely they are taken into consideration. This is mainly a consequence of a prevalent perspective that limits the purpose of technical analysis and the way criteria and methods are selected to choose among alternative projects. Acknowledgment of a perspective that sees the technical process more as part of an argumentative and structuring process can help improve its function and strengthen the overall transportation planning process.

Bibliography

Adams, J. R., and Swanson, L. A. (1976) "Information Processing Behavior and Estimating Accuracy in Operations Management," *Academy of Management Journal*, 19-1, 90-110.

Adler, Sy (1987) "The New Information Technology and the Structure of Planning Practice," *Journal of Planning Education and Research*, 6-2 (Winter), 93-98.

Alexander, Ernest R. (1984) "After Rationality, What? A Review of Responses to Paradigm Breakdown," *Journal of the American Planning Association*, 50-1 (Winter).

Allen, John G. (1985) "Post-Classical Transportation Studies," *Transportation Quarterly*, 39-3 (July), 451-63.

————. (1986) "Public-Private Joint Development at Rapid Transit Stations," *Transportation Quarterly*, 40-3 (July), 317-31.

Allen-Schultz, E., and Hazard, J. L. (1982) "The U.S. National Transportation Study Commission: Congressional Formulation of Policy," *Transportation Policy and Decision Making*, 2, 17-49.

Allison, Graham T. (1971) *Essence of Decision, Explaining the Cuban Missile Crisis*. Boston, MA: Little, Brown.

Altshuler, Alan, with James P. Womack and John R. Pucher (1979) *The Urban Transportation System: Politics and Policy Innovation*. Cambridge, Massachusetts: MIT Press.

American Public Transit Association, Transit 2000 Task Force (1988, October) "Transit 2000: Interim Report," Washington, DC: APTA.

Argyris, Christopher (1976) "Single-Loop and Double-Loop Models in Research on Decision-Making," *Administrative Science Quarterly*, 21 (September), 363-77.

Armstrong-Wright, Alan (1986) *Urban Transit System: Guidelines for Examining Options*, World Bank Technical Paper Number 52. Washington, DC: World Bank.

Atkins, Stephen T. (1987) "The Crisis for Transportation Planning Modelling," *Transport Reviews*, 7-4, 307-25.

Attewell, P., and Rule, J. (1984) "Computing and Organizations: What We Known and What We Don't Know," *Communications of the ACM*, 27-12 (December).

Bardach, Eugene (1977) *The Implementation Game*, Cambridge, MA: MIT Press.

Bay, Paul N. (1984) "Determining Cost-Effectiveness of Transit Systems," *State-of-the-Art Report 2*. Washington, DC: Transportation Research Board, National Research Council.

Benveniste, Guy (1972) *The Politics of Expertise*. Berkeley, CA: Glendesary Press.

Berkman, Leslie (1984) "Bullet Train Data Assailed by Consultant," *Los Angeles Times*, October 26, pp. 1 and 8.

Blanchard, R. D. (1976) "Transportation and the New Planning: Toward a New Synthesis," *High Speed Ground Transportation Journal* (Spring).

Bouchard, Richard J. (1982) "Relevance of Planning Techniques to Decision-Making," *Highway Research Board, Special Report 143*. Washington, DC: Transportation Research Board, National Research Council, 17-19.

Bryson, J. M., and Roering, W. D. (1987) "Applying Private-Sector Strategic Planning in the Public Sector," *Journal of the American Planning Association*, 53-1 (Winter).

Calder, G. (1976) *The Principles and Techniques of Engineering Estimating*. Oxford, UK: Pergamon Press, Ltd.

Catanese, A. J. (1984) *The Politics of Planning and Development*. Beverly Hills, CA: Sage Publications.

Caudill, R. J., Kaplan, R. A., and Taylor-Harris, A. (1983) "Developing Bus Operating Cost Models: A Methodology," *Journal of Transportation Engineering*, 109-2 (March).

Cervero, Robert (1984) "Examining the Performance Impacts of Transit Operating Subsidies," *Journal of Transportation Engineering*, 110-5 (September).

Charles River Associates (1983, August) "Cross Cutting Analysis of Rail Transit Impact Studies in Washington, D.C., Atlanta, and San Francisco." Prepared for the Transportation System Center, Cambridge, MA.

Chomitz, Kenneth M., and Lave, Charles A. (1984) "Part-time Labour, Work Rules, and Urban Transit Costs," *Journal of Transport Economics and Policy*, 18-1 (January).

Christensen, Karen S. (1985) "Coping with Uncertainty in Planning," *Journal of the American Planning Association*, 51-1 (Winter).

Churchman, C. West (1982) *Thought and Wisdom*. The Systems Inquiry Series. Seaside, CA: Intersystems Publications.

Clark, F. D. and Lorenzoni, A. B. (1985) *Applied Cost Engineering*. Second Edition. New York: Marcel Dekker.

Crozier, Michel (1964) *The Bureaucratic Phenomenon*. Chicago: University of Chicago Press.

Dalton, Linda C. (1986) "Why the Rational Paradigm Persists—The Resistance of Professional Education and Practice to Alternative Forms of Planning," *Journal of Planning Education and Research*, 5-3 (Spring), 147-53.

Date, C. J. (1986) *An Introduction to Database Systems*. Fourth Edition. Reading: MA: Addison-Wesley.

Deiter, R. H. (1985) *The Story of Metro: Transportation and Politics in the Nation's Capital*. Glendale, CA: Interurban Press, Interurbans Special 101.

De Leuw, Cather and Company (1976, August) "Santa Clara County Transit District Light Rail Feasibility and Alternatives Analysis: Final Report."

De Neufville, Judith Innes (1987) "Knowledge and Action: Making the Link," *Journal of Planning Education and Research*, 6-2 (Winter), 86-92.

Dorschner, John (1985) "Metrorail: How a Magnificient Idea Became a White Elephant," *The Miami Herald*, September 15, pp. 11-25.

Drake, John W. (1973) *The Administration of Transportation Modeling Projects*. Lexington, MA: D.C. Heath.

Edner, S. M., and Arrington, Jr. (1985, March) "Urban Decision Making for Transportation Investments, Portland's Light Rail Transit Line." Prepared for U.S. Department of Transportation.

Einhorn, H. J., and Hogarth, R. M. (1981) "Behavioral Decision Theory: Processes of Judgment and Choice," *Annual Review of Psychology*, 32, 53-88.

Engineering News Record, various issues, 1970-1988.

Etzioni, Amitai (1988) *The Moral Dimension: Toward a New Economics*. New York: Free Press.

Faludi, Andreas (1987) *A Decision-Centered View of Environmental Planning*. Oxford, UK: Pergamon Press, Ltd.

———. (1973) *Planning Theory*. Oxford, UK: Pergamon Press, Ltd.

Fielding, Gordon J. (1983a) "Changing Objectives for American Transit. Part 2. Management's Response to Hard Times." *Transport Reviews*, 3-4, 341-62.

———. (1983b) "Changing Objectives for American Transit. Part 1. 1950-1980." *Transport Reviews*, 3-3, 287-99.

Flyvberg, Bent (1984) "Implementation and the Choice of Evaluation Methods," *Transportation Policy and Decision Making*, 2, 291-314.

Forester, John (1984) "Bounded Rationality and the Politics of Muddling Through," *Public Administration Review* (January/February).

Frankena, Mark W. (1983) "The Efficiency of Public Transport Objectives and Subsidy Formulas," *Journal of Transport Economics and Policy*, 17-1 (January).

French, S. (1986) *Decision Theory: An Introduction to the Mathematics of Rationality*. London: Ellis Horwood.

Friend and Hickling (1988) *Planning Under Pressure*, Oxford, UK: Pergamon Press, Ltd.

Gakenheimer, Ralph (1985) "An Addendum to "Planning, Organization and Decision-Making: A Research Agenda," *Transportation Research, Part A: General*, 19A-5/6, 535-38.

———. (1984) "Project Programming in Urban Transportation: Methodology prepared for Cairo, Egypt," *Transportation Policy and Decision Making*, 2, 315-34.

———. (1976) *Transportation Planning as Response to Controversy: The Boston Case* Cambridge, MA: MIT Press.

Gakenheimer, Ralph, and Meyer, Michael D. (1979) "Urban Transportation Planning in Transition: The Sources and Prospects of Transportation System Management," *Journal of the American Planning Association*, 45-1 (January), 28-35.

Giuliano, G. (1985) "A Multicriteria Method for Transportation Investment Planning," *Transportation Research, Part A: General*, 19A-1, 29-41.

Gorry, G. Anthony, and Scott Morton, Michael S. (1986) "A Framework for Management Information Systems." In *The Rise of Managerial Computing*, Rockart and Bullen, eds. Homewood, IL: Dow Jones-Irwin.

Hall, Peter (1980) *Great Planning Disasters*. Berkeley and Los Angeles: University of California Press.

Hamer, A. M. (1976) *The Selling of Rail Rapid Transit, A Critical Look at Urban Transportation Planning*. Lexington, MA: D.C. Heath.

Hammond, K. R., McClelland, H., and Mumpower, J. (1980) *Human Judgment and Decision Making: Theories, Methods and Procedures*. New York: Praeger, Hemisphere Publishing.

Harris, Britton (1986) "How to Teach How to Plan." Paper prepared for the Milwaukee meetings of the ACSP, October.

Henry, Claude (1974) "Investment Decisions under Uncertainty: The Irreversibility Effect," *American Economic Review*, 64-6 (December), 1006-12.

Hogarth, R. M. (1980) *Judgment and Choice: The Psychology of Decision*. Chichester, UK: John Wiley and Sons.

Hogarth, R. M., and Makridakis, S. (1981) "Forecasting and Planning: An Evaluation," *Management Science*, 27-1, 115-38.

Holsapple, C.W. (1984) "A Perspective on Data Models," PC Tech Journal (July), 113-141.

Howe, Elizabeth (1980) "Role Choices of Urban Planners," *Journal of the American Planning Association*, 46-4 (October), 398-409.

Innes, Judith (1988) "The Power of Data Requirements," *Journal of the American Planning Association*, 54-3 (Summer).

Jack Ybarra and Associates (1981, October) "Guadalupe Corridor, Phase II, Alternatives Analysis/D.E.I.S.: Summary of Community Participation Program." Prepared for The Santa Clara County Transit District.

Janis, I. L., and Mann, L. (1977) *Decision Making*. New York: Free Press.

Jansen, Eric Williams (1987) "The Charge of the Light Rail Brigade," *San Jose Metro*, August 20-26, pp. 9-11.

Johnston, R. A., Sperling, D., DeLuchi, M. A., and Tracy, S. (1988) "Politics and Technical Uncertainty in Transportation Investment Analysis," *Transportation Research. Part A: General*, 21A-6, 459-75.

Jones, David. (1985) *Urban Transit Policy: An Economic and Political History*. Englewood Cliffs, NJ: Prentice-Hall.

Joint Policy Committee of the Association of Bay Area Governments and Metropolitan Transportation Commission (1979, March) "Santa Clara Valley Corridor Evaluation: Summary."

————. (1978, November) "Santa Clara Valley Corridor Evaluation: Draft Report, Issue for Public Review and Comment."

Kahneman, D., Slovic, P., and Tversky, A. (1982) *Judgment under Uncertainty: Heuristics and Biases*. Cambridge, UK: Cambridge University Press.

Kaplan, M. F., and Schwartz, S., eds. (1975) *Human Judgment and Decision Processes*, New York: Academic Press.

Kaplan, Thomas J. (1986) "The Narrative Structure of Policy Analysis," *Journal of Policy Analysis and Management*, 5-4, 761-78.

Kartez, Jack D. (1989) "Rational Arguments and Irrational Audiences," *Journal of the American Planning Association*, 55-4 (Autumn), 445-56.

Kaufman, J. L. and Jacobs, H. M. (1987) "A Public Planning Perspective on Strategic Planning," *Journal of the American Planning Association*, 53-1 (Winter).

Kelman, Steven (1987) *Making Public Policy: A Hopeful View of American Government*. New York: Basic Books.

Keen, Peter G. W. (1981) "Information Systems and Organizational Change," *Communications of the ACM*. 24-1 (January), 24-33.

Keen, Peter G. W., and Scott Morton, Michael S. (1978) *Decision Support Systems: An Organizational Perspective*. Reading, MA: Addison-Wesley.

Keeney, Ralph L., and Raiffa, Howard (1976) *Decisions with Multiple Objectives: Preferences and Value Tradeoffs*. New York: John Wiley and Sons.

Kellogg (1985, February 19) "Comparative Analysis of the San Diego Trolley and the Portland Banfield Light Rail Projects to Determine the National Policy Impacts and Implications for UMTA Financial and Technical Assistance." Prepared for the Urban Mass Transit Administration.

Klosterman, Richard E. (1987) "The Politics of Computer-Aided Planning," *Transportation Planning Research*, 58-4, 441-51.

Kotz, Nick (1988) *Wild Blue Yonder: Money, Politics, and the B-1 Bomber*. New York: Pantheon Books.

Kouskoulas, Vasily (1984) "Cost Functions for Transportation Services," *Journal of Transportation Engineering*, 110-1 (January).

Krieger, Martin H. (1986) "Big Decisions and a Culture of Decision-making," *Journal of Policy Analysis and Management*, 5-4, 779-97.

Langendorf, R. (1985) "Computers and Decision Making," *Journal of the American Planning Association*, 51-4 (Autumn), 422-33.

Larkey, P. D. (1977) "Process Models of Governmental Resource Allocation and Program Evaluation," *Policy Sciences*, 8, 269-301.

Lindblom, Charles (1959) "The Science of Muddling Through," *Public Administration Review*, 19 (Spring).

Linstone, Harold A. (1984) *Multiple Perspectives for Decision Making: Bridging the Gap between Analysis and Action*. New York: North-Holland.

Lipsky, Michael (1980) *Street-Level Bureaucracy, Dilemmas of the Individual in Public Services*. New York: Russell Sage Foundation.

Mahmassani, H. (1984) "Uncertainty in Transportation Systems Evaluation: Issues and Approaches," *Transportation Planning and Technology*, 9, 1-12.

Mahmassani, H. and Krzysztofowicz, R. (1983) "A Behaviorally Based Framework for Multicriteria Decision-Making under Uncertainty in the Urban Transportation Context," *Environment and Planning B: Planning and Design*, 10, 293-306.

Manheim, Marvin L. (1985) "Research on Planning, Organizations and Decision-Making: An Essential Component of a Transportation Research Program," *Transportation Research, Part A: General*, 19A-5/6, 538-42.

Massachusetts Bay Transportation Authority (1986, September) "Old Colony Railroad Rehabilitation Project: Preliminary Scoping Report." Prepared by Sverdrup Corporation and Cambridge Systematics, Inc.

————. (1986, January) "Old Colony Railroad Rehabilitation Project: Report Number 4, Conceptual Definition of Alternatives." Prepared by Sverdrup Corporation.

————. (1987, October) "Old Colony Railroad Rehabilitation Project: Technical Report, Social, Environmental, and Economic Impact Assessment." Prepared by Cambridge Systematics.

————. (1987a, December) "Old Colony Railroad Rehabilitation Project: Technical Documentation for Report Number 9, Methods and Results: Operating and Maintenance Costs." Prepared by Sverdrup Corporation.

————. (1987b, December) "Old Colony Railroad Rehabilitation Project: Report Number 8, Methods and Results: Capital Costs." Prepared by Sverdrup Corporation.

————. (1987c, December) "Old Colony Railroad Rehabilitation Project: Report Number 9, Methods and Results: Operating and Maintenance Costs." Prepared by Sverdrup Corporation.

————. (1987d, December) "Old Colony Railroad Rehabilitation Project: Report Number 10, Methods and Results: Service and Patronage Impact Assessment." Prepared by Cambridge Systematics.

————. (1984, June) "Old Colony Feasibility Study: Summary Report." Report to the Great and General Court of the Commonwealth of Massachusetts.

Menendez, Aurelio (1986) "Instituciones y Planeamiento: La Controversia sobre las Autopistas en Boston, Toronto y Londres," *Ciudad y Territorio*, 70 (October-December), Instituto de Estudios de Administracion Local, Madrid, Spain.

Menendez, Aurelio, and Cook, Peter (1990) "Transportation Modelling and Institutional Change," *ITE Journal*, 60-1 (January).

Merewitz, Leonard (1972, November) "Cost Overruns in Public Works with Special Reference to Urban Rapid Transit Projects." Working Paper No. 196/BART 8, Institute of Urban and Regional Development, University of California, Berkeley.

Meyer, Michael D. (1978) "Organizational Response to a Federal Policy Initiative in the Public Transportation Sector: A Study of Implementation and Compliance." Unpublished Ph.D. dissertation, Department of Civil Engineering, Massachussetts Institute of Technology.

Meyer, Michael D., and Miller, E. J. (1984) *Urban Transportation Planning: A Decision-Oriented Approach*. New York: McGraw-Hill.

Mintzberg, H., Raisingham, D., and Theoret, A. (1976) "The Structure of Unstructure Decision Processes," *Administrative Science Quarterly*, 21, 245-75.

Moore, Terry (1988) "Planning without Preliminaries," *Journal of the American Planning Association*, 54-4 (Autumn), 525-28.

Morlok, Edward K. (1978) *Introduction to Transportation Engineering and Planning*. New York: McGraw-Hill.

National Cooperative Transit Research and Development Program (1983, December) *Report 4: Improving Decision-Making for Major Urban Transit Investments*. Washington, DC: Transportation Research Board, National Research Council.

Nellis, John (1989) "Contract Plans and Public Enterprise Performance." Policy, Research and Planning Working Paper ???. Washington, DC: World Bank.

Neuberg, L. G. (1986) "What Can Social Policy Analysts and Planners Learn from Social Experiments ?," *Journal of the American Planning Association*, 52-1 (Winter).

Nisbett, R., and Ross, L. (1980) *Human Inference: Strategies and Shortcomings of Social Judgment*. Englewood Cliffs, NJ: Prentice-Hall.

Niagara Frontier Transportation Authority (1976, June) "Metro for Buffalo: Transit Alternatives for the Buffalo-Amherst Corridor, Technical Report." Alan Voorhees & Associates, Inc.

———. (1976, February) "Evaluation of Transit Alternatives: Buffalo-Amherst-Tonawandas Corridor, Staff Conclusions and Recommendations." Metro Construction Division.

———. (1985, May) "Metro Rail and You." Advertising brochure.

———. (1987, May 8) Internal memorandum excerpts.

Nutt, P. C., and Backoff, R. W. (1987) "A Strategic Management Process for Public and Third-Sector Organizations," *Journal of the American Planning Association*, ?-? (Winter).

Obeng, Kofi (1985) "Bus Transit Cost, Productivity and Factor Substitution," *Journal of Transport Economics and Policy*, 19-2 (May), 183-203.

O'Brian, Kreitzberg and Associates, Inc. (1987, October) "Guadalupe Corridor: Program Report." Prepared for Santa Clara County Transportation Agency.

Offner, J. M., Bonamy, J., Brachet, O., and Tachon, M. (1982, November) *Etudes et Decisions, La Ligne C du Metro Lyonnais*, Institut de Recherche des Transports, Rapport de Recherche I.R.T.

Pearman, A. D. (1988) "Scenario construction for transpot planning," *Transportation Planning and Technology*, 12, 73-85.

Pelaum, A. M. and Delmont, T. J. (1987) "External Scanning—A Tool for Planners," *Journal of the American Planning Association*, 53-1 (Winter).

Pfeffer, J., Salancik, G. R., and Lebledici, H. (1976) "The Effect of Uncertainty on the Use of Social Influence in Organizational Decision Making," *Administrative Science Quarterly*, 21 (June), 227-45.

Pickrell, Don H. (1992) "A Desire Named Streetcar: Fantasy and Fact in Rail Transit Planning," *Journal of the American Planning Association*, 58-2 (Spring).

————. (1989, October) "Urban Rail Transit Projects: Forecast Versus Actual Ridership and Costs." Prepared for the Office of Grants Management, Urban Mass Transportation Administration.

————. (1985) "Rising Deficits and the Uses of Transit Subsidies in the United States," *Journal of Transport Economics and Policy*, 19-3 (September).

Pill, Jury (1979) *Planning and Politics, the Metro Toronto Transportation Plan Review*. Cambridge, MA: MIT Press.

Pucher, John (1988) "Urban Public Transport Subsidies in Western Europe and North America," *Transportation Quarterly*, 42-3 (July), 377-402.

Pucher, J., Markstedt, A., and Hirschman, I. (1983) "Impacts of Subsidies on the Costs of Urban Public Transport," *Journal of Transport Economics and Policy*, 17-2 (May), 155-75.

Quade, E. S. (1989) *Analysis for Public Decisions: Third Edition, Revised Edition by Grace M. Carter*. A RAND Corporation Research Study. New York: Elsevier Science Publishing.

Richmond, Jonathan (1982) "The Costly Lure of the Bullet Train," *Los Angeles Times*, September 8, p. II 7.

Ryan, J. M., Emerson, D. J., et al. (1986, September) *Procedures and Technical Methods for Transit Project Planning*. Prepared for the Urban Mass Transportation Administration, U.S. Department of Transportation, review draft.

Saaty, Thomas L. (1980) *The Analytic Hierarchy Process*. New York: McGraw Hill.

Santa Clara County Transit District (1988, July) "Guadalupe Corridor: Cost Report No. 25." Prepared for Santa Clara County Transportation Agency, Gordon Smith, project manager.

————. (1987, February and May) "Light Rail Lines: Your Connection to the Future." Published quarterly.

————. (1987, June) "Guadalupe Corridor: Cost Report No. 14." Prepared for Santa Clara County Transportation Agency, Gordon Smith, project manager.

————. (1987, October) "Guadalupe Corridor: Program Report." Prepared for Santa Clara County Transportation Agency, by O'Brien, Kreitzberg, and Associates, Inc.

————. (1987, October) "Guadalupe Corridor : Cost Report No. 18." Prepared for Santa Clara County Transportation Agency, Gordon Smith, project manager.

————. (1983, September) "Guadalupe Corridor, Busway/HOVway: Response to UMTA Comments on the Supplemental Analysis."

————. (1983, June) "Guadalupe Corridor: Briefing Booklet."

————. (1981, December) "Guadalupe Corridor: Preferred Alternative Report."

Schön, Donald A. (1983) *The Reflective Practitioner: How Professionals Think in Action.* New York: Basic Books.

————. (1971) *Beyond the Stable State.* New York: Random House.

Scott, W. Richard (1981) *Organizations: Rational, Natural, and Open Systems.* Englewood Cliffs, NJ: Prentice-Hall.

Senn, James A. (1984) *Analysis and Design of Information Systems.* New York: McGraw-Hill.

Shangraw, R. F. (1986) "How Public Managers Use Information: An Experiment Examining Choices of Computer and Printed Information," *Public Administration Review* (Special Issue).

Simon, Herbert A. (1976) *Administrative Behavior: A Study of Decision-Making Processes in Administrative Organization,* Third Edition. New York: Free Press.

Smerk, George M. (1987) "Federal Mass Transit Programs, 1984 to 1987," *Transportation Journal* (Winter), 41-53.

————. (1974) *Urban Mass Transportation—A Dozen Years of Federal Policy.* Bloomington: Indiana University Press.

Smith, Gordon (1987) "Light Rail Update: Santa Clara County, California." Paper presented at the American Public Transit Association Rapid Transit Conference.

————. (1986) "Transit Tactics: Keeping Light Rail Moving," *Civil Engineering* (November).

Stanger, Richard, and Darche, Ben (1984) "Development of a Rail Transit Plan and Implementation Strategy for Los Angeles County," *State-of-the-Art Report 2.* Washington, DC: Transportation Research Board, National Research Council.

Stewart, Rodney (1982) *Cost Estimating.* New York: John Wiley and Sons.

Stone, Deborah A. (1988) *Policy Paradox and Political Reason.* Glenview, IL: Scott, Foresman.

Szanton, Peter (1981) *Not Well Advised.* New York: Rusell Sage Foundation and the Ford Foundation.

Tanaka, Josue (1982) "Towards a Syntax of Decision and Analysis Processes: Federal Urban Transport Investment in Brazil." Ph.D. thesis, Massachusetts Institute of Technology, Department of Civil Engineering.

Tomazinis, Anthony R. (1985) "The Logic and Rationale of Strategic Planning." Paper presented at 27th annual conference of the Association of Collegiate Schools of Planning, October, Atlanta.

Transportation Research Board, National Research Council (1989) *Light Rail Transit: New System Successes at Affordable Prices*. Special Report 221. Papers presented at National Conference on Light Rail Transit, May 8-11, San Jose, CA.

————. (1988) *A Look Ahead: Year 2020*. Special Report 220. Proceedings of Conference on Long-Range Trends and Requirements for the Nation's Highway and Public Transit Systems, Washington, DC.

————. (1978) *Light Rail Transit: Planning and Technology*. Special Report 182. Proceedings of conference by the Urban Mass Transportation Administration and conducted by the Transportation Research Board in cooperation with the American Public Transit Association, Washington, DC.

Truelove, P. (1980) "Some Lessons from the Washington Metro," *Transport Policy Decision Making*, 1, 121-32.

Tversky, Amos, and Kahneman, Daniel (1981) "The Framing of Decisions and the Psychology of Choice," *Science*, 211, 453-58. Reprinted in Elster, Jon, ed. (1986) *Rational Choice*. New York: New York University Press, pp. 123-41.

Ungson, G. R., Braunstein, D. N., and Hall, P. D. (1981) "Managerial Information Processing: A Research Review," *Administrative Science Quarterly*, 26, 116-34.

U. S. Department of Transportation (1984) Annual Operating Statistics, Section 15 Data.

U. S. Department of Transportation, Urban Mass Transportation Administration (1984, June) "Guadalupe Corridor Project: Full Funding Grant Agreement."

————. (1981, July) "Guadalupe Corridor, Alternatives Analysis: Draft Environmental Impact Statement." Prepared in cooperation with California Department of Transportation, Association of Bay Area Governments, Metropolitan Transportation Commission, City of San Jose, City of Santa Clara, and Santa Clara County County Transit District.

————. (1977, December) "Buffalo Light Rail Rapid Transit Project: Final Environmental Impact Statement."

————. Massachusetts Bay Transportation Authority (1988) "Old Colony Railroad Rehabilitation Project: Draft Environmental Impact Statement, First Review Draft" (July).

U. S. General Accounting Office (FY1982-87) GAO database, subject areas: Cost Analysis, Cost Control, Mass Transit Funding, Transportation Costs, and Value Engineering.

————. (1987, March) "Grant Formulas: A Catalog of Federal Aid to State and Localities."

————. (1986, September) "Procurement: Selected Civilian Agencies' Cost Estimating Process for Large Projects." Briefing report to the Chairman, Committee on Governmental Affairs, United States Senate, GAO/GCD-86-137BR.

————. (1986, July) "Budget Issues: Cost Escalation on Three Major Department of Transportation Projects." Report to Congressional Committees, GAO/AFMD-86-31.

————. (1984, November) "Greater Use of Value Engineering has the Potential to Save the Department of Transportation Millions in Construction Costs." Report to the Secretary of Transportation, GAO/RCED-85-14.

————. (1983, April) "UMTA could take steps to reduce costs in the development of light rail projects." GAO/B-211567.

————. (1982, December) "Need to Periodically Reassess Mass Transit Construction Projects." GAO/RCED-83-82.

Urban Mass Transportation Administration (1988, February 24) "Grants Assistance Programs: Statistical Summaries." Mimeo.

————. (1984, May) "A Detailed Description of UMTA's System for Rating Proposed Major Transit Investments," Washington, DC: U.S. Department of Transportation.

————. (1980) "Alternatives Analysis Procedures and Technical Guidelines." Draft, Office of Planning Assistance. Washington, DC: U.S. Department of Transportation.

Vaziri, M., and Deacon, J. A. (1986) "Choosing Performance Indicators for Transit Decision Making," *Transport Policy and Decision Making*, 3, 323-40.

Von Winterfeldt, D., and Edwards, W. (1986) *Decision Analysis and Behavioral Research*. Cambridge, UK: Cambridge University Press.

Vuchic, Vukan R. (1981) *Urban Public Transportation: Systems and Technology*, Englewood Cliffs, NJ: Prentice-Hall.

Wachs, Martin (1982) "Ethical Dilemmas in Forecasting for Public Policy," *Public Administration Review* (November/December).

————. (1985a) "Planning, Organizations and Decision-Making: A Research Agenda," *Transportation Research, Part A: General*, 19A-5/6, 521-31.

————. (1985b) *Ethics in Planning*. New Brunswick, NJ: Center for Urban Policy Research.

Walker, Cynthia Ann et al. (1984) "Application of Transit Operating Cost Models," *State-of-the-Art Report 2*. Washington, DC: Transportation Research Board, National Research Council.

Ward, Sol A., and Litchfield, Thorndike (1980) *Cost Control in Design and Construction*. New York: McGraw-Hill.

Wechsler, B., and Backoff, R. W. (1987) "The Dynamics of Strategy in Public Organizations," *Journal of the American Planning Association*, 53-1 (Winter).

Weiner, Edward (1983, August) *Urban Transportation Planning in the United States: A Historical Overview*. Final Report, prepared for the U.S. Department of Transportation, Washington, DC.

————. (1987) "Urban Transportation Planning since the Federal-Aid Highway Act of 1962," *Journal of Transportation Engineering*, 113-6 (November).

Wheeler, D. D., and Janis, I. L. (1980) *A Practical Guide for Making Decisions*. New York: Free Press.

Whitt, J. A., and Yago, G. (1985) "Corporate Strategies and the Decline of Transit in the U.S. Cities," *Urban Affairs Quarterly*, 21-1 (September).

Whitt, J. A. (1982) *Urban Elites and Mass Transportation: The Dialectics of Power*. Princeton, NJ: Princeton University Press.

Wildavsky, Aaron (1979) *Speaking Truth to Power: The Art and Craft of Policy Analysis*. Boston: Little, Brown.

Wohl, Martin, and Hendrickson, Chris (1984) *Transportation Investment and Pricing Principles*. New York: John Wiley and Sons.

Womack, J. F., and Altshuler, A. A. (1979) *An Examination of the Transit Funding Process at the Local Level*. Prepared for U.S. Department of Transportation, Urban Mass Transportation Administration, by the Center for Transportation Studies, MIT.

World Bank (1988) *Road Deterioration in Developing Countries: Causes and Remedies*. A World Bank Policy Study. Washington, DC: World Bank.

Yeeles, M. T., Allport, R. J., and Evans, R. C. (1984, June) "Operating Costs of Mass Transit Systems." Paper presented at World Bank conference on mass transit, Singapore.

Index

Analysis and decision-making,
interaction of, 64-66, 85, 121-2;
institutional actors involved in, 122-
4
Alternatives analysis process:
definition, 7, 14-18; purpose of, 16,
18, 66, 155-7
Argument-oriented paradigm of
planning, 20-21, 22

Boston Case Study: description of,
29-36; characteristics of, 64;
comments on, 36-38; cost estimates
in, 36; data automation in, 85;
decision-making process in, 105;
and estimating approaches, 78, 80;
hindsight into, 168; increases in
preliminary cost estimates in, 91;
organizational issues in, 115
Buffalo's Light Rail Rapid Transit
Project: characteristics of, 64-65;
comments on, 61-63; cost estimates
of, 3, 5; and cost qualifications, 84;
and dealing with uncertainty, 90;
decision-making process in, 107;
description of, 53-61; and
estimating approaches, 77, 79;
hindsight into, 167-8; organizational
issues in, 115

Capital costs of U.S. transit projects,
3-4

Causes of wrong estimation, 1-2
Contingency factors, 92
Cost control, 2, 78
Cost effectiveness: as selection
criteria, 16, 99, 108, 114
Costs: characteristics of, 8; data
automation of, 65, 83-84, 129, 154,
158; data, information, and
methods for estimating, 75, 128-9,
144; definition of, 8
Costs classification, 80-83, 147-8,
153, 158; demand-based, 82-83;
direct-indirect, 80, 82; fixed-
variable, 81; elements of, 92-93

Decision criteria. See Selection
criteria
Decision makers: characteristics and
perceptions of, 114-5, 124; and
information, 114-5, 146, 154
Decision making: decisions within,
104-5; descriptive-prescriptive
perspectives, 99-100; individual-
general perspectives, 99-100; in
private vs. public sector projects,
98-99; interaction with analysis, 64-
66, 85, 121-2; stages, 103; in
transportation planning, 98, 104-12
Design-to-cost approach to estimating,
116-7

EIS (Environmental Impact

Statement), 16, 29, 33, 47, 59
Estimating: approaches to, 77, 86,
  116, 153; automation in, 83-85, 92;
  decision model for estimating, 129-
  42; in private vs. public sector
  projects, 76; purpose, 4; technical
  steps and elements of, 6, 75-76, 86

Financial feasibility, 16, 81
Financial context, 89, 93

Government responsibilities in the
  analysis process, 16
Ground-up estimating approach, 77

Internalization of costs, 116-7, 148,
  160

Level of service, 89

MBTA (Massachusetts Bay
  Transportation Authority), 30-36,
  38

NFTA (Niagara Frontier
  Transportation Authority), 54-62

Old Colony Project, 30. *See also*
  Boston Case Study
Organizational context in estimating,
  101-2, 115-6

Particularistic selection criteria, 103-
  4, 111
Phasing project investments, 79, 92
Productivity performance measures,
  89, 108-12
Project scale, 101

Rational paradigm, 19, 22, 97-98,
  114, 121; alternative paradigms,
  20-21; criticisms, 20
Resource build-up estimating
  approach, 86-87

Santa Clara County's Light Rail
  Project: characteristics of, 64;
  comments on, 50-53; cost estimates

of, 46, 50-51; description of, 39-
  50; hindsight into, 168;
  organizational issues in, 115
SCCTD (Santa Clara County
  Transportation District), 41-49, 53
Scenario design, 92, 158
Section 3 and Section 9 funds, 29
Segmentation estimating approach, 86
Selection criteria, 142-3, 157, 159-60;
  and uncertainty, 126-7, 145;
  universalistic vs. particularistic,
  103-4, 111
Sensitivity analysis, 81, 85, 90-91,
  145-6, 153, 158
Specificity of goals and tasks of
  planning process, 101
Standardization of cost estimating
  process, 78, 101, 159-60

Top-down estimating approach, 77
Transportation planning:
  characteristics of, 98-99, 113-4,
  127-9, 154; data and information
  in, 129; history of, 13-14;
  institutional environment of, 18-19,
  102, 104; time frame and project
  scope in, 128, 144, 157
Transit project planning. *See*
  Alternatives analysis process
Transit projects: role, 32, 40, 54, 64
TSM (Transportation Systems
  Management), 32, 45

Uncertainty: actionable, 126;
  avoidable, 126; and cost
  classifications, 81-82; definition and
  perspectives of, 125, 127;
  inevitable, 126; as issue in
  transportation planning, 18, 64, 89-
  92; as part of proposed analytical
  framework, 144, 153, 157; and
  types of selection criteria, 103
UMTA (Urban Mass Transportation
  Administration): and the Boston
  Case Study, 33-35, 37-38; and
  Buffalo's Light Rail Rapid Transit,
  55-56, 58-60; and consideration of
  financial context, 93-94; and data

automation, 85; and performance
measures as selection criteria, 108;
role in history of transportation
planning of, 28-29; and Santa Clara
County's Light Rail Project, 40-43,
46-47, 52

Value engineering, 147, 159

About the Author

AURELIO MENEDEZ is an infrastructure specialist with The World Bank in Washington, DC. For the past decade he has been involved at the academic and professional level with public transportation planning and decision making in both the developed and developing world. He holds a Ph.D. in urban regional planning from Massachusetts Institute of Technology.